IFLA Publications 118

International Newspaper Librarianship for the 21st Century

Edited by
Hartmut Walravens

K · G · Saur München 2006

IFLA Publications
edited by Sjoerd Koopman

Recommended catalogue entry:
International Newspaper Librarianship for the 21st Century / edited by Hartmut Walravens ;
[International Federation of Library Associations and Institutions]. – München : K.G. Saur, 2006.
– 298 p. : ill. ; 21 cm. – (IFLA Publications ; 118).

ISBN 3-598-21846-X

Bibliographic information published by Die Deutsche Bibliothek
Die Deutsche Bibliothek lists this publication in the Deutsche Nationalbibliografie;
detailed bibliographic data is available in the Internet at
http://dnb.ddb.de.

⊗

Printed on permanent paper
The paper used in this publication meets the minimum requirements of
American National Standard – Permanence of Paper
for Publications and Documents in Libraries and Archives
ANSI/NISO Z39.48-1992 (R1997)

Printed / Bound by Strauss GmbH, Mörlenbach

ISBN 13: 978-3-598-21846-0
ISBN 10: 3-598-21846-X
ISSN 0344-6891 (IFLA Publications)

CONTENTS

Cape Town 2003

PREFACE

This volume consists of presentations at recent events of the IFLA Newspaper Section and documents the variety and intensity of newspaper activities worldwide. Newspapers are still not liked by a large number of librarians and archivists because they are labour and staff intensive, and that means cost intensive. Also, they take a lot of shelf space, they need special treatment for preservation, and they should be microfilmed ...

During the last years a most encouraging development has taken place which seems to release newspapers from their Cinderella position: The progress of digitisation and text management has opened up a promising market. Several major business companies have digitised large amounts of newspapers and are offering newspaper contents to wide audience. Considering that newspapers are among the most important often unique (even if not always reliable) historical source materials the success of such ventures is hardly surprising. Thanks to OCR treatment of the newspaper files people can now find details of their local history and their family easily, not to speak of scholarly purposes. Were newspaper-related subjects avoided by Ph.D. candidates in previous times because the tracking down of individual papers and the reading of many reels of film were estimated as an additional two years of labour, things have become so much easier: newspapers are now among the most preferred sources as the information is available by a mouse click – provided the newspaper was digitised.

The current state of digitisation worldwide is encouraging: After the spectacular success of the Scandinavian TIDEN project, major national projects are under way, especially in Great Britain and the United States. But other countries have been active, too: Estonia and Lithuania have been digitising newspapers, in Latin America the Grand Colombia project was concluded successfully, and China is catching up at an amazing speed. Not to forget Luxembourg where the national papers are currently digitised. The projected 2006 International Digitisation Conference in Salt Lake City, which is co-organised by the Newspaper Section, is expected to provide the latest information both on the current projects as well as the technological progress.

The present volume has two main focuses: regional activities, and current work in the fields of preservation and digitisation. The first subject does not only introduce the newspaper holdings of individual institutions and regions but also gives information about current activities and challenges. It has been part of the Newspaper Section's policy to reach out to other parts of the world and foster cooperation and information exchange with colleagues in other countries. This seems the logical and most efficient way to work towards the preservation of and access to an important part of the world's heritage. The second focus is perhaps a bit more technical as the most advanced means and technologies are monitored and applied towards secure long-term archiving. It may be stated here that the general view of newspaper experts still is that only silver film is a reliable media for archiving. Certainly, experts have not been blind to the progress of digitisation and electronic storage technology. In this context attention may be drawn to the electronic mass storage facility maintained by the National Library of Norway at Mo i Rana where the Newspaper Section organised a preservation seminar in 2005. More security in the transmission and re-copying of the content of electronically stored material may become, at least in part, a rival to traditional long-term preservation media. On the other hand, born digital newspapers can now be preserved in COM format owing to technology developed, among others, by the Fraunhofer

Gesellschaft in Germany. Another essential subject covered in this volume is newspapers and copyright; this is a very complex issue that has drawn much attention in the context of major digitisation projects. Most libraries decided therefore to digitise only materials in the public domain, i.e. newspapers published before approximately 1900. There are a few cases, however, where libraries cooperated with the respective publisher and accomplished successful projects.

This volume comprises presentations given at the Section's events during the years 2003 – 2005, and relate to venues in six countries: Berlin, Buenos Aires, Canberra, Cape Town, Oslo, and Shanghai, thus justifying both the attributes "current" and "international" in the book's title. Papers were included as presented, with only minor technical editing. In a very few cases the English text needed some more editing in order to facilitate readability. A couple of Powerpoint presentations were included even though a text version would have been preferable. As the authors were unable, mainly because of other pressing duties, to provide them, the reproduction of the frames seemed useful because of the information they carry and their – at least to a large degree – self-explicative character.

I would like to thank all the authors for their contributions, Carolin Unger for the layout, and IFLA and K. G. Saur Publishers for their – as always – excellent cooperation.

Berlin, Nov. 4, 2005   Hartmut Walravens

DEVELOPMENT OF ELECTRONIC PERIODICALS AT THE BIBLIOTHÈQUE NATIONALE DE FRANCE : Digitisation of French daily newspapers from Mid 19th Century to 1944

Pascal Sanz

Director of the department Droit, Economie, Politique,
Bibliothèque nationale de France
Paris, France

The Bibliothèque nationale de France (BnF) keeps a vast collection of French and foreign newspapers : end 2004 it includes some 60,000 retrospective or running titles. But it is of course the collection of French newspapers that the BnF considers its duty to preserve and to develop. Therefore it seemed quite natural as well as justified that the library should digitise a crucial selection of this important newspapers collection in order to give better access for researches in almost all kinds of social and human sciences : daily newspapers. To introduce the digitisation programme I want to give a short presentation of the BnF's holdings of French newspapers : it will be the first part of my paper. In the second part I shall point out technical and scientific choices of the Newspaper Digitisation Programme. My conclusion will deal with future prospects of developing and enlarging this programme.

1. The French Newspaper Collection at the Bibliothèque nationale de France

There are different ways of classifying French newspapers (the INSEE newsprint list, the classification of the Bureau for Justification of Newsprint Circulation (OJD), etc.). Having this in mind one may divide the newsprint into some great categories :

- National newspapers comprise :
  - political and general information newspapers including dailies (such as *Le Temps*, *Le Figaro* or *L'Humanité*) and weeklies
  - illustrated people magazines with serial stories and strip cartoons such as *Le Petit Journal* launched by Moïse Millaud in 1863 at an issue price of 5 centimes
  - gossip papers and satirical papers
- Regional and local newspapers : big regional dailies with several local editions (ex. : *Ouest France*), local weeklies
- Overseas newspapers from the former French colonies and territories (for instance *La Dépêche algérienne* or *L'Echo d'Oran*) as well as newspapers from the present DOM-TOM (French overseas administrative departments)
- Specialised newsprint including in particular women's magazines (ex : *Le Petit courrier des dames*), leisure magazines, newsprint on finances, law, sport, etc. (ex. : *L'Auto*)
- Reading newsprint including, among others, childrenís magazines, youngstersí illustrated periodicals (ex. : *La Semaine de Suzette*), newspapers for the leisure market, religious newsprint, associations' periodicals

- Free newspapers
- Government publications : official gazettes, local council bulletins, etc.
- Alternative press

The word press covers indeed a great variety of publications and newspapers holdings are to be found in all BnF's collection departments. However, the department Droit, Economie, Politique keeps the majority of the library's newsprint holdings. In fact, when the library moved from the Richelieu site to the new building 8 years ago, this recently created department became the principal heir of the Periodicals department which disappeared in so far. Within the department Droit, Economie, Politique the Newsprint office (Service de la Presse) and the Government Publications office (Service des publications officielles) are in charge of most of the newspaper holdings. Just a few totals to give you an idea of the extent of the holdings :

Current entries into the stacks (in paper format)

Daily newspapers and large size periodicals of general information contents or concerning law, finances, politics, as well as periodical government publications.

Different entry modes to the stacks :

- Most titles by legal deposit, including also some foreign titles
- Expensive acquisitions (subscriptions)
- Gifts
- Exchanges

At present the total number is 832 titles of which 225 daily newspapers. On average more than 7300 issues arrive every month. The yearly increase of the holdings covers 200 linear meters (ml) plus 40 linear meters of periodical government publications forming a subset to the newsprint collection.

The Retrospective Collection (in paper format)

It includes two groups.

Periodicals (allotting the call numbers Jo, Gr fol-Jo, JoB and JoA) up to end 1990 including more than a 100,000 titles : local publications, technical journals, extremely varied magazines.

Some samples :

- Regional and local newspapers (including former French territories such as Algeria).

  Thus we have as well *L'Abeille des Vosges* (Jo-11021) as *Le Progrès de Sétif* (Jo-88403);
- Professional newsprint : *L'Industriel forain* (Jo-8942) or the *Bulletin des fruits et primeurs* (Jo-31150) ;
- Trade-union or association bulletins such as *L'Auto-tram de Paris* (Jo-30242) or *La France mutilée* (Jo-25331) ;
- Children's magazines (ex.: *Les Belles images* Jo-55958).

Large size periodicals and/or daily newspapers kept by the former Periodicals department. In this collection you find the holdings of the *International Herald Tribune* (Pb-1751 bis) or of the daily *Les Echos* (Lc2-6878).

Microfilmed periodicals belonging to this closed collection are not available in paper format as the majority of the holdings are no more stored on the François Mitterand site but forwarded to the library's Technical Centre in Bussy-Saint-Georges for preservation.

The Newspaper Microfilm Collection

If not otherwise stated the entire Newspaper Microfilm Collection, formerly kept in the Periodicals department, moved into the department Droit, Economie, Politique (under the call number Micr D or Mfilm + the call number of the original holding in paper format). This collection counts up to some 2200 titles (or call numbers). At the time it was moved to the new site, it included round 75,000 reels. It comprises the great national retrospective or current newspaper titles (all the dailies from the 19th and 20th centuries) and a large choice of past or running regional newspaper titles or newspapers from the former French territories.

The yearly increase of new microfilmed titles counts some 5500 reels including

- Current microfilming of several national dailies (*Le Monde, Le Figaro, La Croix, L'Humanité...*) and regional dailies (PQR = Presse régionale quotidienne). To be precise, with regard to regional newspapers with multieditions the BnF purchases or makes the microfilm of all the editions but in paper format the Library only keeps the main edition. Since 2004 the preservation of these regional dailies is shared with the public libraries in charge of the Printers' legal deposit ;
- Retrospective microfilming. As to very brittle holdings they must be restored partially or totally by thermosizing before filming.

In 2004, 229 newspapers holdings were microfilmed that way, which means some 400,000 frames.

2. The 2005-2009 Digitisation Programme of Retrospective National Daily Newspapers

Within this group, since mid-19th century, the highly circulated daily newspapers have attracted not only journalists' articles but also contributions from politicians, writers, artists, researchers. They all got hold of this media whose vast circulation was unknown until then, in order to publish essais, reviews, debates and novels. The quality and the variety of these contributions explain why newspapers from the 19th century to mid-20th century form an unrivalled supply to the study of the political, social, scientific, literary and artistic life. However, material pressure due to preservation and access to the paper format or to the microfilm has resulted in an underdevelopment of the newspapers as a purpose for historical studies or, more generally, as a research aim. The digitisation of collections of newspapers and magazines therefore contributes to exploit such information collections in an still unequalled way. This programme was defined and launched last year (2004). It is a five-year programme (2005-2009) which finally started in the beginning of 2005.

Selecting of the collection

The BnF decided to digitise twenty-one French nationally circulated newspapers as well as the supplements to six of those papers, from the first published issue up to 1944. These are:

- *La Croix*

- *Le Temps*
- *Le Figaro* (+ literary supplements)
- *L'Humanité*
- *Le Petit parisien* (+ weekly supplement)
- *Le Matin*
- *Le Siècle*
- *La Presse*
- *Le Petit journal* (+ weekly supplement)
- *L'Action française*
- *L'Univers*
- *Le Gaulois* (+ weekly supplement)
- *Le Rappel*
- *La Lanterne* (+ weekly supplement)
- *Gil Blas* (+ weekly supplement)
- *La Justice*
- *L'Intransigeant*
- *L'Aurore*
- *Le Constitutionnel*
- *L'Echo de Paris*
- *Le Journal des débats*

Some of these dailies which started mid-19th century stopped publishing long before 1944. Other titles disappeared during the Second World War. A few titles which continued to be published during the war stopped precisely in 1944. And some others are still running. As a matter of fact the digitisation is starting with these newspapers : *La Croix* (1883 -), *L'Humanité* (1904 -), *Le Figaro* (1826 -). Those titles as well as *Le Temps* (1861-1942) should be totally digitised before the end of 2006.

Besides the historical caesura of 1944 the choice of this deadline has allowed us to make an agreement quickly and easily with the administrations of the still running newspapers which rightfully could aim at digitising and putting online commercially their collections of the last sixty years. It also was agreed that the limit of 1944 should form a mobile barrier which may go up a year each year. This means that the BnF gradually will be able to give access on line of the following years.

For the time being, 27 newspaper titles (from the first published issue up to 1944) represent 3.2 million pages.

Digitisation methods and formats

As a first step of the Programme it was decided to use image digitising of this vast collection.

Two reasons were pointed out :

- The image mode is very well controlled today and less expensive than the text mode

- Research workers using retrospective newspapers need to see (even if they have also other needs) the articles in their original aspect and background, their page-setting and their reference to illustrations, etc.

Pages are digitised from the original newspaper and preserved in non compressed TIFF format which is considered to be the most reliable for long-term preservation while the circulation will be in JPEG format on the BnF's website in its digital library *Gallica*.

The digitisation will be carried out by three digitisation lines :

- 2 lines within the BnF : one at its Centre in Sablé which is already set up and on work, the other one at the library's technical Centre in Bussy-Saint-Georges which is being set up now ;
- after inviting bids a third line committed to a provider off site who will also work within the library on the Bussy-Saint-Georges site.

If access to the facsimile image of each page is absolutely necessary to most research workers, we also know that they want to dispose of other access methods : all the possibilities of full text search, the facilities of hypertext navigation, etc.

In order to offer such possibilities the second stage of BnF's programme is to prepare the conversion of the original digitisation product in image mode to a digital collection which will be accessible in text mode after having been treated by Optical Character Recognition (OCR) software.

Access and navigation methods and functions

The collection of the digitised newspapers will be accessible either through the BN-Opale Plus catalogue which clearly points out the documents available in an electronic version, or by searching directly in the *Gallica* database.

The search functions of the documents were firstly dealt with in a compilation of informations and experiences from some big libraries having already carried out a digitisation programme on line of a newspapers collection (Australia, Austria, USA, Norway, New-Zealand, United Kingdom). All this information was then studied by a working group including members of the different relevant departments of the BnF. Moreover, a survey was set up consisting in interviews with a range of research workers using newspapers in the reading rooms in order to get a real idea of what they need in this field. At present the following functions have been held up :

- search by date : access through a calendar (year/month/day) ; « kiosk » function (ex. : all the newspapers of a given day) ;
- full text search with possible segmentation (especially isolating of a given article on a full text page) ;
- within the same issue : logical consultation of the layout (like using a railway plan) is needed to know about the structure of an issue ; advertising of pagination so as to find one's way in this structure ; zooming of an extract to facilitate reading ;
- the possibility of navigating from one issue to another within the same title.

Funding

The estimated amount of the costs of digitisation in image mode of the complete collection is 3.5 million Euros. It includes particularly :

- salaries and national insurance contributions to members of BnF's staff in charge of this work (control, completing and preparing of the holdings ; working of the 2 lines within the house)
- costs of data storage
- providing committed to the sub-contracting off site (third digitisation line ; special work on the access method to the digitised collection)

The amount of 3.5 million Euros is entirely supported by BnF's proper budget which especially is supplied with grants from the Ministry of Culture and Communication. In order to start the second stage of the work – passing over to text mode – the BnF is looking actively for supplementary funding, in particular through sponsoring and partnership. The first financial support to the BnF for this part of the 5 year digitisation programme has come from the Senate which decided to make a grant of 150,000 Euros per year during three years (2005-2007), a total of 450,000 Euros.

3. Future prospects of developing and enlarging of the Programme

From now on several tracks of enriching and enlarging of this newspaper digitisation programme are already explored or future plans are taking shape. The working tracks often implicate to co-operate with other libraries or, as far as running titles are concerned, with thenewspapers themselves.

Completing of the initial collection and its enriching through historical factors

When some issues are lacking in BnF's holdings or if the physical condition of the documents make it difficult to carry out proper digitising the BnF tries to find these issues in other libraries or, in some cases, it may be necessary to apply to the newspaper administrations whenever the newspapers are still running. Beyond this completing, researches could be undertaken so as to find and digitise former censored articles of the relevant newspapers from brush proofs (last proofs before final printing of the newspaper) generally kept in some newsprint archives.

Enlarging by Including Regional Daily Newspapers

An agreement has already been made with the administrative staff of the regional daily *Ouest France* (the largest circulated French newspaper) so that the BnF may digitise and put online the former title of this daily, *Ouest-Eclair* (1899-1934, main edition).

The opening of BnF's digitisation programme to regional daily newspapers (PQR) will truly not remain at that stage. Co-operative prospects with libraries in some regions and, once more, with the newspaper administrations themselves are in preparation. For instance, in the region Champagne-Ardennes, the digitisation of the regional daily *L'Union* as well as of the other titles of its group (*L'Est-Eclair*, *l'Ardennais*) is studied at the moment jointly by the administrative staff of the newspaper, by the three main public libraries in the region (Châlons-en-Champagne, Reims, Troyes) and by the BnF. This co-operative effort may also concern a certain number of retrospective local newspapers, especially in the department Aube.

Enlarging to specialised collection of rare documents

Besides specialised journals which are already digitised in the Gallica database (ex. *Le Journal des économistes*, an important monthly economic journal from mid-19th century to 1940), collections of very specialised newspapers which are rare and of great historical value, will also be digitised and put online. As an example the BnF and the Bibliothèque de Documentation Internationale Contemporaine (BDIC) have undertaken a shared digitisation programme of their respective and complementary holdings of the « trench newspapers », that means newspapers written and carried out by the soldiers themselves in the trenches in Eastern France during the First World War.

Addition of tools to facilitate researches

When the time has come, we shall study the possibility of digitising existing tools (such as tables, indexes, newspaper yearbooks) in order to link them to the collection of digitised newspapers. For instance, we think of the tables of the daily *Le Temps* or of the subject file of the newspaper *Le Matin* which is examined by a research worker right now. In this field the carrying out of a major project would represent a capital tool for the newspaper history and for the history in general : the digitisation of the Bibliography of the French political et general information newspapers (Bibliographie de la presse française politique et d'information générale or BIPFPIG) which identify and locate such newspapers in libraries and archives in France, department by department. The digitisation Programme of retrospective newspapers now undertaken by the BnF will bring up its first results in the beginning of 2006. As we have already noted, the programme can only be imagined in co-operation with certain newspapers and certain libraries in France.

It is clear that it falls particularly well in with an international co-operation. At least two axes of partnership and opening are taking shape from now on :

- the French speaking dimension, in particular with the future prospects of connecting BnF's Programme and the initiative of the National Library of Quebec (whose director is a member of BnF's Scientific Council) concerning digitisation of newspapers from both countries ;

- the European dimension, with the project aiming the creation of a European digital library supported by the European Union and several member countries, in which, according to us, newspapers should hold an essential position.

LES DÉVELOPPEMENTS EN MATIÈRE DE PÉRIODIQUES ÉLECTRONIQUES A LA BIBLIOTHÈQUE NATIONALE DE FRANCE:
La numérisation de la presse quotidienne française du milieu du XIXème siècle a 1944

Pascal Sanz

Directeur du Département droit, économie, politique,
Bibliothèque nationale de France, Paris, France

La Bibliothèque nationale de France (BnF) possède un ensemble de presse française et étrangère extrêmement important, comptant, fin 2004 quelque 60 000 titres morts ou vivants.. Mais c'est, bien entendu, tout d'abord à l'égard de sa collection de titres de presse français que la BnF estime avoir un devoir de sauvegarde et de mise en valeur. Il était donc tout à fait légitime autant que naturel que la bibliothèque choisisse, dans cet ensemble considérable, de numériser un corpus crucial pour la recherche dans pratiquement tous les domaines des sciences de l'homme et de la société : la presse quotidienne . Pour présenter ce programme de numérisation, je commencerai par présenter rapidement les collections de presse française de la BnF : cela constituera la première partie de cet exposé . Puis, dans une deuxième partie, j'indiquerai quels sont les choix scientifiques et techniques du chantier de numérisation de la presse. Je conclurai en évoquant les perspectives d'évolution et d'élargissement de ce programme.

1. Les collections de presse française de la Bibliothèque nationale de France

Il existe différentes classifications de la presse française (nomenclature INSEE des produits presse, classification de l'Office de justification de la diffusion, etc.). S'inspirant de celles-ci on peut diviser la presse en quelques grands ensembles :

* la presse nationale, qui comprend :
    - la presse politique et d'information, regroupant quotidiens (comme *Le Temps*, *Le Figaro* ou *l'Humanité*) et hebdomadaires
    - la presse populaire fortement illustrée et comportant romans-feuilletons ou bandes dessinées, comme *Le Petit Journal* lancé au prix de 5 centimes par Moïse Millaud en 1863
    - la presse d'échos et la presse satirique
* la presse régionale et locale : grands quotidiens régionaux à éditions locales (ex : *Ouest-France)*, hebdomadaires locaux
* la presse d'outre-mer qui concerne les anciennes colonies et ex-territoires français (citons *La Dépêche algérienne* ou *L'Echo d'Oran*) ainsi que les actuels DOM-TOM
* la presse spécialisée comprenant notamment la presse féminine (ex :le *Petit courrier des dames*), la presse de loisirs, la presse économique, juridique, sportive (ex : *L'Auto*), etc.
* la presse de lecture dont font partie, entre autres, la presse enfantine, la presse des jeunes

ou les illustrés pour la jeunesse (par exemple *La Semaine de Suzette)*, la presse d'évasion, la presse religieuse, la presse associative

- la presse gratuite
- la presse de type publication officielle : journaux officiels, bulletins municipaux, etc.
- la presse alternative

La notion de presse recouvre donc une très grande variété de publications et on retrouve des fonds de presse dans tous les départements de collections de la BnF. C'est cependant au Département droit, économie, politique que se trouve concentrée la plus grande partie d'entre eux. En effet, au moment du transfert des collections de l'ancien bâtiment de la rue de Richelieu, il y a huit ans, ce departement nouvellement créé s'est trouvé être le principal héritier du Département des périodiques, qui disparaissait en temps que tel. Au sein du Département droit, économie, politique, ce sont le Service de la presse et le Service des publications officielles qui détiennent la majorité des collections de presse.

Quelques chiffres pour donner une idée de l'ampleur de ces collections :

Entrées courantes en magasin (support papier)

Il s'agit de quotidiens ou de périodiques de grand format, d'information générale ou relevant des disciplines droit, économie, politique ainsi que des publications officielles périodiques.

Les différents modes d'entrée en magasin sont :

- le dépôt légal pour la très grande majorité des titres, y compris pour des titres étrangers
- les acquisitions onéreuses (abonnements)
- les dons
- les échanges

Le tout représente actuellement 832 titres dont 225 quotidiens. Plus de 7300 fascicules sont reçus en moyenne chaque mois. L'accroissement annuel s'élève à plus de 200 mètres linéaires (ml) auxquels s'ajoutent environ 40 ml de publications officielles périodiques constituant un sous-ensemble de la presse.

Fonds clos (support papier)

Il comprend deux ensembles.

Les périodiques (cotés Jo, Gr fol-Jo, JoB et JoA) allant jusqu'en 1990 inclus, le tout représentant plus de 100 000 cotes. Il s'agit de publications d'intérêt local, de revues techniques ou de magazines d'une extrême diversité.

Quelques exemples :

- la presse régionale ou locale (incluant les anciens territoires français comme l'Algérie).

   Ainsi, nous avons aussi bien *L'Abeille des Vosges* (Jo-11021) que le *Progrès de Sétif* (Jo-88403) ;

- la presse professionnelle : *L'Industriel forain* (Jo-8942) ou le *Bulletin des fruits et primeurs* (Jo-31150) ;

- les bulletins syndicaux ou d'associations comme *L'Auto-tram de Paris* (Jo-30242) ou *La France mutilée* (Jo-25331) ;

- les revues pour la jeunesse (*Les Belles images* Jo-55958) .

Les périodiques grand folio et/ou quotidiens précédemment conservés au Département des périodiques. On trouve ainsi dans ce fonds la collection de *l'International Herald Tribune* (Pb-1751 bis) ou du quotidien *Les Echos* (Lc2-6878).

Dans ce fonds clos, les titres qui ont été microfilmés ne sont plus communicables sous leur forme papier et, dans la très grande majorité des cas, les collections elles-mêmes ne sont plus conserves dans les magasins du site François Mitterrand mais ont été envoyées au Centre technique de Bussy- Saint-Georges.

Fonds de microfilms de presse

Le fonds de microfilms de presse précédemment conservé au Département des périodiques a été déménagé, sauf exception, dans le Département Droit, économie, politique : (cotés Micr D ou Mfilm + la cote papier d'origine). Ce fonds représente environ 2200 cotes et comprenait plus de 75 000 bobines lors de son déménagement. On y trouve les grands titres de presse nationale ancienne et courante (tous les grands quotidiens des 19ème et 20ème siècle) et une large sélection de titres régionaux morts ou vivants ou de presse des anciens territoires français.

Pour les nouveaux titres de microfilms l'accroissement annuel (Micr D et Mfilm Jo) s'élève à environ 5500 bobines comprenant,

- le microfilmage courant de plusieurs titres de presse quotidienne nationale (*Le Monde, Le Figaro, La Croix, L'Humanité* ...) et de presse quotidienne régionale (PQR). Précisons que pour les titres de PQR à éditions multiples, la BnF achète ou fait réaliser le microfilm de toutes les éditions alors que pour le papier elle ne conserve que l'édition principale et que depuis 2004 la conservation de la PQR est partagée avec les biblio-thèques municipales en charge du dépôt légal imprimeur ;

- le microfilmage à titre rétrospectif. Pour les collections en très mauvais état, on est obligé de restaurer partiellement ou intégralement les fascicules par thermocollage avant de pouvoir effectuer la prise de vues.

En 2004, c'est ainsi 229 titres qui ont été microfilmés : pratiquement 400 000 images.

2. Le programme 2005-2009 de numérisation de la presse quotidienne nationale rétro-spective

Dans cet ensemble, la presse quotidienne à grand tirage, dès le milieu du XIXème siècle, a drainé, à côté des articles des journalistes, les contributions des hommes politiques, des écrivains, des artistes, des savants, qui se sont emparés de ce média à la diffusion sans précédent pour publier essais, critiques, tribunes et romans. La qualité et la diversité de ces textes font de la presse du XIXème et de la première moitié du XXème siècle une source incomparable pour l'étude de la vie politique, sociale, scientifique, littéraire et artistique.

Et pourtant, les contraintes matérielles de conservation et de consultation du papier ou du microfilm ont entraîné une sous-exploitation de la presse comme objet d'histoire et plus largement comme objet de recherche. C'est pourquoi la numérisation des corpus de jour-naux et magazines apporte des solutions, jusqu'à présent inégalées, d'exploitation de ces corpus documentaires.

Ce programme a été défini et décidé l'an dernier (2004). Il s'agit d'un plan pour cinq ans, 2005- 2009, qui a effectivement commencé début 2005.

Le choix du corpus

La BnF a décidé de numériser vingt et un journaux français de diffusion nationale et les suppléments de six d'entre eux, de leurs origines respectives à 1944. En voici la liste :

- *La Croix*

- *Le Temps*

- *Le Figaro* (+ supplément littéraire)

- *L'Humanité*

- *Le Petit parisien* (+ supplément hebdomadairc)

- *Le Matin*

- *Le Siècle*

- *La Presse*

- *Le Petit journal* (+ supplément hebdomadaire)

- *L'Action française*

- *L'Univers*

- *Le Gaulois* (+ supplément hebdomadaire)

- *Le Rappel*

- *La Lanterne* (+ supplément hebdomadaire)

- *Gil Blas* (+ supplément hebdomadaire)

- *La Justice*

- *L'Intransigeant*

- *L'Aurore*

- *Le Constitutionnel*

- *L'Echo de Paris*

- *Le Journal des débats*

Certains d'entre ces quotidiens, nés entre le milieu et la fin du XIXème siècle ont cessé de paraître bien avant 1944. D'autres ont disparu pendant la seconde guerre mondiale. Quelques-uns, qui s'étaient maintenus pendant la guerre ont, précisément, disparu en 1944. Quelques-uns, enfin, sont des titres toujours vivants et c'est par eux, d'ailleurs que nous commençons la numérisation : *La Croix* (1883-), *L'Humanité* (1904-), *Le Figaro* (1826-). Ces trois titres ainsi que *Le Temps* (1861-1942) devraient être entièrement numérisés d'ici à fin 2006.

Outre la césure historique que représente l'année 1944, le choix de cette date limite a permis de trouver très rapidement et facilement un accord avec les directions des journaux vivants, qui peuvent aspirer très légitimement à numériser et mettre en ligne commercialement leurs collections des soixante dernières années. Il est convenu avec eux que cette limite – 1944 – constituait une barrière mobile, qui pourra s'élever chaque année d'un an, c'est à dire que la BnF pourra, si elle le souhaite, fournir ensuite progressivement l'accès en ligne aux années suivantes.

Pour le moment, des origines jusqu'en 1944 donc, le total des 27 titres représente 3,2 millions de pages.

Les modes et formats de numérisation

Il a été décidé de numériser, dans une première étape, ce très important corpus en mode image et ce pour deux raisons :

- parce que cette technique, très bien maîtrisée, est beaucoup moins coûteuse que la numérisation en mode texte,

- parce que les chercheurs qui ont recours à la presse rétrospective ont besoin (même s'ils peuvent avoir aussi d'autres besoins) de consulter les articles dans leur forme originale, avec leur contexte, le mise en page, le rapport aux illustrations, etc.

Les pages des journaux sont numérisées à partir des originaux et conservées en format TIFF non compressé, jugé le plus fiable pour la conservation pérenne, tandis que la diffusion se fera au format JPEG, sur le site web de la BnF, dans sa partie bibliothèque numérique, « Gallica ».

La numérisation sera effectuée par trois chaînes de numérisation :

- 2 chaînes internes à la BnF, dont une sur son site de Sablé, déjà installée et qui a commencé à produire et l'autre au Centre technique de Bussy-Saint-Georges, en cours d'installation,

- une chaîne confiée, après appel d'offre, à un prestataire externe, mais qui sera installée également dans les murs de la bibliothèque, à Bussy-Sait-Georges.

Mais nous savons bien que, si l'accès à l'image en fac-similé de chaque page est indispensable à la plupart des chercheurs, ceux-ci souhaitent également disposer d'autres modalités de consultation : toutes les possibilités de la recherche plein texte, les facilités de la navigation hypertextuelle, etc.

Afin d'offrir ces possibilités, la Bnf se prépare donc, dans une deuxième étape, à convertir le produit de la numérisation originale en mode image en un corpus numérique accessible aussi en mode texte, après utilisation d'un logiciel de reconnaissance optique de caractères (OCR).

Les modes et fonctionnalités d'accès et de navigation

Le corpus de presse numérisée sera accessible soit à travers le catalogue Bn-Opale Plus, qui signale clairement quels sont les documents faisant l'objet d'une version électronique, soit en interrogeant directement la base *Gallica*.

Les fonctionnalités de consultation des documents ont d'abord fait l'objet d'un recueil d'informations et d'expériences auprès d'un certain nombre de grandes bibliothèques ayant déjà engagé un programme de numérisation et de mise en ligne d'un corpus de presse (Australie, Autriche, Etats-Unis, Norvège, Nouvelle-Zélande, Royaume-Uni). Les informations ainsi recueillies ont ensuite été étudiées par un groupe de travail comprenant les différents departments concernés au sein de la BnF. De plus une enquête par entretiens auprès d'un échantillon de chercheurs utilisateurs de la presse dans les salles de lecture de l'établissement a été menée, afin de disposer d'une connaissance plus fine de leurs propres souhaits en la matière. A l'heure actuelle, les fonctionnalités suivantes ont été retenues :

- recherche par date : accès par un calendrier (année/mois/jour) ; fonction « kiosque » (exemple :tous les journaux d'un jour donné) ;

- recherche plein texte avec possibilité de segmentation (notamment, isolement d'un article donné dans une page en plein texte) ;

- au sein d'un même fascicule : consultation du chemin de fer, pour connaître la structure du numéro ; affichage de la pagination, pour se repérer dans cette structure ; zoom sur un extrait, pour en faciliter la lecture ;
- au sein d'un titre : navigation d'un fascicule à l'autre.

Le financement

Le coût de la numérisation en mode image pour l'ensemble du corpus a été évalué à 3,5 millions d'euros. Ce coût recouvre notamment :

- les salaires et charges des agents de la BnF affectés à cette tâche (vérification, complètement, préparation des collections ; fonctionnement des deux chaînes internes),
- le coût du stockage des données,
- les prestations confiées à la sous-traitance externe (troisième chaîne de numérisation ; certains travaux relatifs au mode d'accès au corpus numérisé).

Ce coût de 3,5 millions d'euros est financé entièrement sur le budget propre de la BnF, lui même principalement alimenté par les subventions annuelles que lui attribue le Ministère de la culture et de la communication.

Pour engager la deuxième phase de travaux – le passage au mode texte – , la BnF recherché activement des financements complémentaires, notamment via le mécénat et le partenariat. Le premier soutien financier ainsi obtenu par la BnF lui est accordé par le Sénat, qui a decide d'apporter au plan quinquennal de numérisation de la presse une dotation de 150 000 euros par an pendant trois ans (2005-2007), soit 450 000 euros au total.

3. Les perspectives d'évolution et d'élargissement de ce programme.

Plusieurs pistes d'enrichissement et d'élargissement de ce plan de numérisation de la presse sont d'ores et déjà explorées ou se dessinent en perspective. Souvent, ces pistes de travail impliquent une coopération avec d'autres bibliothèques ou, pour les titres vivants, avec les journaux eux-mêmes.

La recherche de l'exhaustivité du corpus initial, son enrichissement d'éléments historiques.

Lorsque certains fascicules manquent à la BnF ou se présentent dans état physique permettant difficilement la numérisation dans de bonnes conditions, la BnF recherche ces fascicules dans d'autres bibliothèques ou, dans certains cas, auprès des journaux eux-mêmes.

Au delà de ce travail de complètement, un travail de recherche pourrait être mené pour retrouver et numériser, à partir des morasses, c'est à dire des dernières épreuves avant impression du journal conservées dans certaine archives de presse, les articles censurés, à certaines époques, pour les titres concernés.

L'extension à la presse quotidienne régionale

Dès à présent, un accord a été conclu avec la direction du Quotidien régional *Ouest-France* (le plus gros tirage de la presse française) pour que la BnF numérise et mette en ligne l'ancêtre de ce titre, *Ouest-Eclair* (1899-1934, édition principale).

Vraisemblablement, l'ouverture du programme de numérisation de la presse de la BnF à la PQR n'en restera pas là. Des perspectives de collaboration avec des bibliothèques de certaines regions et, encore une fois, avec certains journaux, sont à l'étude. Par exemple, en Champagne-Ardenne, la numérisation du journal régional *L'Union* et des autres titres de son groupe (*L'Est-Eclair*, *L'Ardennais*) est actuellement étudiée conjointement par la direction de ce journal, les trios principales bibliothèques municipales de la région (Châlons-en-Champagne, Reims, Troyes) et la BnF. Cette coopération pourrait aussi porter sur un certains nombres de titres rétrospectifs locaux, notamment dans le département de l'Aube.

L'extension à des corpus spécialisés de documents rares

A côté de titres de revues spécialisées qui se trouvent déjà numérisées dans la base Gallica (exemple : *Le Journal des économistes*, grand mensuel d'économie du milieu du XIXème siècle à 1940) des corpus de presse très spécifiques, rares et d'une haute valeur historique seront également numérisés et offerts à la consultation en ligne. Par exemple, la BnF et la Bibliothèque de documentation internationale contemporaine (BDIC) ont entrepris la numérisation concertée de leurs collections respectives et complémentaires de « Journaux de tranchées », c'est à dire les journaux rédigés et réalisés par les soldats eux mêmes dans les tranchées de l'Est de la France, pendant la Première Guerre mondiale.

L'adjonction d'outils facilitant la recherche

Il s'agira, le moment venu, d'examiner la possibilité de numériser des outils existants (tables, index, annuaires de la presse) et de les mettre en relation avec le corpus de presse numérisée. Nous pensons, par exemple, aux Tables du *Temps* ou au fichier par sujets du journal *Le Matin*, sur lequel travaille actuellement un chercheur.

En la matière, la réalisation d'un projet majeur constituerait un instrument capital pour l'histoire de la presse et l'histoire tout court : la numérisation de la Bibliographie de la presse française politique et d'information générale (BIPFPIG), qui identifie et localise dans les bibliothèques et archives, département par département, la presse de cette nature.

Le chantier de numérisation de la presse rétrospective, désormais engagé par le Bibliothèque nationale de France et dont les premiers résultats seront visibles dès le début 2006, ne se conçoit déjà, comme on l'a vu, que dans une coopération avec certains journaux et certaines bibliothèques en France.

Il est clair qu'il se prêterait particulièrement bien à une coopération internationale. Au moins deux axes de partenariat et d'ouverture se dessinent dès à présent :

- la dimension francophone, avec notamment la perspective de la mise en relation du programme de la BnF et de l'initiative de la Bibliothèque nationale du Québec (dont la directrice siège au Conseil scientifique de la BnF) en matière de numérisation de la presse des deux pays ;

- la dimension européenne, avec le projet de création d'une bibliothèque numérique européenne, soutenu par l'Union et plusieurs de ses pays membres et dans laquelle la presse devrait, selon nous, tenir une place capitale.

10 BILLION WORDS: THE BRITISH LIBRARY BRITISH NEWSPAPERS 1800-1900 PROJECT

Some guidelines for large-scale newspaper digitisation

Jane Shaw

The British Library, London, UK

Abstract

The British Library (BL) decided that comprehensive chronological coverage across the whole of the nineteenth century was the key to their project, and as the holder of the ‹master collection›, the real challenge would be to convert a large volume of text into a searchable online resource knowing that very little is out there in terms of «mass of content».[1] The lessons learnt half way through the ‹British Newspapers 1800-1900› (BN) project argue that in order to digitise a large volume of historic newspapers to the highest possible quality, it is necessary to take the planning time to know the characteristics of your source material and to adequately resource your team from the outset. Existing agreed standards for digitisation from microfilm are defined but not fully followed.[2] The BL therefore set about to establish some standards for filming for large-scale newspaper digitisation and guidelines for best practice.

Problems with both the source material and the digitisation process prompted certain decisions. These decisions included:

- *Setting aside very poor condition volumes.*

- *Condition survey/assessment of source material to act as a benchmark.*

- *Refilming as a platform for digitisation, filming one page per frame to ensure a consistent look.*

- *Only digitising from microfilm for speed, consistency and cost.*

- *Human intervention to aid condition checks, page by page collation and simplified article zoning.*

- *Open source software solution that can be repurposed*

Other points that have been considered in depth are the design of an interface for access to newspapers, how much metadata should be incorporated, and what kind of searches should be enabled.

Introduction

This paper derives from a series of reports commissioned by our funder JISC (Joint Information Systems Committee) and from our experience of developing ‹British

---

1 See OCLC.
2 For a full description of this issue, see: *RLG Guidelines for Microfilming to Support Digitization*, January 2003. See also, IFLANET, Newspapers Section, *Microfilming for Digitisation and Optical Character Recognition*, December 2002.

Newspapers 1800-1900 Project.› (BN) The paper attempts to answer some basic questions about the practical and technical processes involved in the creation of a mass of searchable online newspaper content from microfilm images. Will the entire content of each newspaper be digitised, such as adverts, pictures or only selected articles? What navigation tools will be available; (will readers be able to ‹turn pages›, will there be keyword searches?) What is the impact of using microfilm produced for one purpose i.e. preservation, for another purpose – digitisation? How does pre-sorting, testing and benchmarking the source material, set the foundations for unimpeded online access to previously difficult-to-access material? The paper reports on how realistically we planned the project. It describes our decision-making and the cost components for filming to high technical quality standards to yield high quality digitial images and improved OCR.

Background

Early in 2004, the British Library secured funding from JISC.[3] Under the Digitisation Programme, funded with a £10 million grant from the Comprehensive Spending Review, JISC enabled a small number of large-scale digitisation projects that would bring significant benefits to UK Further and Higher Education communities, one of which is British Newspapers 1800-1900 (BN) project.

The JISC selection criteria for funding under the Digitisation programme were:

• The materials should be of broad disciplinary interest and form a coherent theme or themes.

• A small number of large-scale projects should be funded that would not be possible without an investment of this size.

• The materials would need to be fully compatible with the common information environment.

• The materials would need to meet rigorous quality-assurance standards and be of value to the wider post-16 education community.

The project was funded to deliver the following – the scanning of the entire microfilmed content; article zoning and page extraction; OCR of the page images; and the production of the required metadata. The main objectives are to digitise up to two million pages of British national, regional and local newspapers, the majority from new microfilm and to offer access to that collection via a sophisticated searching and browsing interface on the Web.[4] This will include names and dates, obituaries, advertisements, regional perspectives and local perspectives to national news.

Aims of the project and how they have guided the selection of newspaper titles

Both the overall goal of the project;

• to provide a mass of historic newspaper content on the web for full text searching by academic communities;

---

3 The JISC agreed to support the project from April 2004 to September 2006 at a total cost of £2,022,131. See: http://www.jisc.ac.uk
4 BL Business Plan, 14 October 2003.

And the main aim,

• to digitise up to 2 million pages of out-of-copyright UK printed material, regional and local newspapers, the majority from new microfilm and to offer free access to that collection via a sophisticated searching and browsing interface on the web

have not changed in the last year. The project plan however does differ from the original business case in the following main areas;

1. The balance of new filming has increased from 50% to 90%, to enable consistency of images.

2. Filming one page per frame for optimum digitisation.[5]

3. Introduction of an in-house Quality Assurance Team to prepare and repair the volumes, collect both issue level and condition level metadata and filter out duplicates, variants; and identify missing pages, issues, and the last timed edition at the start of the project.

4. Placing an academic User Panel at the core of the project to steer selection of newspapers and advise on the website design.[6]

5. Introduction of two Pilots to survey the physical characteristics of the nineteenth century newspapers, to agree on a methodology for the supply of microfilm and to confirm that specifications are yielding the desired end product, including image quality and OCR results.[7]

Selection Constraints

The original business plan included a preliminary list of many titles, at least 160; split into London national dailies and weeklies; English regional dailies and weeklies; Home Countries newspapers (Scottish national, Scottish regional, Welsh, Northern Irish) and ‹specialist sub-clusters›. For copyright reasons, and to keep within the scope of the original project brief, only dates between 1800-1900 were selected. However, in the early stages of the selection, additional constraints arose. Owners of incorporated[8] titles still publishing could have objected even if pre-1900 issues are clearly out of copyright. Owners of titles still publishing may be digitising or have plans to digitise their back runs (e.g. *Guardian, Daily Telegraph*) and it would not make economic sense to duplicate their efforts.

Surprisingly, very little information was available about how many pages each title represented and in order to keep to the project schedule a decision was made to start with a Pilot of a discrete specialist sub-cluster such as the Chartists followed by the first work batch which included obvious titles (e.g. *Examiner, Morning Chronicle, Graphic*). At the same time, an audit into the pagination and condition began of further likely candidates for selection from the preliminary list.

Notwithstanding the above constraints, the User Panel still decided to assess the value of all of the titles from the original list (the long list) from the perspective of potential usage by the HE/FE community.

---

5 There is variable density within images and within exposures on existing two pages per frame films.
6 Although a complete beginner would have been a useful member to advise as a layperson who just wants to browse.
7 Reference: Jane Shaw, *JISC Development Programmes, January 2005 Progress Report*
8 Newspapers published in the nineteenth century can be incorporated in extant newspapers

From the User Panel's prioritised list, a ‹wish list› emerged which was sub divided into coherent bundles or work packages. Four work packages have been selected to date and comprise approx. 2 million pages in total. The Work Packages follow a logical mix of UK wide coverage and nationals with regionals. Work Package 1 includes the Pilot work (The Chartist sub-cluster), plus three national titles – a daily, a Sunday and a weekly review. Work Package 2 extends the coverage to include three regional titles, North of England, far South West and central. Work Package 3 continues the national press with one Sunday, one daily, introduces Scotland and Ireland and continues with the English regional press. Work Package 4 continues to extend UK coverage, with Ireland, Scotland and Wales and enhances the English regionals.[9]

Online Consultation and User's Needs

The relevance to actual or potential users needs has been determined not only by an academic panel to inform the selection, but also validated through the exercise of an online questionnaire.

An online consultation with the wider academic community took place during February - March 2005, specifically on the titles to be included within the BN project and also to ascertain what titles should be included if future funding became available either to extend the BN project or pursue new projects. 195 people replied and of these, the majority were from librarians and lecturers working mainly in Universities and FE colleges, with a spread of researchers, students, managers and teachers. Surprisingly, 13% were replies from USA.

The questionnaire asked users to rank in order of priority for digitising (1 = strongly disagree, 5 = strongly agree), the titles from the long list in the business plan. In addition, we asked them to offer comments on any other titles they may want which were not listed.

Overall, it was clear that the replies endorsed the approach for UK wide coverage and the methodology adopted (i.e. a framework of national titles and countrywide coverage with the breadth and depth to form a virtual key to provincial newspapers in any medium). It was also clear that the omission of newspapers from Eire was causing concern.[10] This is being re-evaluated by JISC.

Some Portraits of Newspaper Titles Selected

Morning Chronicle: A London daily. Under the editorship of John Black, the young Charles Dickens was a reporter, and Thackeray worked as an art critic.

---

9   See Appendix 1 for our list of selected titles.
10 E.g. *«This is a long overdue project, which has the capacity to transform research on this period. It will make a big difference to Open University history teaching. Ideally, the papers chosen will offer a good geographical, political and chronological spread.»* *«Given that newspapers such as the Limerick Chronicle or the Cork Examiner or the Dublin papers of the 19th century were in cities that were part of the United Kingdom, why are none such newspapers included in your project? From an historian's point of view, such an omission is highly illogical and produces an unrepresentative selection. Any chance a few of the major Irish papers might be included in this very interesting and highly promising project?»* *«Digitized newspapers are a wonderful resource for History departments. They facilitate independent research and learning, which all of us encourage, via a format, which students enjoy. This is especially welcome given the pressure on library books and journals following increases in student numbers in recent years.»*

Reynolds Newspaper: Achieved sales of more than 350,000 by the early 1870s. In origin a radical newspaper, it remained in control of the Reynolds brothers until 1894.

Poor Man's Guardian: founded by Henry Hetherington in 1831 to further the cause of universal suffrage and the trade union movement. Offices raided in 1835 by courts and their presses seized and destroyed.

Cobbett's Weekly Political Register: William Cobbett founded this paper in 1802, to further his parliamentary career. Tory in outlook initially but gradually became more radical.

Birmingham Daily Post: The Birmingham Daily Post was launched in 1857 by Irishman John Frederick Feeney as a Monday to Friday Paper of four pages and priced at one penny. It is still published.

Belfast Newsletter: founded in 1737, for almost two hundred years the Henderson family was closely associated with the newspaper. It is still published.

Copyright

The BL is in continual discussion with publishers, including newspaper publishers, on a range of IPR issues, covering the life cycle management of information – from acquisition to access to preservation.

The Library policy is to proceed with the agreement of rights holders and their representative bodies. In the case of newspapers, recent discussions with newspaper publishers and updated legal advice to the Library means that for this project, the starting point is that no newspaper less than 100 years old will be digitised for access by HE and FE.[11]

How the Project was shaped by problem solving

Deliverables

The project will deliver up to 2,000,000 pages, totalling approximately 10,000,000,000 words from British newspapers 1800-1900. This equates to around 40 titles.

The digitisation process will deliver an archival master file for each page, in TIFF format, version 6.0. These files will be scanned effectively at a resolution of 300 dpi, 8-bit greyscale.[12]

The service images will be created after the process of article zoning and OCR. The service copies will be delivered as greyscale hybrids, TIFF version 6.0, and as JPEGs. Many of the newspaper titles were filmed on acetate and before National Preservation Standards were adopted systematically (1990). In order to yield highest quality images and to save on costs in the longer term, best practice was to control the quality of the microfilm from the start and to aid elimination of many postproduction queries. Thus reducing QA workload and providing the supplier with a uniform benchmark and a consistent look.[13] The addition-

---

11 The Chair of the User Panel has suggested that ‹Holes in the Selection Process› could be addressed by a longer term licensing agreement such as buying in other licensed sources and by creating relationships with commercial companies.

12 This is less than the 400dpi that the Library of Congress recommends. BL chose 300 dpi because a higher resolution only gives a significant increase in file size, particularly for greyscale and OCR quality does not improve above 300 dpi, and that on-screen resolution is usually between 72 and 100 dpi.

13 It also placed the responsibility for the later quality assurance squarely with the supplier.

al work of collating duplicates and missing pages, condition survey work and collecting issue level metadata was seen to be the more effective and of best value in the longer term for microfilm scanning.

If organisations do not want to refilm and decide to use their existing stock, because it is more time efficient or within policy, there is still likely to be a cost, at the end of the process and more under the control of the suppliers. Disbinding the newspapers was not an option and when new state of the art Zeutschel microfilm cameras were introduced into the BL Microfilm Unit, the project benefited from new technology by re-filming bound volumes using spine bars as needed, and not under glass. The Library is not trying to correct the printer's errors or areas of missing text. Facsimile images stored as greyscale master files can easily be repurposed and/or disaggregated for many future projects. BN project team decided it would be valuable if the information could be viewed in context, as originally published, and with a full-page image.[14] In addition, the three selection criteria of: complete runs of each newspaper, UK wide coverage and spanning the whole of the nineteenth century would provide substantial access to news stories by ‹simple› search terms.

The project is not about digitising eighteenth century issues or variant editions, nor are the rich resources of British Colonial newspapers included. Only the latest timed edition of each issue is being filmed and some occasional supplements e.g. «*The Graphic*» *Stanley Number,* 30 April 1890. BL made these decisions in order to keep duplication of effort to a minimum and to include the maximum number of original pages in our two million total. The User Panel created by the Project also decided that it wished to have as much coverage of different newspapers as possible. This is preferred to including variant editions.

From other digitisation projects in the BL, there is an awareness of issues surrounding both the preservation and digitisation of newspapers, and knowledge of strategies for digitizing them. This paper describes how the BN project team made an informed decision about the appropriate strategy for this particular project. The density of nineteenth century texts makes machine identification of breaks between articles a more difficult task thus requiring a balance between automatic metadata generation and human intervention. Working with a supplier with many years experience, the BL took the view that human intelligence would give the best quality result and therefore shaped the project around computer assisted/human intelligence throughout the whole cycle.

Due to the shape of the project the per page cost for digitisation is estimated at,

100% dupe from existing film = 75 p per page

100% new filming = 98 p per page

Moreover, this is in line with the original budget, (£1 per page).

Physical Characteristics of the source material, underlying problems and how these could affect the digitization process

BL holdings of Newspapers

In common with other large collections of historic newspapers, BL's holdings are predominantly bound together in volumes. Generally, this was seen to be the best method to pre-

---

14 This decision was revisited and is discussed in detail under Digitisation Issues.

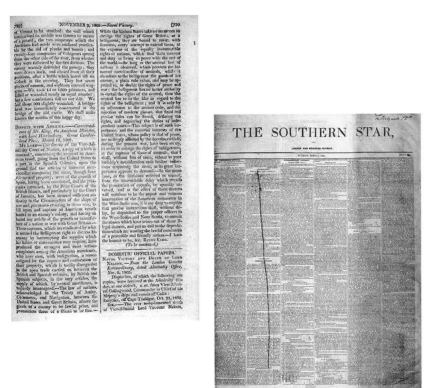

serve them against the effects of long-term handling. Due to the nature of the bindings, some volumes are very tightly bound and others have started to disintegrate leading to damage around the edges of the pages and consistently within the end papers.

There are two problems due to the way the newspapers are bound, the text being bound into the spine and the curvature of the papers towards the spine. Text can be lost during filming due to gutter shadow, text can be skewed, and this may affect the percentage of the last column that can be OCR-ed. Other examples of problems the OCR will have to overcome include; problems with «set through», (able to see the printing on the reverse of the page through the paper), often due to poor quality paper, heavy inking or a combination of the two, and printers errors due to paper slippage or creased/folded paper causing breaks in the font during printing. The OCR engines could have problems in overcoming these errors and in recognising complete words.

A further complication is, duplicate issues and variant editions are usually bound in together and different titles can be mixed in the same volume. For this project, only using the last timed edition, variants and duplicates had to be weeded out. We decided to hand weed at the initial preparation stage rather than later pre-or-post scanning.

Early nineteenth century newspapers reveal a significant amount of printer's errors, (e.g. a page creased during printing results in text loss when the crease is ironed out). There is also the appearance of the hyphenated word, mainly found at the end of 2 column newspaper texts.[15] Formats and structure change frequently and unexpectedly, from a 4-page issue to a 6-page issue, the order of the content often switched, the appearance of the «editorial essay» invested with the signature of the editor and sudden style changes from a «Two-Penny Trash» to a broadsheet. They represent a rich resource in the history of print and the development of radical argument and opinion is reflected through innovations in typography and layout. They also represent a significant challenge to the OCR, which prefers even text layout, even tone and larger print. We did not accept significant loss of text from gutter shadow or uneven density film from old laminated pages.

BL holdings of Microfilm

It is within BL policy to use existing film and to complete gaps in master negative or dupe runs, to avoid double handling of the collections. However, a high proportion of the BN selected titles are on early acetate. The worse the condition of the film, the longer it takes to copy, thus reducing output and increasing unit costs.[16] In addition, the existing microfilm is too variable for a steady workflow, comprising acetate, pre National Preservation Standard polyester, post standard polyester and post 2004 new camera standard and there may be additional quality problems and post production costs due to this mix of unsuitable film. Overall, the BL decided that managing complicated workflows due to the different speed work steams to match the mix of variable film, could lead to unacceptable delays and compromised quality.

The existing stock of film may include duplicate issues and all variant editions for any bound title, as historically this was haphazard and the current policy is to film the latest timed edition, which is in accordance with the project. A scanning operator would have to learn which parts of the film to scan and which to ignore. To overcome these problems, the BL decided that for this digitisation project, where condition and binding of the material allows, the BL Microfilm Unit on the new cameras would film most newspapers in-house. Most of the pages have been clipped to keep them flat during filming. This may look odd and appear as black if we are presenting a facsimile image of the page to users. Nearly every reel has a splice and this is because of missing pages identified at the checking stage of production or retakes due to various technical problems. These have been areas of concern.

---

15 Particularly relevant to *Cobbett's* and *The Examiner* where the page layout is two columns per page and words are hyphenated at the end of the line rather than a larger than usual space being left and the full word printed on the next line. What will the OCR software make of both the layout of the page and the way the words are split?

16 The Burney Newspapers project proved it was possible to scan from older acetate, but with a high production cost.

Data Capture Sources

STATE	CONDITION	DECISIONS				
Microfilm Poor Quality	Newspaper Good	Refilm	Dupe	Scan	Enhance	
Microfilm Good Quality	Newspaper Poor	Dupe	Scan	Enhance		
Microfilm Poor Quality	Newspaper Poor	Set Aside	Select another title			
Microfilm Good Quality	Newspaper Good	Dupe	Scan	Reject	Refilm	Rescan
Microfilm Good Quality	Newspaper Good	Dupe	Scan	Enhance		

Reduction and Resolution

When filming the volumes the lowest possible reduction has been used, for example the *Pall Mall Gazette* was filmed at a reduction of 12x. Further to this, it is important to keep the same reduction throughout an entire reel. However, this has not always been possible due to some titles containing fold out illustrations within the pages. The wide range of titles selected, mean that some of the physically larger volumes have been filmed at a higher reduction, up to 20x in some cases. It is worth noting that we have only used full reductions (i.e. no half reductions used).

Despite the concerns over using high reductions, we are achieving some very good resolution figures. In some cases readings of 140 LPM (lines per millimetre) are being regularly achieved, this is further enhanced by tight control of density readings.[17]

Procurement

Due to the likely cost of the digitisation contract being over £153,376 we were subject to OJEU procurement rules which is a lengthy process involving much learning.[18] The whole process took approximately one year, from request for proposals through to signing of contract.

---

17 The resolution used is a minimum of 115 LPM (lines per millimetre) and the reduction is set by the material that is being filmed, although the material is filmed at the lowest possible reduction, depending on the size of the original. We have pages that vary from A4 through to broadsheet. The quality control is done frame by frame for image quality, with each roll tested for resolution and density using a microscope and densitometer. We also use a Quality Control Sheet for each roll of film that documents all the technical information for that roll and any future generations.

18 The Official Journal of the European Union, an advertisement is placed inviting interested companies to complete and submit a questionnaire. A very thorough RFQ, or request for proposals, produced 26 expressions of interest, from which a short-list of six potential suppliers was made and three companies went through to Best and Final Offer stage (BAFO).

All of the potential suppliers offered us the suggestion of later high-level conversion. They could all scan and OCR the pages, scan OCR with highlighting of searchable terms, scan, OCR highlighting and viewing the page, but only one could scan, zone, OCR, check and repair zoning and re-key headlines as necessary within a reasonable budget. There was no ability anywhere to present a «completely» clean OCR file.

Learning from the first year of Operation

What we would do again and what we would do differently if we were to start again.

* Preparation is the key: in depth survey and assessment of the physical characteristics of source material to set a benchmark for later QA.

* Page counting and weeding out of duplicate issues and variant editions necessary to produce our work packages and monitor progress against our overall total.

* The format of a long run will often change during a century, so page counting is vital to understand the structure of a long run.

* Place a User Panel, at the core of the project, to act as ambassadors and take ownership.

* Define criteria for selection early on to guide User Panel deliberations.

* Intellectual Property Rights – address issues early, take a robust and consistent approach and maintain an ongoing dialogue with the newspaper industry.

* Conduct an online consultation with user communities during the funding process. A large potential list of titles meant we could not focus.

* User Panel preselected our potential 2 million pages, followed by an online consultation that did not suggest completely new and untried titles apart from Eire ones, so work could start.[19]

* Consider concept of ‹Set Asides› – titles too fragile to film as benchmarks for the future. Tolerate and accept gaps in full runs and do not seek to fill these until later on.[20]

* Consider the quality of your microfilm [refilming a proportion of your content will add value in the longer term] in order to adapt many of the risks around heterogeneous originals and variable quality microfilm which should in turn aid image capture.[21]

* The BL's collection of nineteenth century newspapers is in better shape than predicted, less than 2% unfit to film. However, due to the mechanical processes of scanning (too slow and too harsh for vulnerable fragile source material) it was decided to digitise from microfilm.

* Manage future expectations through online endorsement of titles lists by user communities.

* Aspirational production targets do not work. Sustainable targets based on real work done to date should be regularly reviewed and reprofiled as necessary to forecast trends.

---

19 It could be argued that the consultation should have happened earlier, before the Pilot began, but this was prohibited by the possibility of IPR challenges and conversely the best time to consult with the larger communities could be seen to after piloting some of our assumptions.

20 There have been very few poor condition volumes set aside so far, less than 2%, considerably less than forecast in the business plan. We were able to redeploy conservation money into funding a QA team and refilming.

21 BL benefited from new technology. Better images from new cameras because lighting is consistent, the gutter of tightly bound volumes is handled via beds that can be raised and the pages are not filmed under glass, just clipped where necessary.

- Use «Doubles» or intentional second exposures as a quality assurance technique, after weighing this up in relation to efficient workflows.[22]

Some Digitization Issues

What standards?

We are following some rigid standards e.g. METS, a metadata encoding and transmission standard and BSI standard for microfilming.[23] We believe we will have well formed metadata using people working with original pages and from good quality microfilm, which provides authentication.

The BL requires Dublin Core descriptive metadata records compliant to the British Library Application Profile (BLAP) with the elements encoded as XML and finally an OAI-PMH data provider service as a means to meet our interoperability requirements.

Levels of metadata

There will be four structural levels, title, issue, page and article. Within the title level metadata, there is any changes to the title, publication date, type and sub collection all captured captured by the BL QA team. Issue level metadata comprises, issue number, printed date, normalised date, number of pages and reel identity number.

Additonal metadata that will be provided in the XML files includes:

- Date of Issue in standard ISO format.
- Quality rating, (A, B, C) on condition of original material.
- BL copyright statement.
- BL copyright year.
- Conversion credit.
- Placeholder tags for table and illustration credits.
- Placeholder tags for author names.

Greyscale Hybrids versus bitonal

Pages scanned as 8-bit greyscale appear softer, with finer detail and subtler greys, particularly beneficial for text and illustrations and truer-to-source archival images. Speckling interference is reduced, superior deskewing and a higher OCR accuracy with a resolution of 300 dpi.

The project is developing a new product, a hybrid image, to optimise the quality of the images as well as the text. Text areas are converted to bitonals, sharpened using an enhanced version of IZ-Image, and saved to greyscale along with untouched greyscale images of illustrations. These reconstructed hybrids are the service copies that will be accessed via the website. The main disadvantage of this method is a ten-fold increase in

---

22 This is a requirement of BL standards, that the page to be doubled is filmed at the normal exposure and then filmed at the new exposure. The digitisation supplier has the job of choosing the best quality image post scanning.

23 BS ISO 4087 (1991)

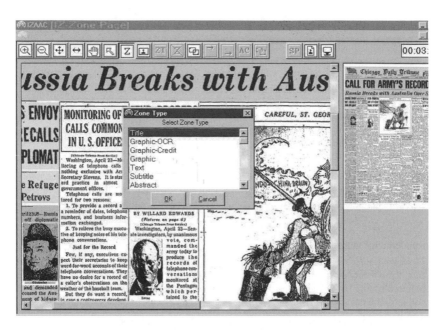

Selecting the 1st zone of an article

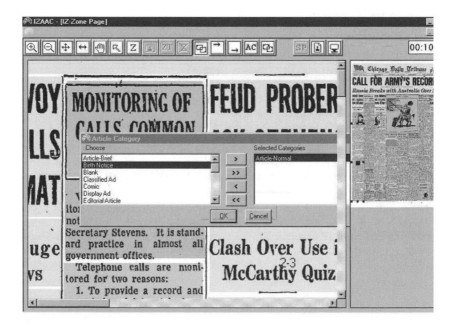

Assigning article category

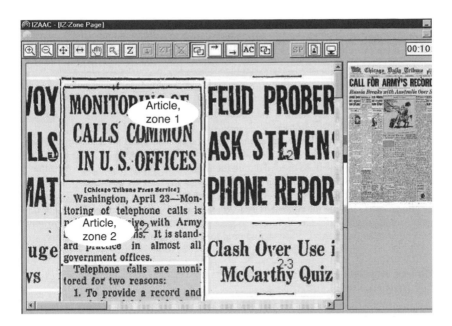

Selecting zones in reading order

Linking of multi-page articles

image size, which could increase our storage costs and cause problems for 56k modem users. As future users will be mainly broadband and costs are acceptable, the project team accepted the concept of greyscale hybrids.[24]

Of course, there needs to be an exact concordance between the master file and service copy images

Cropping

We felt there was a need to balance legibility and completeness and for the master files to represent as accurately as possible the visual content in the original pages. An object image or archival master file will be created during the initial scan from the microfilm by cutting the black borders away from the entire imaged object on a frame-by-frame basis. The page image, to be used for the full-page service copy, is created by cropping the object image to a uniform border around the content of each page, thus removing any unsightly clips or targets. Any impression of scale or changes to page sizes could be lost due to this uniformity, but on the other hand, this method should produce images optimised for web delivery.

Hit term Highlighting

The project does not want to have inaccurate word highlighting and hence a poorer user experience. This will be displayed on the page and is under development now.

Articles without titles

An instance where this is prevalent is in categories such as advertisements, notices, obituaries etc. It was decided that where a category cannot serve as a title, a title would be constructed from the first couple of lines of text.

Deskewing

The human eye will simply address this. Images are de-skewed until they appear straight to the inspector and as very image is inspected prior to OCR this is acceptable. In addition, greyscale images can be corrected up to 10 degrees of skew, whereas bitonal images with as little as 1 degree can affect the quality of the OCR levels.

Article vs. page level

Page images will consist of both articles with search terms highlighted, once completed and full pages. Users will be able to view the page images associated with any of their search matches.

---

24 An idea currently under discussion is for users to be able to view the uncorrected OCR text to «repurpose» within their Virtual Learning Experience (VLE)

Recommendations for Subject Categories

With such a mass of words to search on and an unprecedented degree of crossreferencing the project is also providing users with straightforward article categorisation, allowing a way into the material to enrich searching by key words.

Our recommendations for subject categories are,

1. News (Domestic); items relating to the UK

2. News (Foreign); items relating to the rest of the world

3. Advertisements & Notices; ranging from items for sale to situations vacant to Public notices. Differentiated from news items by format.

4. Arts & Popular Culture; Reviews of books, music & the theatre. Poems and serialised fiction. Items relating to travelling shows & fairs.

5. Births, Deaths & Marriages; announcements made regarding each.

6. Obituaries; specific items relating to the death of someone with a biography of that person.

7. Court & Society; relating to the Royal family and the aristocracy.

8. Crime and Punishment; Reports from the various courts, sessions and assizes.

9. Commerce; business and shipping news, market & Stock Exchange Tables.

10. Letters; usually written to the Editor and printed in part or in full.

11. Sports; items covering a range of sporting topics.

12. Editorial/Comment; items usually, but not exclusively written by the editor on a particular topic or topics.

13. Miscellaneous; items that do not fit the above.

14. None; Default category.

15. Illustrations: without captions.

Steps in the Production Process

The simple steps in the project that the BL is following and hopes will enhance access to historical newspapers are,

1. Condition survey: of holdings of source material to understand the structure and to identify underlying problems. Tight bindings causing gutter shadow, how to handle foldouts and supplements, duplicate issues included in films, titles split across different reels and mixed in with other titles.

2. Collation: The results of the survey were collated and used to aid the selection process and the procurement of a supplier. These results included the number of pages per issue, the differences between nationals and weeklies, changes to structure across full runs, page layout, fonts across the century and the general condition of the microfilm stock.

3. Selection: A list of titles was selected using simple straightforward criteria endorsed by the user communities.

4. Microfilming: Tightly bound volumes, poor condition volumes, and sub standard microfilm were treated on a case-by-case basis as to whether to ‹set aside› the sub standard volume or microfilm or to work with them.

5. Microfilming: A quality assurance system was built using the results of the surveys at the start of the project and tolerances set for ‹set asides›, clarity and legibility.

6. Microfilming: A decision was taken on how much to refilm if at all following microfilm quality levels which had been agreed.

7. Batch Definitions: Assumptions were tested in two pilots, one for each work stream and that each were large enough to deliver valid results.

8. Procurement: In order to grow a critical mass of historic newspaper content in the future, both nationally and internationally we knew we had to procure an open source technical solution.

9. Digitisation: scanning from microfilms; generation of greyscale images, QC, perform manual cleanup or not, QC, archive master files.

10. Digitisation: run IZ-Image character sharpening, load complete issue, zone and categorise articles, QC.

11. Digitisation: link multi-page articles, perform OCR and clean up fielded metadata, generate deliverables.

Costs

How much will it cost an institution or an individual to use? The current proposal under consideration is that the project is looking at ‹free access› to everyone on the Web after Spring 2007, so usage may be free.

Future and Legacy

Will the online ‹stock› be expanded in the future? Due to copyright and IPR issues, it is likely that future projects will select older materials that are out of copyright. There is an urgent need for some form of register or information network of what has been selected for digitisation and what has been worked on that can be checked against before other libraries start to digitise their collections. With the data created from this project, the BL will be in a good position in future projects to predict what the cost per page will be as all the costs in our project have been analysed.

Summary

The BN project team has spent the last year assessing each of the selected newspaper titles and their associated microfilms for the purpose of digitisation; selecting a final list of up to 40 titles, which were endorsed via an online consultation with academic communities, and appointing a digitisation supplier. The in-house teams have prepared and filmed 650,000 pages since October 2004 and are on course to have completed 1 million frames by September this year. Both the Quality Assurance (QA) and Microfilm Unit (MU) teams work to daily and weekly targets. [25]

The coming year (until September 2006), will see a change of focus, with the start up of both digitisation and website development work streams in parallel with the inhouse preparation and filming work.

---

25 See Appendix 2.

The project will continue to follow a rolling review methodology[26] within a subset of PRINCE 2,[27] where we are learning about the source material and the technology as we progress. A User Panel having finished their selection task, have changed role to driving and defining potential user's needs, and commented on the design of the website, prior to an early release of a demonstrator for testing early in 2006.

A phased release of the website is likely to begin in September 2006.

BL have also placed human input at the core of the project by introducing a quality assurance team to screen out duplicate issues and variant editions, harvest issue and condition level metadata before filming. In addition, collaborating with an academic User panel to steer which 2 million pages out of a possible 200 plus million to select for digitisation.

The consistency of this approach extends to the choice of supplier, whose content extraction methodology uses computer assisted/human intelligence and has innovated in article categorisation and keyword indexing. What users will have are:

- full text searching of 2 million pages of newspaper texts.

- the ability to search individual newspapers by date.

- like-for-like comparisons of the same subject's treatment by different titles.

- browsing forwards and backwards through a selected issue.

- images of the original pages to read in the usual way.

- it should be possible to save and build searches, to aid in course teaching and collaborative working.

- display of the results of searches at the article level within the context of the original page.

- the ability to search advertisements, obituaries etc.

- the ability to download text versions of the original pages.

- An anticipated 80% accuracy on the OCR conversion.

Value can be added to variable source material in less than pristine condition and even with a poorly printed original, you should still aim for the best image you can get.

In conclusion, the BN Project is an initiative which has already enhanced the Library's understanding of many issues that digitisation raises. The BL looks forward to its successful conclusion, and, most importantly, that the content will find a wide audience.

---

26 This is the JISC preferred methodology for their projects.
27 PRINCE 2 is a product based project management methodology.

CONNECTING TO THE PAST – NEWSPAPER DIGITISATION IN THE NORDIC COUNTRIES

Majlis Bremer-Laamanen

Helsinki University Library, Mikkeli, Finland

Newspaper collections are targets that have a great demand on the Internet from researchers as well as the public at large. Our digitised historical newspaper collections and the born digital ones are connecting the users to places, questions, nations and human life over centuries. Incidents from the past are suddenly easily accessible. The past is living in the present.

Today I will talk about newspapers in Finland. I will also give an update on the Historical Nordic Newspaper Project – one of the pioneers in digitising historical newspapers.

Newspapers

Newspapers are perhaps astonishingly, still the most important media in Finland. The Norwegian national library tells us that Norway is the country with the largest newspaper reading population. We can say that newspapers have a very high status in all the Nordic countries.

All over the world newspapers have adjusted to new sources of media like radio, movies and television. Today they face «ghosts» like the Internet. How much will the new Internet behaviour interfere with the life of today?

Way of life in Finland

The average use of newspapers in Finland is almost an hour per person per day and it has not diminished.[1]

The daily paper is a way of life. It is delivered to your front door in the morning, to be enjoyed with a cup of coffee or tea. It gives the reader a moment of peace and comfort together with the national and local news before the day starts. Free newspapers are delivered on the subways and trains on your way to work.

Media channels

The look and feel of many newspapers have changed in appearance to a modern outlook, tabloid format, actively reaching out to its customers and the youth at schools, delivering information, science, leisure and advertisements. Surprisingly perhaps, the heavy users of computers are heavy newspaper readers. Over ninety per cent of young Finns read a newspaper each week.[2]

---

1 www.sanomalehdet.fi/en/tietoa/index.html, page 2
2 www.sanomalehdet.fi/en/tietoa/index.html, page 3

Newspapers are the media channel that daily is best reaching the Finns. Hence, over half of all money spent on advertising is in the newspaper business. It is for example the major channel for information on stock exchange today.[3]

Newspapers are the most important research media for research in Finland. They are the prime source of investigation in more than half of the research projects in Finland and almost in half in Sweden. They are used as source material for research in the fields of media, history, political science, sociology, pedagogy, art, business, natural sciences and technology.[4]

As such the interest in our historical newspapers is high. Newspapers are the most used individual group of the Finnish national collection.

The role of online newspapers

Online newspapers are produced all over the world, also in the Nordic Countries. These papers are usually available via the National Libraries. We have about one hundred news-paper titles on the web among the 900 periodicals in Finland.

Surprisingly the role of the Finnish online paper is to support the paper version. Thus their monetary importance is still quite low. These papers are improving and the overall devel-opment in knowledge society will influence their use. Also paper look-alike editions of newspapers are available on the web in Finland since 2002.[5]

Converting large volumes today

John S. North's description of newspapers is relevant and sheds some light on the reasons for the rather late start for newspaper digitisation projects.

«Periodicals bibliography is a much neglected field, for understandable reasons. First, it is massive: periodicals easily outdo monographs in sheer volume of publication. Second, no clear definition of a periodical is generally accepted, and the working definition varies from library to library. Third, any one periodical is likely to change in some of its primary bibli-ographical elements from issue to issue (title, subtitle, format, editor, publisher, proprietor, frequency, printer, size, etc.). Moreover, periodicals are often considered ephemeral: stale news, cheap popular information, trivial records. In short, throw-aways. They are often poor quality paper, arriving in libraries unbound and in endless irregular succession, so are unwieldy to shelve and catalogue, and are seldom to be found in complete runs, seldom well indexed. They are the nightmares of librarians and bibliographers.» (John S. North: *The Waterloo directory of Scottish newspapers and periodicals 1800-1900*)

The newspaper holdings have been considered a nightmare for digitisation as well. The size of newspapers grew in the late 1900th century to four times the size of a tabloid of today. The poor print, the poor quality paper and the use of Gothic Fraktur and Roman text in the Nordic countries made a challenge for digitisation. Even more of a challenge was the Optical Character Recognition needed to make the text searchable from the image of the paper.

Digital newspaper projects are a new hot topic in Europe and around the world. The British Library is going to digitise and give free text search to 2 million pages. Austria and Estonia

---

3 *Hufvudstadsbladet*, 2005, April ; www.sanomalehdet/en/tietoa/index.fi, page 3
4 www.sanomalehdet.fi/suomenlehdistö/fi
5 www.sanomalehdet/en/tietoa/index.shtml, page 4

are well under way with their newspaper projects. The United States (The Library of Congress) is planning newspaper projects. So is also the National Library of Australia.

The Nordic Historical Newspaper Project – TIDEN

One pioneer in the field is the Nordic TIDEN project, starting in 1998 and launched on the web http://tiden.kb.se in 2001.

The libraries participating were the Royal Library of Stockholm, the National Library of Norway and the State and University Library of Århus. The coordinator for the project was Helsinki University Library, the Centre for Microfilming and Conservation.

The aim of the TIDEN-project was:

- to test criteria for microfilm as a platform for digitisation and full text search

- to build production lines for the digitisation of newspapers

- to integrate the digitisation to the libraries ordinary functions

- to give a continuous widening access to newspapers out of copyright

Today the amount of online pages has risen from 400,000 at launch to 1,6 million. In Finland, Sweden and Norway full text search is available.

Automation

When dealing with large collections like newspapers the production has to be as fully automated as possible. This was one of the aims when TIDEN started. The possibilities to do so are far better today than five years ago. Today we are changing our half automated processes to a faster automated process. We are working together with the Royal Library of Sweden to test and enhance their line and our production line. The Centre for Microfilming, Conservation and Digitisation of the Helsinki University Library – the National Library of Finland is situated in a smaller town Mikkeli in Eastern Finland. The Norwegian National Library in Mo and Aarhus Staatsbibliotek will also be able to follow up our results.

The process

The first step in the production line is the digitisation of newspapers, from microfilm or from the original. Newspapers have been a main target for the reformatting programmes in Finland, Sweden, Norway and Denmark since 1950. This makes it possible for us to use microfilm as intermediary for digitisation if the film quality is high enough.

The process of digitising newspapers includes

Microfilming	refilming the newspapers if the quality of the present microfilms is not good enough
Digitisation	scanning of the microfilms; in black and white or grey scale
OCR	conversion of the images to text files; requires many adjustments and training of the software.
Identification	of the title, issue, date, pages and attachments requires some human treatment
Database import	by a separate software

IFLA Guidance

When using microfilm as intermediary the quality of the original newspaper and the micro-film is the key to success.

Some advice is given in *Guidance on the best practice for microfilming of newspapers in preparation for possible future digitisation*. 2003. English, French, Spanish and Chinese versions are available on the IFLA-net.

The Guidance was based on the information gathered within the TIDEN project.

Information is also available on the TIDEN web-page at http://tiden.se.

Goals today

Our goals in Finland are to require:

- an industrial production environment
- an automated optical character recognition (OCR) of both Fraktur and Roman text even within a page
- highest possible quality
- highlighting of search words on the newspaper page
- cost effectiveness
- speed of the process
- xml-METS-standard (Library of Congress)

The results of the OCR-conversion in Finland and Sweden have shown that there are several factors influencing the quality of the conversion, the most important of them being the text font, language and reduction rate. From the very start of the TIDEN-project it was obvious that a hundred per cent OCR conversion is impossible. Due to the old language and the great mass of text proofreading was not our way to enhanced search. It was thus decided that the ASCII versions of the text would be used for searching purposes only.

The basic tool for the users was the digital facsimile of the original pages. A retrieval ware with fuzzy search possibilities was chosen in Sweden and Finland to identify the search words even if one to three letters would differ from the word sought for. The search tool processes the words as bit-strings and uses pattern recognition to find matches.

The speed and automation of the production environment is essential when comparing the process 5-8 years ago to the possibilities today. The automated processes offer the coordinates to each word in the paper. Thus users get better service as the words are highlighted. Other improvements are available. Images are of a better quality as the microfilm scanners and the OCR-software are able to handle greyscale images automatically. Previously, Roman text had to be especially trained for the OCR-software.

Now we are looking at a breakthrough where the text is interpreted automatically.

There are interesting vendors offering reasonable production automation environments on the market. Helsinki University Library and the Royal Library of Sweden tested one of them in 2004. The test period gave us very good information about the key issues for the new production line when carrying out a request for tenders.

If a suitable production environment could be established, we would like to use it for other digitised collections as well.

Connecting the past

In digital futures the digital collection management will be an exiting challenge. It is not enough to digitise our collections and put them on the web with enhanced search possibilities. The infrastructure around our collections is changing fast as well as the expectations of our users. We have to improve access in various ways, including automatic translation to our old holdings, including meeting places for users. We have to connect them to other people, to holdings in other heritage sectors and so on. We do have to make the decisions on the roles of libraries. We have to decide which services are free and which are not.

Today the Historical Newspaper Library in Finland has found its place. It is highly regarded among researchers especially in the field of history and languages. It has also found its way to the public at large via information in the media and from person to person. Many a person is doing some genealogy with the help of the newspaper library from home. Finnish immigrants are using the library, finding information on their families leaving Finland, following them to their new country. Last year 150,000 visits were recorded and 1,8 million pages were searched for. Still, we have to extend the use to education in schools.

People are very enthusiastic about the library. It is easy to use in its Google-like approach.

The users want more and we will try to meet their needs.

One future aim has been to coordinate search to the Nordic historical digital newspaper library. Perhaps also that could be a nice challenge for the future.

TRENDS OF NEWSPAPER DIGITIZATION IN CHINA

Yang Bin

Datum Data Company, Beijing, China

Abstract

As a representative of a leading data capture service provider in China, Datum Data Company, I am honored to be here and would like to thank IFLA for giving me the opportunity to share my thoughts with you today. Most of our recent work has been digitization of newspapers, including many historical newspapers, and books. I will first provide an overview of the latest trends of newspaper digitization in China. Then I will talk about technical challenges in newspaper digitization as well as the technical expertise of Datum Data Company

Continuing the theme of our presentation in this conference last year, I would like to provide an overview of the latest trends of newspaper digitization in China.

Trend No. 1: Rapid market growth in newspaper and library digitization

With the increasing awareness of the benefits from newspaper digitization, a growing number of news organizations are willing to make the investment. During the course of last year, we digitized more than 500,000 pages with over 3 billion characters.

We believe the digitization market will continue to grow for many years to come.

Trend No. 2: Emerging need for digital data transformation

The Founder publishing system – used by the majority of Chinese newspapers and books – is mainly designed for printing purposes, as opposed to data retrieval. Also, some newspaper advertisements provided by clients are in various formats and need to be reprocessed. Therefore, there are many technical challenges for adding the retrieval database.

Trend No. 3: Increasing usage of rough precision digital data

A growing number of clients choose to use PDF format, especially Double-layer PDF (images for reading, text for retrieving); DJVU format is often adopted in book digitization. These are examples of the increasing usage of rough precision text.

Trend No. 4: Increasing richness of annotation information

More and more clients choose to use rich annotation information. There is an increase from 3-4 annotation items previously to more than 10 annotation items. The following is a typical list of annotation items:

Newspaper name
Issue
Source

Title
Subtitle
Author
Date
Edition number
Edition of name
Column
Context
Types
Classification
Illustration
Illustration author
Illustration caption
Other comment

Trend No. 5: Increasing usage of statistical analysis

Special attention is paid to the usage frequency of popular words or phrases.

Trend No. 6: Internet-based data process

Because high-speed Internet access is readily available, an increasing number of data processing operations are conducted remotely, and data are transferred / exchanged via the Internet. Datum has established a dedicated web server for secured clients' data exchange.

We have digitized over 80 Chinese newspapers. Here are a few examples:

- *Hong Kong Ta Kung Pao* (http://www.takungpao.com) – full-text and full-image database of articles dating back to 100 years ago
- *Tibet's Daily* (http://www.tibetinfor.com) – multi-language (Chinese and Tibetan) full-text database of articles dating back to 45 years ago
- *Shanghai Wen Hui Bao* (http://www.whb.com.cn) – full-text database of articles dating back to 61 years ago
- *Shanghai Xin Min Wan Bao* (http://www.xmwb.com.cn) – full-text database of articles dating back to 70 years ago
- *People's Daily Overseas Edition* (http://www.rhwx.com) – full-text database of articles dating back to 15 years ago
- *Harbin daily* (http://www.harbindaily.com) – full-text database of articles dating back to 55 years ago

Here are the top challenges in Chinese newspaper digitization:

Challenge 1: complex layouts and mixed traditional and simplified Chinese characters

Typical layouts of a historical regional newspaper are as follows:

- Early 1950s – vertical stroke in traditional Chinese characters; complex format

- Mid 1950s – horizontal stroke in traditional Chinese characters
- Mid 1950s to End of 1960s – primarily horizontal stroke in mixed traditional and simplified Chinese characters; simple format
- 1970s to 1980s – type printing with different versions of simplified Chinese characters; simple format
- 1980s to 1990s – laser illumination; various formats
- Late 1990s to now – digitized data

Challenge 2: Severely damaged paper copies of historical newspapers

Paper copies of historical newspapers are often fragile, stained, and blurry. It is difficult to process and protect these paper copies.

Challenge 3: Huge amount of data

On average, we need to digitize over 100,000 pages for a regional newspaper. The size of delivered data with images is around 200GB, not to mention the huge amount of data generated during the process of digitization. If the delivered data is in PDF format, the size is even larger.

Challenge 4: Requirement of high data accuracy from clients

With the development of digitization, clients' requirements for accuracy are increasing. The error rate must be less than one ten thousandth for general context; one hundred thousandth to one millionth for important articles; one hundred thousandth for titles and names of the authors; and 0 for important names and addresses.

Challenge 5: Various types and incomplete original data

Original data are usually dispersed in various media (such as paper copies or digital data) and in various formats (such as PS, PDF, txt.). Some information is often missing in the original PDF pages, such as special symbols, graphs, tables, or advertisements. Txt files are often corrupted and lacking important articles.

I would like to talk about Datum's technical expertise, which enabled us to overcome many challenges in newspaper digitization and provide excellent services to our clients.

1. OCR technology

Datum is one of the few data capture service providers that use OCR technology in all phases of the data-processing operations. We deployed a precise pipeline data-processing factory based on Datum owned OCR technology. Our operation line can also integrate with other commercial OCR software.

2. Multi-Language Digitization Process

Datum is capable of processing data in many languages with high accuracy. We have extensive experience in digitization of documentations, newspapers, and books in various languages, including Chinese, English, French, Germany etc.

3. ISO9001 2000 certified quality-control process

Datum has developed a unique and ISO9001 2000 certified quality-control method, which enables us to guarantee the integrity, accuracy and uniformity of clients' data. Our superior quality-control process is the primary reason for our successful bid as Johnson & Johnson's service provider.

We have implemented the following new technologies:

- The recognition technology for degraded images
- Indexing technology

  Establish a universal database for the reference of general key words – clients can access the database anytime; establish a linkage among specified glossaries.

- Information retrieval from multi-database with multi-language cross-reference on a single platform

Datum has participated in the China-US joint Million Book Digital Library Project. This project will be completed next year. The Digital Library will be available in many universities.

Combining our technical expertise, the low-cost of Chinese labor force, and the convenience of high-speed Internet access, Datum can provide excellent digitization services to libraries worldwide. This is a true e-commerce.

http://www.datum.com.cn/
http://www.datumdata.com/
E-mail: Zhangyuzhi@datum.com.cn or   byang@vip.sina.com

IFLA SECTION ON NEWSPAPERS

Hartmut Walravens

Berlin State Library, Germany

In spite of its long and distinguished history IFLA has not focused its attention on newspapers. It was perhaps twenty years ago when a group of newspaper experts established a Round Table on Newspapers. Membership was informal, and colleagues met during the General Conferences. It was in 2002 that IFLA urged all Round Tables and discussion groups to make up their minds whether they wanted to become a section, assuming that their work was permanent, or be disbanded after two years. Serious newspaper work is more urgent than ever, and so the decision was easy: Since then there has been a Newspaper Section, at first ad interim, and as of 2005 as part of the normal IFLA routine. Thus Newspapers have become independent from their former parent body the Serials and Continuing Resources Section. There is a certain difficulty, however: There are few newspaper experts worldwide, and for a number of them it is impossible to attend the World Library and Information Congress, for lack of funding. So after a while it may become difficult to find suitable officers, not to speak of committee members!

Scope

The Section is concerned with all issues relating to newspapers in libraries and archives, including acquisition and collection development; intellectual and physical access; storage and handling; preservation of newspapers and their contents; interlibrary lending; and the impact of digital technologies on all of these.

As a new section we need membership

- institutional membership (IFLA members)

- nominations for members of the Section (newspaper experts)

The Section meets during the annual IFLA General Conference (World Library and Information Congress). It organises an event at this Congress, usually three presentations, often relating to the host country. The main business meeting takes place usually in spring and is combined with an international newspaper conference in order to promote outreach and cooperation. In addition the Section

- runs projects

- organises conferences (like IFLA Satellite Meetings)

- works out guidelines and publications

Current Activities

The 2004 Buenos Aires event focused on the subcontinent and offered three papers which led to vivid discussions. About 100 people attended the meeting; people apparently realized the importance of the subject for the region where libraries are notoriously underfunded and the preservation of and access to such materials is a major challenge. These are the titles of the contributions:

Alfonso Quintéro: *Digitalización de la Prensa Latinoamericána del Siglo XIX* (Digitalización de la prensa de la Gran Colombia 1820 a 1830)

Jorge Orlando Melo: *El Periodismo Colombiano antes de 1900: Colleciones, Microfilmaciones y Digitalizaciones*

Adán Benavides: *Las Noticias de Ayer para el Mañana: la Preservación de la Periódicos Mexicanos, 1807-1929*

We hope that the contacts established with ABINIA and the University of Texas may lead to a lasting cooperation.

The preparations for the 2005 Oslo event are completed:

The general theme is Digital Newspaper Projects in Europe, and three speakers have been recruited. In addition the Section is taking the opportunity of visiting the modern storage and processing facilities of the National Library of Norway and organizes a two-day symposium as a satellite meeting: Arctic Circle Preservation Meeting (Mo i Rana, Norway). Aug. 11-12, 2005 (together with the IFLA Preservation Section). In order to have a fruitful meeting, the number of participants have been limited to 30.

The previous Satellite Meeting took place in Berlin, and it focused on Newspapers in Central and Eastern Europe. It was an attempt to cover the whole field of newspaper development in the region, from the effect of the political and economic changes on newspaper publishing to access and digitization issues. The proceedings of the meeting were published in the IFLA Series.

For 2006 an International Digitisation Conference is projected to take place at Salt Lake City in order to profit from the considerable experience collected on the subject at the University of Utah. It is also a follow-up to the WLIC 2005 in Oslo where the Section will deal with the European experience. 2006 seems good timing for such a conference because both in the UK and the US major national progammes are now under way, and so first results may be reported and discussed at Salt Lake City.

Following its (recent) tradition the Section will also hold its 2006 business meeting at Salt Lake City. It has certainly be a funding issue for Section members to attend both the WLIC and the business meetings. On the other hand, the time slots at WLIC do not offer enough time to discuss all the current challenges and programmes. So it seems that those members who have other IFLA commitments will receive funding to attend WLIC while some other will receive support to attend the business meetings, especially when they are combined with international conferences.

This has been the case in recent years, and highly successful events took place in Cape Town (South African Library) in 2003, and the Shanghai Library (Shanghai tushuguan) in 2004. The present conference is the opportunity to extend the Section's activities to Australia and Oceania, and tap the region's expert newspaper knowledge.

A Hands-on Seminar on Newspaper Digitisation was conducted by the Centre for Microfilming and Digitisation of Helsinki University Library in 2003. It was a highly successful experience for eight participants to go through all the practical steps of digitisation, from the preparation of newspapers for microfilming, the filming itself, the processing of the data, the OCR application and the final steps until loading the files on the net. This unique seminar deserved to be repeated, especially as new software for text management is now being used, improved OCR software at hand. Thus major projects could be prepared more efficiently instead of leaving it to individual project managers to learn on the job first.

Publications

The Section has been good at publishing results of its work: *Guidelines for Newspaper Preservation Microfilming* were a major landmark when published. In the meantime both the technological development and the general trend towards digitisation might be an incentive to make slight revisions. In a way, the supplementary *The Guidelines for Microfilming for Digitisation and Optical Character Recognition* filled the gap already – it is quite obvious that the digitisation and OCR results depend heavily on the quality of the original microfilming.

The Sections *Newsletter* is published once or twice a year, depending on the information officer's time and capacity. There have also been several monographic publications:

Proceedings of the IFLA Symposium Managing the Preservation of Periodicals and Newspapers. Bibliothèque nationale de France, Paris, 21-24 August, 2000. Edited by Jennifer Budd, IFLA-PAC. München: Saur, 2002. 175 p. (IFLA Publications; 103)

Newspapers in International Librarianship. Papers presented by the Newspaper Section at IFLA General Conferences. München: K. G. Saur, 2003. 260 p. (IFLA Publications; 107)

Newspapers in Central and Eastern Europe. Zeitungen in Mittel- und Osteuropa. Papers presented to the Newspaper Section at the IFLA Post Conference, Berlin 2003. München: K. G. Saur, 2004. 251 p. (IFLA Publications; 110)

A new publication plan is to assemble the major contributions to the Section as a follow up to the 2003 volume. This would include also presentations from the Section's international conferences.

Projects are important but often difficult to undertake, for lack of funding. IFLA is in no position to provide adequate funding, and the Section members, of course, also have their day jobs. Nevertheless there are some official Section projects:

- African Newspapers (results of a survey), prepared by Else Delaunay.

- Basic Newspapers Handbook (currently no funding available). This would be highly desirable but has to be shelved, unfortunately.

- Newspaper Internet Links. This was started by Sandra Burrows, and it is intended to add to her data from other regions and language areas.

Cooperation

The Section is interested in extending its cooperation with other organisations. For obvious reasons it shares interests with IFLA PAC and the Preservation Section. Over the years contacts with ICON (International Coalition on Newspapers, Center for Research Libraries, Chicago) have been fruitful even if no direct cooperation project was started.

Germany

The major newspaper collections are kept in archives, not in libraries. Only one library – the Berlin State Library – has a separate newspaper department.

The legal deposit is with the regional libraries, not with the national library. The national library collects only major papers and those only in microform.

2005 marks the 400th anniversary of newspapers in Central Europe. A number of events are scheduled, e.g. a major conference at Mainz. The Berlin State Library is also preparing one (Nov. 2005).

A major newspaper cataloguing project is going on in Munich: newspapers in Bavarian libraries and archives are catalogued and listed in the German Union Catalogue of Serials (ZDB)

Finally a newspaper digitisation project is started (University of Bamberg, and Berlin State Library) – the press correspondence from Bismarck's times, a unique copy was found at the Berlin State Library. It is, however, a relatively small project and in no way comparable with the major Scandinavian, British and Austrian projects.

Current newspaper work is stimulated by the Newspaper Working Group (AGZ) which meets in spring and in autumn. The last meeting took place in Dresden and focused on electronic newspapers. The next one is scheduled for May to be held in Greifswald (on the Baltic coast) and will deal with the role of regional newspapers. There will be more than 30 participants while the more topical Dresden theme drew almost 60 people.

NATIONAL PLAN FOR
AUSTRALIAN NEWSPAPERS PROJECT

About the Project

The National Plan for Australian Newspapers (NPLAN) is a cooperative initiative established by the Council of Australian State Libraries (CASL) involving all State and Territory Libraries and coordinated by the National Library of Australia. The Plan was established in the early 1990's in recognition of the importance of newspapers as primary sources of historical information and a growing concern about the status and preservation of Australian newspapers.

The Plan aims to give all Australians access to the nation's rich newspaper heritage by locating, acquiring, preserving and making accessible all newspapers ever published in Australia. Under NPLAN each State and Territory Library is assuming primary responsibility for the newspapers published in their jurisdiction. Partners include the National Library of Australia, State Library of New South Wales, State Library of Victoria, State Library of Western Australia, State Library of South Australia, State Library of Queensland, State Library of Tasmania and the Northern Territory Library.

Strategies:

Strategies being undertaken as part of NPLAN include Acquisition, Public Access and Information, and Preservation programs. Each of these programs is outlined below.

Acquisition Program

One of the aims of the NPLAN project is to ensure that all partners collect hardcopies of newspapers published within their jurisdiction and identify, locate and collect missing issues.

For the purposes of NPLAN, a newspaper is defined as a publication issued on a regular basis designed to be a primary source of written information on current events connected with public affairs; either local, national, and/or international in scope.

A newspaper usually has the following characteristics:

- It is originally printed on newsprint
- It does not have a cover
- It has a masthead
- It has a format of not less than four columns per page
- It is usually A3 or greater in size

Legal Deposit

Legal Deposit is a statutory provision which obliges publishers to deposit copies of their publications in designated deposit libraries to ensure long term preservation of the publications for the use of future generations. In Australia, Legal Deposit is covered by both Commonwealth and State legislation and extends to newspaper publications.

However, not all issues of Australian newspapers, particularly early newspapers published prior to the introduction of Legal Deposit legislation, may be held by the appropriate libraries.

NPLAN partners are keen to locate missing issues of newspapers, as well as newspapers reflecting Australia's cultural diversity written in English or other languages, so as to ensure the long term preservation of a comprehensive collection of Australian newspapers.

Missing issues may be stored in private homes, community organizations, newspaper offices and local authorities. Listed below are some of the newspapers for which State and Territory Libraries would like to locate missing issues:

- *Bendigo Advertiser*, 1853-1856 (VIC)
- *Bulong Bulletin and Mining Register*, 1890s (WA)
- *Catholic Standard* (Hobart), 1937-1940 (TAS)
- *Daily Commercial Advertiser and Shipping List*, 1891 (NSW)
- *The English and Chinese Advertiser*, Ballarat, 1856-1858? (VIC)
- *Huon Times*, 1913-1916 (TAS)
- *Illustrated Adelaide Post*, any after 1874 (SA)
- *Nord Australische Zeitung,* 1875-1939 (QLD)
- *Northern Standard*, 1934 (NT)
- *Palmer Chronicle*, 1870s (QLD)
- *Swan River Guardian*, 1836 (WA)
- *Truth* (Adelaide edition), any before 1941 (SA)
- *Uralla Times*, 1880, 1901-1903, 1907-1956 (NSW)

If you can help please contact the appropriate NPLAN partner representative.

Public Access and Information Program

NPLAN partners aim to preserve at least one hardcopy of each Australian newspaper while ensuring ongoing access to the information content (see http://www.nla.gov.au/nplan/index. html, Preservation program). Another important aim is to ensure that information about Australian newspapers is nationally accessible. Individual NPLAN partners record information about their newspaper holdings on their online catalogues which can be accessed through their websites (see Contacts). Online catalogues of many other Australian libraries can also be searched via the internet (see Australian Libraries Gateway).

In addition to recording information about their own holdings of hardcopy, microfilm and digital newspapers on their own catalogues, NPLAN partners (and many other Australian libraries) contribute records to the National Bibliographic Database which is available via the KINETICA service. This integrated online database which is widely available nationally, provides access to bibliographic records and Australian library holdings including newspapers. This database can be used to identify libraries across Australia who have hardcopy, microfilm and digital copies of newspapers and to verify bibliographic information. The

National Bibliographic Database also potentially acts as a nationally accessible register of microform masters.

Many current Australian online newspapers are listed and are accessible through the Australian Newspapers Online website.

In the future it is intended that this NPLAN website will be further developed as a forum for partners and other community members to communicate and exchange ideas relating to the location, acquisition and preservation of Australian newspapers.

Preservation Program

The overall aim of the NPLAN project is to preserve all Australian newspapers and to ensure the public has adequate access to them. Many newspapers from the mid-1850s are printed on chemically unstable ground wood pulp paper, which deteriorates rapidly with age and use. As a means of ensuring the longevity of Australian newspapers and ongoing access to their information content, NPLAN partners aim to:

• Retain as long as feasible one hardcopy of every newspaper in their jurisdiction

• Create/purchase an archival-standard master microfilm reproduction of every hardcopy newspaper in their jurisdiction for permanent preservation

• Create/purchase at least one microfilm reproduction of every newspaper in their jurisdiction for public use

On the following website http://www.nla.gov.au/nplan/index.html you can find more information:

• About Preservation of Australian Newspapers.

• About the History of Australian Newspapers

• About Overseas National Newspaper Preservation Programs:

- United Kingdom

UK NEWSPLAN – contains information relating to the preservation of local newspapers throughout the United Kingdom and is a co-operative program between the Heritage Lottery Fund and the UK Newspaper Industry.

See also the British Library – provides background information, publications, reports and a bibliography relating to the UK NEWSPLAN program.

- United States

United States Newspaper Program – funded by the National Endowment of the Arts with assistance by the Library of Congress, this site describes the United States newspaper preservation program and lists program participants.

See also the Library of Congress – describes the United States Newspaper Program and its aim to preserve newspapers published in the United States from the eighteenth century to the present.

National Digital Newspaper Program (NDNP) – a partnership between the Library of Congress and the National Endowment for the Humanities

- About Historical Newspaper Projects:

Digital Access Initiatives from Around the World

Historical Digital Newspapers: Articles and Collections – lists various digital historical newspaper collections and projects being undertaken around the world.

- Australia

Australian Cooperative Digitisation Project: Australian Periodical Publications 1840-1845 – a digital library of Australian journals including newspapers that began publication between 1840-1845.

- The Netherlands

Metamorfoze Preservation Initiative – focuses on the preservation of books, periodicals, manuscripts and newspapers of Dutch origin from the period 1840-1950 and is co-ordinated by the Koninklijke Bibliotheek (The Netherlands' National Library).

Digitisation of Newspapers: The Roaring Twenties – contains digitised images of three Dutch newspapers from the period 1920-1929 and is hosted by the the Koninklijke Bibliotheek (The Netherlands' National Library).

War & Revolution. Digitisation from microfilm from Dutch newspapers 1910-1919 – a summary of a digitisation project to be undertaken by the Koninklijke Bibliotheek (The Netherlands' National Library) using three Dutch national daily newspapers.

- New Zealand

National Library of New Zealand: *Papers Past – New Zealand Newspapers and Periodicals* – undertaken by the National Library of News Zealand, this site brings together digital images of thirty nineteenth century newspapers and periodicals.

TIME'S PIVOTAL POINT – PRESERVING THE PAST FOR THE FUTURE – NOW

Heather Brown and Andy Fenton

*Ms. Brown is Preservation Manager of the State Library of South Australia,
Mr. Fenton is Managing Director of New Zealand Micrographic Services Limited*

Introduction

We are at this conference precisely because newspapers contain unique information and knowledge.

Within a short space many of us will have moved from our current positions; over more time our collecting institutions will change; governments will come and go; political boundaries will change; funding will wax and wane. Ultimately one of the few things that will last will be the knowledge and the information that we preserve for future generations.

This knowledge is part of national and regional cultural heritage. Ultimately it is part of the cultural memory of the whole world.

In newspapers there is a unique cultural synthesis of the so-called ‹big picture issues› and the everyday stuff of life – what Indian author Arundhati Roy has evocatively described as *The God of small things* (Roy 1997). From regional and national perspectives on international events, to the opinions expressed in ‹letters to the editor›, to advertisements of wares for sale, radio and television programs, to the so-called ‹hatch, match and dispatch› classifieds, newspapers provide a unique sociological perspective and commentary; a graphic insight into history, that continues to fascinate historians, sociologists, genealogists, fashion designers, students and the ‹general public›, decades after they are first published.

It is no coincidence that the State library of South Australia chose the prominent head of a newspaper empire to officially open its building. One of the more popular exhibitions simply contains images taken from South Australian newspapers over time, counter-pointed against a timeline of significant cultural and social events.

Of course, we cannot preserve everything. Preservation is about making choices and Ross Harvey has covered key issues relating to selection for preservation.

Preservation as a risk management issue

The major theme of our paper is that preservation of newspapers is also a risk management issue. (Adams, Hart, 2004) Right now, we are standing at a pivotal point. On one side is the imperative to provide access to this information, both now and for the future, while on the other is the imperative to preserve in order to provide the access. There is a symbiotic relationship between the two.

Our theme is that a risk management perspective is a useful tool in maintaining a sustainable balance between these two imperatives. In this context we are talking about long term preservation risks.

There are a number of significant risk factors that have major consequences for the long term preservation of newspaper heritage.

Among these long term key risks are:

1. Inherent nature of the materials

   • hard copy newspapers are produced on ‹poor› quality paper which will deteriorate and become brittle over time due to the lignin content

   • digital repositories of newspapers need to be systematically backed up, refreshed and/or migrated to ensure their ongoing accessibility

2. Quality. Surrogate copies of these newspapers, principally in microfilm but also now increasingly in digital formats, have not always been created to quality standards.

3. Storage. As Henry Snyder has vividly described, the physical storage of the originals and microfilm copies has not always been managed to ensure their long term access. This also includes issues relating to poorly processed microfilms and the storage of older acetate films. More recently the risks relate to the storage of digital copies. We are aware of at least one Australian newspaper agency that has forever lost a portion of its digital newspaper database during the 1990s. This story would not be unique in the region.

4. Bibliographic tracking of originals and surrogates. As the IFLA-PAC newspaper programs reflect, the systematic listing of newspapers and surrogate copies – microform and digital format – is critical to managing their long-term access and preservation. This role has traditionally been the province of national and state libraries and has been undertaken to varying degrees of success to date. While we are not cataloguers or database managers, we are familiar with the complexity of tracking newspapers that have common titles, different editions and frequent title changes, and undergo mergers and splits. Without clear national and regional union lists of the newspapers and holdings in all their formats, there will be the risk of duplication and at the worst – the potential loss of cultural heritage.

These risks are not new. Like motifs, they run through most of the literature about newspapers, microfilming and digitising over the past 15 years.

One of our key themes is that these key risk factors will need to be addressed as part of any broad regional strategies to preserve and provide access to newspapers in the future.

Risk management and microfilm

In our respective roles as a preservation manager in a state library and as a director of a preservation microfilming and digitising company, we both strongly advocate the advantages of preservation microfilm as a prudent risk management strategy for the ‹now›.

In this context we are referring to preservation microfilm that is produced to well-established, rigorous international quality assurance standards. The IFLA Guidelines for Newspaper Preservation Microfilming and Supplement: Microfilming for Digitisation and Optical Character Recognition are based on such standards (IFLA 1996, 2002). Most of the people in this audience will be aware of the long life expectancy of preservation microfilm. Simulation tests demonstrate that microfilm produced to these standards has an estimated life expectancy of up to 500 years if it is stored according to the recommended environmental conditions. While many countries in the region aim to keep the originals for as long as possible, this will inevitably become more difficult over time. In a significant number of cases, preservation microfilm will last long after the originals have crumbled to dust.

In 500 year's time all that will be needed to read the newspapers on microfilm is a simple magnifying glass.

In comparison digital information is transient, and currently at least, requires frequent intervention to ensure accessibility in relation to rapid changes in software and hardware. In 500 years' time the likelihood of being able to access today's digital files will be extremely limited unless these files have been continually migrated/refreshed/emulated.

As Ross Harvey has highlighted the issue of whether preservation can be considered as a preservation mechanism is heavily debated. The conclusions reached by the recent ARL paper on Recognizing Digitization as a Preservation Reformatting Method (Arthur 2004) have been hotly debated within the international preservation community. Indeed the very same report states that standards and guidelines for long term preservation are still in the developmental stage, that issues of technological obsolescence need to be addressed and that management and storage costs are not fully known (Adams 2004).

‹...*indeed we expect digital formats will be very unforgiving of neglect during periods when some content has lower perceived value, or when financial resources prevent adequate attention.*› (Hart 2004)

In other words, the jury is still out.

From a risk management perspective, both the likelihood and consequences of loss of digital information are significant.

Paolo Usai, the Director of Australia's Screensound, raised some important points in relation to systems for preserving digital information at the international Web Archiving Conference in November 2004. (National Library of Australia 2004)

As he called for future systems of preservation that:

- do not require frequent updates
- have their own metadata
- are not reliant on electricity to make them accessible,

one cannot help but recall the microfilm and the simple magnifying glass.

At the same time microfilm has some clear limitations. Its strict linear nature can make it tedious to access and black and white microfilm does not reproduce photographs well and generally not colour.

Digitisation and access

Indisputably, digitisation is the key to enhanced access. Digitisation has increased our means to make our collections of newspapers more readily accessible through the world wide web and also by adding advanced search features such as OCR to access the text information within.

The hybrid approach

Right now, by combining the approaches of digitisation and microfilming, it is possible to get the best of both worlds. Right now, we are advocating that microfilm is the prudent medium for long term preservation, and digitisation the medium for access.

Preservation microfilming reduces the potential of significant risk of loss inherent in both the nature of the acidic hard copy papers and in the digital repositories which need to be systematically backed up, refreshed and/or migrated to ensure their ongoing accessibility.

Microfilm then becomes an integral step in the expanding future of newspaper digitisation programs.

In looking at the hybrid approach the primary method to date has been to film first and scan from the film. This approach supports the goals of the *IFLA Newspapers Section Strategic Plan* (IFLA 2004) especially Professional Priorities:

- (g) Preserving our intellectual heritage, and

- (i) Promoting standards, guidelines and best practice.

It is clear from the content and debate covered at the Business meeting held immediately prior to this Conference that the heart and passion so evident in the heritage micrographics' industry over the years is alive and well in the Committee Members of the IFLA Newspapers Section.

Andy's company, New Zealand Micrographics, has been involved in some major newspaper projects such as:

- The Maori Language Newspapers Project (Niupepa). Conversion of 19th and 20th Century newspaper images from microfilm to digital, and Maori language OCR

- The Hawaiian Language Legacy Programme. Conversion of 19th Century newspaper images from microfilm to digital, and Hawaiian language OCR.

Both of these very popular projects were collaborative initiatives and involved microfilm of varying vintage and quality, scanned with OCR in mind. Both were hosted with Greenstone Digital Library Software developed by New Zealand's University of Waikato – which was recently featured in the latest IFLA Newspapers Section Newsletter.

A third project New Zealand Micrographics has had heavy involvement in over the past few years is:

- Papers Past 2002, 2003, 2004 and 2005 – Conversion of pre-1905 newspaper images from microfilm to digital, with a view to future OCR

Ross Harvey has remonstrated the benefits of Papers Past a short while ago, whilst Dave Adams and Clark Stiles described this National Library of New Zealand initiative in good detail yesterday.

This Conference is very much about sharing knowledge. Other examples (of a variety of projects) where you might be able to compare notes with your peers when considering a digitisation project can be found at http://ndf.natlib.govt.nz .

These newspaper scanning projects in particular gave the company ample opportunity to review its microfilming practices with a view to improving their potential for scanning.

Microfilming for digitisation

Andy has noted some distinct differences in his company's approach to that recommended by the Research Libraries Group's Guidelines for microfilming for digitisation, (Meyer 2003) and to a lesser extent the IFLA Newspapers Section's Microfilming for Digitisation and Optical Character Recognition – Supplement to Guidelines (IFLA 2002).

Andy supports the caveats of ‹the commonsense approach› in the IFLA document. The following is a brief summary of where his practical experience intersects with this Supplement and he welcomes further feedback or debate on these issues.

The scope of the IFLA Supplement identifies that it reflects the ‹present situation› (in fact ~2002) and both documents imply current microfilm can be ‹an efficient and economically favourable intermediary in a digitisation programme if this aspect is considered during the microfilming process.› Andy contends that historical microfilm (produced purely with the intention of preserving the intellectual content of the document) can offer the same benefits.

Since Cornell University's seminal work in the mid-90's regarding its Digital to Microfilm Conversion Project (Kenney 1996), technology has advanced so that the current crop of microform scanners are quite capable of rendering sufficient detail from reasonable film, as opposed to having to go (back) to the original.

This is an area ripe for further research and development, in doing this we must endeavour to compare the scan systems on a ‹level playing field›.

In an age when the best chance of funding for preservation microfilming projects is for custodians to insist it is part of a digitisation project – as a prudent risk management feature – it is sadly ironic that the bulk of the recommendations in the IFLA Supplement, if taken up, will add significant costs to the imaging budget, through slower filming rates, increased preparation time, more difficult quality control and so on.

As technology in scanning has advanced, Andy's belief is that we should put our energies into the production of the traditional quality microfilming practices – that is consistent density, excellent resolution (and the use of the ‹Quality Index›) and good tonal representation of pictorial content …. and let the microform scanner & software manufacturers worry about automated detection of images from microfilm. Do not spend hours collating documents into uniform blocks, leave in-film targeting in situ and do «duplicate (intentional second) exposures».

Despite some misgivings about some of the recommendations, we concur with the final paragraph of the IFLA Supplement:

‹*Do it once, do it right. Technology will surely remove [and is removing] some, if not all, of our present obstacles. If a quality program for microfilming is established as a part of the library strategy, it will make things easier for the future digitisation activities. Microfilming should be considered as a part of the library's digital [or ‹imaging›] program.*› *(IFLA 2002)*

This risk-averse initiative I think we should all endorse.

Both of these guidelines have been produced to identify to traditional microfilmers the ‹tips and tricks› that may assist automated scanning of rolls of microfilm.

However there is good news. With recent technological advances in scanning there is now less need to make a number of the recommended modifications to microfilming practices. It is likely that these can be more easily handled by the microform scanning staff, in conjunction with microform QA staff if necessary.

Andy has taken up the challenge by Robin Dale, Editor of the RLG Guidelines, to share his practical experiences in our part of the world – and welcomes the opportunity to discuss them with you further.

He would like to propose two suggestions for further research and development:

1. Consider the use of notches or small holes to identify areas of potential difficulty on the film. These could be relatively easily detected as part of the scan process and files annotated accordingly for closer scrutiny.

2. Consider the use of colour microfilm, as suggested in Goal Six of IFLA Newspapers Section Strategic plan 2004-2005. However, develop this program alongside the production of a 2nd generation Preservation Duplicate Master as an ‹extended-term› greyscale polyester microfilm. Logically, with modern papers, we might consider the production of COM colour film using files direct from the publisher, if they can be formatted to suit the COM machines of the time, or scanned direct from the originals.

COM as a hybrid imaging technology

One alternative to scanning from microfilm is to digitise first (or perhaps take ‹born-digital› material) and output that to microform via a Computer Output to Microform (COM) device. Today it is often a viable method of hybrid imaging, certainly with commercial documents.

Interpretation of the quality of the COM image is difficult to assess in the context of image quality using traditional microfilming methods.

Andy's experience is that he increasingly finds himself relying the modern equivalent of traditional microfilming ‹Quality Index› methodology; that is to ‹read the fine print›! If the output COM film can resolve a four point font then it has passed a reasonable test for resolving power. Of course, an assessment should not be made without reference to the original document and the scanned image first.

One of the main barriers to COM for newspaper imaging is the issue of resolution and tonal representation. In short COM devices struggle to render fine detail of large format material well on 35mm film.

Andy believes it is fair to say the same applies to newspapers – both old and new. We can achieve good results scanning older newspapers and outputting the digital images to COM, albeit scaling may be necessary.

However the cost of scanning and handling often-frail documents in the first instance is often too expensive. Wide-format sheet-fed scanners shine too much light through the page increasing the problem of bleed-through and necessitating the backing of the newspaper pages. Thus a (slower) overhead scanner (perhaps a hybrid scanner/microfilm camera) may have to be used, these are becoming more widespread, but are invariably more expensive to operate.

In short traditional filming methods are often cheaper, even when scanning film thereafter is included. With the recent technological advances in scanning microfilm, comparative quality can be achieved.

In the past five years, for modern ‹born-digital› material, the issues are somewhat more complex. Proprietary print file formats were initially a problem; nowadays a PDF file is easy to produce by a willing printer/publisher for use on the COM device, but coordination can be difficult when a newspaper uses more than source to produce its publication – which may consist of the main body of news, advertising & classifieds, glossy or magazine inserts, leaflets etc

Another complexity is that colour photographs embedded in the files can be difficult to render on monochrome microfilm on some recorders.

On the other hand, a key benefit of COM is the ability for metadata captured at or during the scan process to be inserted in each frame if desired.

Digital to microfilm conversion is a seductive area in its infancy, rapidly attracting worldwide attention that is ripe for further research and development. A few micrographic bureaux in the region are already working in this area.

Andy summarises: ‹As someone who earns his income far more readily from digitisation than microfilming I could not put my hand on my heart and risk a preservation imaging solution that only involves digitisation. Most of you in this audience are stewards of significant cultural collections, and until we reach the pivotal point when digitisation longevity issues will be resolved it behoves us to not rest on our laurels and promote the ‹access› solution as a likely long-term keeping solution.›

As Alan Smith, the Director of the State Library of South Australia recently commented: *‹Our greatest ambition as stewards and custodians of our respective nations' documentary heritage is to pass the collection on to the next custodian better than we received it ourselves, ...whilst providing access is essential – too much access may deny future access...›* (Smith 2005)

Training and quality assurance

Training in quality assurance is also critical to ensuring that the information and knowledge is preserved for the future to the highest level.

Within the region the National Library of Australia's PADI (Preserving Access to Digital Information) site provides a valuable educational framework and signpost relating to digital preservation issues.

Within the Asia-Pacific region we are both actively involved in working with like-minded organisations to deliver training to support quality filming and digitizing at the ‹hands-on› practitioner-level and also at the ‹project management/quality assurance› level.

For example, along with representatives from the Australian National Library, state libraries and archives and microfilming industry, we are both members of the Australian Course Advisory Panel that will approve the re-accreditation of the new competency-based Certificate IV in Preservation Microfilming (NTIS website). This specialised course has been taken up outside Australia and ensures that microfilming practitioners have the requisite skills and knowledge of ‹best practice› techniques and international standards and guidelines, including digitising from microfilm.

IFLA – PAC, the National Library of Australia and the State Library of South Australia recently collaborated to produce training materials in preservation microfilming which have been distributed throughout the Asian-Pacific region, again with the aim of skilling practitioners in quality preservation microfilming (Brown 2003).

Singapore National Archives is emerging as a regional training centre and we have recently worked with them to provide training workshops about microfilming and digitisation quality issues to practitioners and project managers. Participants from Singapore, Brunei, New Zealand, Thailand and Vietnam attended.

In the recent past SEACAP (Southeast Asian Consortium for Access and Preservation) has highlighted the need for quality assurance in preservation microfilming and systematic bibliographic tracking of surrogates. The proceedings of its February 2000 International Meeting on Microform Preservation and Conservation Practices in Southeast Asia, at Chiang Mai University are available from the SEACAP website.

Training such as this within the region reduces the risks of poor quality preservation microfilm and digital imaging – and ensures that both access and preservation needs are met for the future.

Standards and guidelines

The ongoing revision of standards and guidelines is an integral part of risk management. We have already referred to recent technological advances in scanning that are resolving some of the issues raised in the IFLA and RLG Guidelines discussed.

Within the region, a number of the delegates at this conference participate in the review and development of standards and guidelines through membership of the Australia & New

Zealand Standards Committee for Micrographics and Image Management, and as we have also been doing over the past year with the National Archives of Singapore and the Singapore Code of Practice.

Standards and best practices do exist for the creation of digital master files, but the same cannot be said for the long term care of these files. *‹Since such practices are still in their infancy, it is not really feasible for a large number of the cultural heritage community to accept digitization as a viable preservation method. It would be more prudent to wait until the field is more stable.›* (McAlister 2004)

Quality assurance auditing

In a related quality assurance area we have also been involved in conducting a series of audits on the micrographic and digital imaging systems at the Singapore National Archives, one of the major microfilming and imaging agencies in the region. Auditing is another tool for ensuring that systems are continuing to work to requisite quality assurance levels and is linked back to their role in maintaining the identity, integrity and quality of the copy as a trusted source of the cultural record.

In turn this has parallels with the recent push for certification of ‹trusted digital repositories›, which was highlighted by Robin Dale from the Research Libraries Group at the Web Archiving Conference.

Conclusion

Right now we stand at a pivotal point.

A point of rapid technological advances in digitisation that are simultaneously greatly enhancing access, and yet are also beguiling.

Paolo Usai, the Director of Australia's Screensound summed up the risks at the international Web Archiving Conference in November 2004 with his comment:

‹If there is too much emphasis on access instead of preservation we lose balance and our cultural assets›.

Our theme is that NOW is the opportunity to balance the two. We are at the pivotal point of rapidly expanding newspaper digitisation programs. We are also at a point where there is the potential to virtually and seamlessly link national and regional bibliographic lists via the world wide web.

Right now an integrated risk management approach gives the opportunity to balance preservation and access. Such an approach links back to the four key risk factors:

1. inherent nature of the materials

2. quality

3. storage

4. bibliographic tracking of originals and surrogates.

A balanced risk management approach can be achieved through:

- hybrid technologies, using microfilm as the preservation platform and digitisation for access

- training and the promotion of quality assurance systems such as auditing

- ongoing development and review of standards and guidelines

- national and regional coordination of physical and virtual storage of the originals and microfilm and digital surrogates

- further development and virtual linking of national and regional lists of original newspapers and their microform and digital surrogates

- further national and regional cooperation and coordination to preserve and provide access to regional newspapers.

This is what stewardship is about. As Colin Webb summarised at the International Web Archiving Conference (National Library of Australia 2004) it is doing the best we can with what we can achieve and being watchful and active.

We are all stewards of the region's newspaper heritage. And we believe that a prudent risk management approach, doing the best we can in the NOW helps achieve this balance. No one said it would be easy. ‹*Stewardship is easy and inexpensive to claim; it is expensive and difficult to honor, and perhaps it will prove to be all too easy to later abdicate.*› (Lynch 2004)

Time's pivotal point is NOW.

Resources are limited. The risks are higher than some might appreciate. The consequences of loss are significant. Time is rapidly running out. And the balance between preservation and access is always dynamic.

References

Adams, D et. al. 2004, Addressing a risk perspective when considering digitisation as a preservation reformatting method: a response from «down under» *Microform and Imaging Review* vol. 33 no. 4, Autumn pp188-189.

Arthur, Kathleen et.al. 2004, *Recognizing Digitization as a Preservation Reformatting Method*. Prepared for the ARL Preservation of Research Library Materials Committee. (http://www.arl.org/preserv/digit_final.html)

Brown, Heather 2003, *Training in Preservation Microfilming*. 13 volumes. National Library of Australia, Canberra. (http://www.nla.gov.au/preserve/trainmat.html)

Drake, Karl-Magnus, *Report on preliminary testing on COM systems* [Metamorfoze conference] (http://www.kb.nl/coop/metamorfoze/expert/drake.pdf)

Hart, Andrew 2004, A critique of «Recognizing Digitization as a Preservation Reformatting Method» *Microform and Imaging Review* vol. 33 no. 4, Autumn pp184-187.

Hawaiian Language Legacy Programme http://nupepa.org

Kenney, Anne & Chapman, Stephen 1996, *Digital Imaging for Libraries and Archives*, Cornell University Library Department of Preservation and Conservation, Ithaca, NY

IFLA Newspapers section

- 1996, *Guidelines for Newspaper Preservation Microfilming*

- 2002, *Microfilming for Digitisation and Optical Character Recognition: Supplement to Guidelines*

- *IFLA Newspapers Section Strategic plan 2004-2005*

Langendoen, Andrea 2004, The Metamorfoze Preservation Program *Microform and Imaging Review*, vol. 33 no.3, pp110-114.

Lynch, Clifford, 2004 in *RLG DigiNews* 15 August 2004 v8 no.4

The Maori Language Newspapers Project (Niupepa)

McAlister, Sheila & Trinkaus-Randall 2004, «Wouldn't it be prudent»: Digitization as a Preservation Reformatting Method *Microform and Imaging Review* vol. 33 no. 4, Autumn pp181-183. http://www.nzdl.org/niupepa

Metamorfoze team 2004, Digitization as a Preservation Method-Comments from the Netherlands *Microform and Imaging Review* vol. 33 no. 4, Autumn pp191-194. See also Metamorfoze

Meyer, Lars & Gertz, Janet, 2003 *Guidelines for microfilming to support digitisation*. Research Libraries group, Mountain View, California. Available online at http://www.rlg.org/preserv/microsuppl.pdf

National Library of Australia

- Web archiving Conference November 2004

- NPLAN National Plan for Australian Newspapers

- PADI (Preserving Access to Digital information)

National Library of New Zealand. Papers Past website

National Training Information Service (NTIS) website. Provides details of the Australian course Certificate IV in Preservation Microfilming.

New Zealand Micrographics

Roy, Arundhati 1997, *The God of Small Things*, Flamingo, Hammersmith, London.

SEACAP (Southeast Asian Consortium for Access and Preservation) 2000, *Proceedings of the International Meeting on Microform Preservation and Conservation Practices in Southeast Asia: Assessing Current Needs and Evaluating Past Projects, February 21-24, 2000*, Chiang Mai University, Chiang Mai. (Available from the SEACAP website)

Smith, Alan 2005 Interview. State Library of South Australia, 18 February 2005.

PRESERVATION OF NEWSPAPERS IN THE INTERNATIONAL CONTEXT

Marie-Thérèse Varlamoff

Director IFLA PAC

Abstract

IFLA Core Activity on Preservation and Conservation (PAC) has one major goal : to ensure that library materials, including newspapers, will be preserved in accessible form for as long as possible. Newspapers being the primary record of events that shape our communities they represent an important part of our global memory that cannot be ignored. As a follow-up of the Symposium co-organized by IFLA and the Bibliothèque nationale de France in Paris, August 2000, PAC launched a survey on the state of preservation of African newspapers. Results being scarce and incomplete, it was decided, with the help of the IFLA Section on Newspapers, to launch a second, more narrowly-targeted survey, to determine which titles to select and where were the gaps in the collections. According to answers a strategy for future actions will be implemented in collaboration with foreign libraries having similar holdings and reformatting resources. Another example of international co-operation deals with the digitization of the 19th century Latin American press, focusing on the work done by ABINIA (Latin American national Libraries Association) and the National Library of Venezuela in rescuing the press of the Great Columbia, 1820-1830. The choice between microfilming and digitization as a reformatting process depends on the goals to be reached (preservation and/or access), on the country concerned, on the resources available, now and in the future. Co-operation between PAC and the IFLA Section on Newspapers is a prerequisite for the success of any international project.

I am very grateful to the Section on Newspapers and particularly to Hartmut Walravens and Ed King for having given me the opportunity to participate in this international conference at the National Library of Australia. All the more since the NLA is hosting one of the Regional PAC Centers. A great thanks too to Jan Fullerton for inviting me.

I assume that you all know IFLA (the International Federation of Library Associations and Institutions) but you might not know what PAC stands for. PAC means Preservation and Conservation and it is one of the five Core Activities of IFLA. PAC was officially created during the IFLA meeting in Nairobi in 1984 to focus efforts on issues of preservation and initiate worldwide cooperation for the preservation of library materials. But the PAC program was effectively launched in Vienna during the Conference of the Directors of National Libraries. Contrary to other IFLA Core Programs, PAC has been originally conceived in a decentralized way : a Focal Point, hosted by the Bibliothèque nationale de France in Paris to manage activities and Regional Centers responsible for their choices and policies. There are now twelve Regional Centers, six of them were created in 2004. The Regional Center for Pacific and South East Asia, located here in Canberra and directed by Colin Webb was created in 1989 and has been very active ever since, especially in the fields of microfilming, disaster preparedness and digital preservation, this last item being its pole of excellence. The other Regional Centers are respectively located in Paris, Moscow, Tokyo, Beijing, Cape Town, Porto Novo (Benin), Washington, Trinidad & Tobago, Caracas, Rio de Janeiro, Santiago de Chile.

IFLA PAC has one major goal: to ensure that library and archive materials, published and unpublished, in all formats, will be preserved in accessible form for as long as possible according to the following principles :

- preservation is essential to the survival and development of culture and scholarship – this is particularly true for newspapers and periodicals;

- international cooperation is the key – we shall deal with this issue later;

- each country must accept responsibility for the preservation of its own publications.

As I said PAC is concerned by the preservation of all library documents in all formats, which explains why our prior concern focuses on fragile documents, hence on newspapers. Newspapers represent huge collections, which, for various reasons – diminishment of budget, lack of human resources or carelessness – tend to be incomplete. The fragility of newspapers holdings is not to be depicted. Everyone knows that because of their size and because of the acidity of the paper used, newspapers, especially ancient newspapers, are difficult to handle and each consultation worsens their state of preservation. Being the source of undeniable richness for historians, newspapers pertain to our global memory and their preservation is certainly a duty for all librarians and archivists.

1. Surveys on the preservation of African newspapers

1.1 First survey

The reason why I am here has to be sought for back in August 21-24, 2000 when the IFLA Conference in Jerusalem was followed by an international symposium on «Managing the Preservation of Periodicals and Newspapers». This symposium, held eleven years after the first symposium on the subject organized at the Library of Congress in Washington, was co-organized by the Bibliothèque nationale de France and IFLA Section on Preservation and Conservation, IFLA PAC Core Activity, IFLA Section on Serial Publications and IFLA Round Table on Newspapers. Proceedings have been edited by IFLA PAC and published as an IFLA Publication (103) by SAUR. The idea for this symposium originally came from the IFLA Section on Preservation and Conservation to promote the preservation of serial publications, including those in electronic form. At the end of the symposium there were discussions and the African participants called attention to the particularly serious situation of periodicals and newspapers conservation in Africa.

As Chair of the organizing committee and director of IFLA PAC I immediately proposed that a survey be conducted among African national libraries and national archives. The purpose was not to launch one more survey but first to try and make the inventory of the main titles owned by each institution and to find out missing issues. After gathering the answers we expected to be able to see whether other institutions preserved the same title(s) and were susceptible to fill in the gaps by producing duplicates (microfilms or CD ROMs). IFLA PAC wrote the questionnaire, in English and French, and sent it, on behalf of JICPA (the Joint IFLA/ICA Committee on Preservation in Africa) to all African national institutions. Questionnaires were sent in March 2001 and answers requested no later than July 2001.

Unfortunately very few replies had reached us by then and we had to send a reminder with another dead line: November 2001. By that time we had only received 25 answers and it became obvious that we could not draw a clear picture of the situation. The questionnaire dealt with the following topics: information about the institution and description of the collections (catalogue, number of titles, names of titles of national interest), questions about preservation issues (storage, state of conservation of the collections, restoration of and access to the originals, environmental conditions), reformatting (microfilming or digitization, reading equipment) and communication.

1.2 Second survey

A certain misunderstanding and confusion resulted from the responses. It was agreed, in collaboration with the Section on Newspapers, to undertake a new inquiry. The form established by Else Delaunay was printed on a single sheet in English on one side and in French on the other side. It focused on the most basic questions concerning newspaper holdings in the various institutions to be contacted. A letter was sent together with the form explaining that only newspapers published in Africa should be listed . The new questionnaire was mailed using IFLA PAC mailing list (especially for archives) and to the British Library list. The questionnaire was also mounted on the IFLANET. Main questions dealt with collecting policy (comprehensive or selective), permanent retention (all African newspapers, regional newspapers, national newspapers, local newspapers, microfilms), shared preservation with other institutions, limited retention period, disposal after microfilming. Institutions were asked to join a list of their newspapers holdings with first and last date of publication.

In July 2003, 125 questionnaires were sent to national archives and libraries and a few university libraries in 47 countries. Only 7 answers were received by November 2003. A reminder was sent to 99 libraries and 31 answers were received by January 31, 2004, which represents a total of 38 answers (or 30,89%). As a whole answers to this second questionnaire were much more precise and accurate than those of the first survey but were not sufficiently explicit to implement a strategic project.

1.3 Third questionnaire

This is why Else Delaunay prepared another form focusing on a microfilming project: asking which title was to be microfilmed in priority, the reasons for such a choice, bibliographical information, storage conditions, condition of conservation of paper and which institutions in the country conserved the same title and could fill in the gaps for missing issues. The same questions were asked for a second title. There were also questions about other titles and existing or needed reading equipment for microfilms. Last questions concerned storage facilities of films and master negatives. This third round lasted three months (July-September 2004) and concerned 31 institutions, out of which only 17 answered.

1.4 What shall we do next ?

This brief historical overview of what has been done in five year time proves how difficult it is to conduct surveys and to implement projects on an international scale. Reasons for that are multiple. Countries involved in such projects are sometimes too many and it becomes difficult to have each one of them react and answer according to a same scheme. There are also cultural and linguistic differences, but most of all economic discrepancies : lack of resources and lack of staff can make any form of co-operation difficult if not impossible. In the case of this particular survey difficulties also arose because, generally speaking, and I would not like to appear politically incorrect, preservation in Africa is a newer concept than in Western countries for instance. Africa has long had an oral tradition, which can partly explains why the preservation of African documentary heritage lacks behind. At the same time, as publishing activity is still low in most of the African countries and as the preservation of archives has not been steadily taken care of, it is of the utmost importance that newspapers holdings that reflect the daily life of the country, the region or the city, be preserved or rebuilt. This is why it is now necessary to list the titles indicated as to be saved in priority, to look out for complete collections or microfilms of the same titles conserved in other institutions.

Next step will be to find money in order to microfilm these titles, so as to fill in the gaps in the collections that are incomplete. The IFLA Section on Newspapers and IFLA PAC will have to build up a project proposal and find donors: a hard task, all the more since we shall also have to establish priorities between countries and titles. But we are determined and, time permitting, we should be able to succeed, provided that African institutions recognize the necessity of becoming active partners and not only grantees. Provided also that institutions in developing countries are willing to contribute. We know that we shall meet some difficulties with the choice of the process: microfilm v/s digitization, most donors being now in favor of this new process, which is perhaps not the best to be recommended for Africa if we consider the lack of equipment to read CD ROMs or to access the internet. Anyhow, it is essential that, in the case of a microfilming process, masters be conserved in storage facilities that comply to the environmental principles in force, which means that they probably should be kept abroad and only copies will be used for access in Africa.

2. A Latin American experience

In Latin America another kind of project concerning the Nineteenth Century Press Rescue was implemented in the nineteen nineties and completed in 2004. Considering the risk of irreparable damage or even disappearance of newspapers collections due to the instability of the medium and the existing limited preservation capabilities, ABINIA (Latin American National Libraries Association) approved a project set up by the National Library of Venezuela to rescue the nineteenth century press, a project which became a pilot project of UNESCO Memory of the World.

• The project was divided into three phases

• Creation of a catalogue so as to create a data base to be used by researchers.

• Training in microfilming so as to assure the reproduction of nineteenth century press

• Indexing and digitization of the most representative newspapers in order to publish a CD ROM, facilitating access to information by researchers.

The first two phases were successfully completed and a computerized union catalogue of nineteenth century newspapers was developed and is available on microfilm in the National Library of Venezuela and in several other institutions. At the same time training activities were set up and the National Library of Venezuela organized a microfilm workshop in six different Latin American countries. Thanks to UNESCO contributions, the CD ROM *Nineteenth Century Latin American Press* was edited, presenting almost 9000 bibliographic references and digitized images corresponding to a period of one year's circulation of the most important newspaper from each of the fourteen countries.

In fact the objective of the project was to digitize the most important nineteenth century Latin American newspapers so as facilitate their access either through a CD ROM or on-line.

2.1 Grand Columbian Press Project

A project funded by the Andrew W. Mellon Foundation (200,000 US$) and agreed in 1996 was implemented in 1997 by the National Library of Venezuela under the direction of the Director of technical services who was also IFLA PAC Regional Director for Latin America. The purpose was to edit a CD ROM on the *Grand Colombian Press, 1820-1830* containing images from one representative newspaper from each of the participating countries, that is : Venezuela, Colombia, Ecuador, Panama, Peru and Bolivia.

The first step was the acquisition of the equipment and software. A scanner for 16 and 35mm microfilms was bought. The scanner had to be adapted to a computer and to the software «Paint Pro Shop and Imaging» and a CD Recorder. The difficulties in the setting up of the scanner lasted more than one year and the equipment ready for use only in January 1999. Additional softwares (including Adobe Photoshop) were acquired in 1999. In 2002 it was decided to buy an additional computer to make easier the processes of entering the records, image manipulation and quality control. But there were difficulties with the purchase of the computer which was one year delayed and not in use before September 2003.

Training and hiring of human resources was another aspect and problem of the project. In 1997 seven civil servants were trained to use the equipment. In September and November 1999 project Director attended two digitization meetings in the US, one presented by the Northeast Document Conservation Center in Nebraska and the second one given by the University of Cornell in New York. The person in charge of the digitization process went to the University of Colima, Mexico, to observe the complete process from digitization to the edition of the CD ROM.

Hiring historians to compile indexes, a transcriber and a graphic designer proved to be difficult, because of the high turnover.

Each National Library selected the most representative Grandcolombian newspapers in its country. But, due to the limitations imposed by the CD ROM capacity only five titles were chosen, which represented 3,542 images.

The indexing process was much slower than the digitization. Because of the decision (recommended by Hans Rutimann from the Mellon Foundation) not to apply Optical Character Recognition (OCR), it was decided to comprehensively index all the information contained in the five selected newspapers in order to achieve retrieval of pertinent and complete information by means of name, geographic and subject indexes. The indexing process meant a meticulous reading of each page in order to extract the necessary information to complete 26 different fields in each record. There were not enough specialists of the period who could work continuously on the project, hence the delay in completing the work, which could not be achieved before January 2003.

The quality control process revealed the non-existence of some scanned images and the repetition of others. The substitution or inclusion of images could not be done until the scanner was repaired in April 2003.

A prototype of the CD ROM was received in September 2003, but did not include the final corrections in the data base. Unfortunately, for various reasons the project director and the project coordinator had to leave the National Library and at the same time the National Center for Paper Conservation began its move to a new site in Caracas. Both these situations brought new delays in the project. A new director was hired for the Conservation Center in 2004 and pending activities were resumed after the scanner, which had been slightly out of use because of its move, was repaired. A specialist had to be hired to make it work again.

Both ABINIA and its constituting national libraries supported the project initiated and completed by the National Library of Venezuela. It is an excellent example of a fruitful, though very difficult, co-operation. Although the most important newspapers from participating countries had been identified, few newspapers were already microfilmed. The National Library of Venezuela had to microfilm from facsimile editions or duplicated rolls of microfilm positives sent by the participating libraries. The project was the first of its kind. It served as a trial and showed how difficult it was to find qualified staff for indexing and also to select and train adequate technicians. Moreover , acquiring the right equipment, making it work properly on a regular basis is another difficulty, each failure implying long delays in the completeness of the project.

Such projects gathering different countries and different institutions are too often hindered by the lack of experience in handling new technologies, by the lack of knowledge concerning the conditions in partner institutions and a naive desire of perfection or of exhaustiveness. Projects, and above all international projects should take into account the extreme variety of the various components and keep in mind that the more partners you have, the more different they are, the longer the project will take.

3. Do international projects have a future?

Which lesson to learn from these two examples ? Shall we consider international projects as the panacea or as an endless endeavor full of traps. Of course, as the director of an international program with twelve relaying centers all over the world I would be tempted to blindly promote the idea that international projects are worthwhile. Unfortunately a rather long experience has made me more cautious. As a conclusion I shall try to list reasons why some projects never succeed or remain incomplete. Causes for failure, or for success, may be organized in different categories:

3.1 Project itself

- *Object and goal of project:* the object of the project must be clearly defined and have a precise goal

- *Size of project:* too big of a project is necessarily doomed to fail. Ambitious projects will have a better chance of success if they are revised and cut down.

- *Coverage of project:* the same rule applies to the coverage of the project which should not include too many participants and in the case of an international project too many countries.

3.2 Project management

- *Partnership:* partners selected for participation in the project should be reliable and willing to fully co-operate on a well-balanced basis.

- *Leadership:* the institution or organization which takes the responsibility of the leadership of the project must be fully conscious of the overload of work it represents. Moreover it must establish friendly though strict and firm contacts with project partners. Managerial skills and a strong knowledge and respect of financial accounting rules are required from the leader.

- *Sponsorship:* no project can succeed without funding. Fund raising is a difficult task, especially for libraries (museums or cultural events – dance, performances…– attract sponsors more easily). The selection of concerned potential sponsors is fundamental. The project proposal must be presented with care and preciseness, indicating goals, partners, existing resources, budget needed and calendar. Once the sponsor found the project leader must do his(her) best to stick to the agenda and to the different phases of the project. The sponsor should never be deceived but on the contrary always informed in case something is going wrong. It is a question of confidence.

3.3 Resources and workload

- *Equipment:* special projects require special equipment. Be conscious that equipment purchased abroad may take a lot of time to arrive and when it breaks there may be major difficulties for repairing it (spare parts or technicians may have to come for miles away). New technologies are certainly attractive but not always compatible with the existing resources in staff and equipment of the institution entitled to do the work.

- *Staff:* high staff turnover is to be envisaged and represents a major difficulty in respecting deadlines. Do not ask the existing staff to work for the project without diminishing their daily usual work. If you do not have in your teams the adequate specialists to run the project, either train those in your staff who are volunteers or hire specialists for the length of the project.

- *Money:* if your project has been well prepared you should not run out of money. Nevertheless unexpected events may require some flexibility in financial outcomes and you may be force to either slightly diminish the coverage of the project or to suppress some of the final products.

3.4 Degree of knowledge and capability

- *Scientific knowledge:* beware of hiring or selecting too scrupulous staff who, on account of exhaustiveness or perfection, will spend hours on operations that should last minutes.

- *Technical ability:* most projects, especially those including new products, require the assistance of skilled and trained technicians. Be aware the rapid evolvement of technology necessitates a permanent updating of those technicians.

3.5 Unforeseen events

- difficulties and delays in acquiring equipment or in hiring and training appropriate staff;

- equipment out of order and difficult to replace or repair on the spot;

- political changes in the management of the institution leading to redundancy;

- economic recession;

- disasters of all kinds.

3.6 Heavy administrative mechanisms

- in hiring appropriate staff for instance;

- financial complexity for purchasing equipment abroad.

3.7 Communication and transportation

- different languages and absence of a common language in use among all partners;

- lack of communication between partners;

- long distances between partners and lack of easy transportation;

- absence of rapid communication networks (e-mails, fax, telephone, regular mails) between all partners.

Despite all this, I remain convinced of the importance and the necessity of building projects together. «L'union fait la force» as we say in French. Moreover we cannot but observe that being and acting «global» is now the rule. Let us not be afraid of setting up and proposing projects with an international component. The IFLA Section on Newspapers, whose members come from so many different countries and the IFLA PAC Core Activity, with its twelve Regional Centers all over the world must join their expertise and knowledge in order to implement, propose and achieve joint projects. The survey on African newspapers requires a follow up and we need the support of you all to succeed in this endeavor.

CANADIAN DEVELOPMENTS FOR THE DIGITIZATION OF NEWSPAPERS

Sandra Burrows

Newspaper Specialist, Library and Archives Canada

Abstract

Canadian researchers generally feel that of all of the wealth of material that could be on Canadian web sites, newspapers would be the easiest to digitize and search. Vast parts of newspaper collections, such as photography collections and birth, marriage and death notices have already been scanned and indexed. These parts have seldom been taken directly from the printed or the microfilm editions. Rather, genealogical societies and a consortium of contributors undertaking historical projects usually scan existing word documents and finding aids, in the case of genealogical information, and contact prints or scrapbooks in the case of newspaper photographs with added historical arrangement and context.

Holistic digitization is much more problematic. The questions of copyright, storage, access, editions, cost recovery are among a few that will be addressed at the end of this paper. Generally, Canadian newspaper digitization projects, in particular, those undertaken by Library and Archives Canada are thematic digitization projects. To be more specific, newspapers have been used to enhance and illustrate particular themes in the Canadian experience such as hockey, weather disasters or the opening of the west. This paper examines a few of these projects, as well as the present and future direction of digitization projects at Library and Archives Canada. It also presents a general overview of other projects across Canada and concludes with a review of issues in the digitization of newspapers.

Background

In October 2002, Library and Archives Canada convened a national consultation to examine the issue of a national strategy to strengthen access to Canadian newspapers online. In addition to discussions on «born-digital» newspapers and access to these, the consultation participants also considered the issue of digitization of Canadian newspapers already existing in other formats, primarily print and microfilm. Organized in association with the Canadian Initiative on Digital Libraries (CIDL), the Canadian Newspaper Association (CNA), and the Association for Canadian Studies (ACS), the consultation drew together experts in the fields of newspaper publishing, micro graphics, preservation, digitization, information dissemination, librarianship, archival science and scholarly and genealogical research. The consultation's outcomes included an impassioned plea for larger-scale full-text digitization of newspapers, a call for Library and Archives Canada to exercise leadership in ensuring long-term access to Canadian newspapers online and a multi-stakeholder approach to a national strategy. More details on this initiative are available in *Making Known a National Collection of News Media in Canada: a report to the China Newspaper Seminar Tuesday, March 30, 2004*, available at http://www.ifla.org/VII/s39/conf/Sandra1.pdf

National programmes

In the 1980's, Canada, Britain and the United States embarked on separate yet similar national programs for their respective newspaper heritage. There are variations according to country, yet the goals are the same: 1) to identify newspapers (titles and holdings); 2) to preserve them; and 3) to make them accessible. Twenty years later, all three countries have virtually met the first goal of identification and description. The second goal, preservation, requires a greater investment of time and resources. For newspapers, the accepted preservation medium is microfilming and preservation microfilming is continuing at varying levels of intensity.

In Canada, heritage institutions, consortia, commercial micropublishers and newspapers themselves do preservation microfilming. Library and Archives Canada acquires newspapers on microform partly through legal deposit for post 1988 papers for which more than four microfilm copies are produced and partly through purchase. The collection now numbers over 300,000 reels.

In conjunction with identification and preservation, all three countries turned to the third goal: making the content of newspapers accessible. When the national programs began in the 1980's, accessibility meant indexing selected content; in the current context, accessibility means digitization and full-text searching.[1]

At present, negotiations are underway to position Library and Archives Canada as a key player in making Canadian newspaper content accessible. As in many countries, legal deposit does not apply to digital content on the web. Library and Archives Canada, however, a «single, modern-knowledge institution» has extended legal deposit to online publications and to a sampling of Web sites. The Library and Archives Act and its related regulations, and a major initiative on the development, management and care of LAC's digital collection, will allow us to explore agreements with newspaper publishers to make known more newspaper content.[2]

Library and Archives Canada Web Sites with Canadian Newspapers

Several thematic projects on Library and Archives Canada website have significant newspaper components. For finding aids, there is a Newspaper page that includes a list of Canadian newspapers on microfilm and a Checklist of Indexes to Canadian Newspapers. The thematic sites include:

Canadian Illustrated News 1869-1883: Images in the News / Les nouvelles en image at: http://www.collectionscanada.ca/cin/

Impressions: 250 years of printing ...in the lives of Canadians / 250 ans d'imprimerie dans la vie des canadien(ne)s at http://www.collectionscanada.ca/2/10/

Special Editions of Canadian Newspapers at http://www.collectionscanada.ca/newspapers/index-e.html

---

1   The above information under Background is taken from the Draft *Centre for Newspapers and News in Canada: a document for discussion* by [Library and Archives Canada] Management Board. January 2005 by Mary Jane Starr, Director-General, Centre for Newspapers and News in Canada. (Ottawa: Library and Archives Canada, 2005), pages 2-3

2   *Performance Report for the period ending March 31, 2004.* The National Library of Canada and National Archives of Canada Performance Report for the period ending March 31, 2004, was tabled in Parliament on Thursday, October 28, 2004.

Éditions spéciales de journaux canadiens at http://www.collectionscanada.ca/journaux/index-f.html

Engine of Immortality: Canadian newspapers from 1752 until Today / Moteur d'immortalité : les journaux canadiens de 1752 à nos jours at http://www.collectionscanada.ca/halifaxgazette/

The Anti-slavery movement in Canada / Le mouvement antiesclavagiste au Canada Backcheck: a Hockey retrospective / Regard sur le hockey at http://www.collectionscanada.ca/hockey/ and *Celebrating Women's Achievements / Femmes à l'honneur : leurs réalisations* http://www.collectionscanada.ca/women/ or http://www.collectionscanada.ca/femmes/

Other Web Sites for Canadian Newspapers Online

There are other major web initiatives whereby Canadian newspapers are scanned and their content is available: *Paper of Record, Pages of the Past (the Toronto star)* and *Globe and Mail: Canada's Heritage from 1844*. Library and Archives Canada has site licences (licences based on the number of users an institution serves and the number of concurrent users) through their Intranet pages to all three of these products. An Ontario product, HALINET, although not solely a newspaper digitization source, provides a large number of digitized community newspapers on its local education pages.

All three major web products originated from Cold North Wind, Inc. which was established in 1999. Its first paper was the *Melbourne Port Phillip Herald*. In 2002, Cold North Wind, Inc. acquired the non-exclusive rights to scan and index the Canadian Library Association's microfilm, which covered titles from every province and territory from the late 1700's to 1930. Since then, some community newspapers' complete runs on microfilm have been added up to at least 2001. Titles are added frequently. Subscribers may access the product through their library's site licence or individually whereon they are charged for a monthly or yearly subscription. *Paper of Record* offers full-text and date searching and pages can be viewed, saved, printed locally, or high-quality prints ordered and sent by email to another site. Search words are located through an OCR process (which is also available for purchase by media companies) and highlighted. As with any digital product, the images on *Paper of Record* are only as good as the microfilmed product from which they are scanned. Not surprisingly, *Paper of Record* has encouraged preservation microfilming in order to ensure a high-quality product and further preservation of the original formats. Searchers are also able to contribute to the prioritization process by commenting on the newspapers or newspaper pages (as some scanning is incomplete) that they would like to see done. *Paper of Record* also has a featured paper, a featured historical subject with a number of scanned newspaper from a recognized expert source of news on it and a *This Week in History Section*. *Paper of Record* now includes over 500 newspaper titles from 16 countries comprising 8 million pages of newspaper images.[3]

The *Toronto Star: Pages of the Past* was the first digitized newspaper in the world[4]. At a rate of one million pages per month, the paper has been digitized from 1894 now up to 2002

---

3   *About Paper of Record* http://paperofrecord.com/Default.asp and Cold North Wind, Inc http://www.cold-northwind.com/ *Who We Are* pages as well as notes from the lecture by Bob Huggins, President and CEO of Cold North Wind at: *Canadian Newspapers Online: A National Consultation: toward a national strategy to strengthen access to Canadian Newspapers Online*. Speaker Notes. Ottawa: National Library of Canada, 8 October 2002.

4   Notes from the lecture by Bob Huggins, President and CEO of Cold North Wind at: *Canadian Newspapers Online: A National Consultation: toward a national strategy to strengthen access to Canadian Newspapers Online*. Speaker Notes. Ottawa: National Library of Canada, 8 October 2002.

(two year, 1892-1894, are not available except for the first issue, November 3, 1892 as the originals were not available at the time of filming). The newspaper pages in *Pages of the Past* are high-resolution scans that average 700KB each. Subscriptions through the Torstar Syndication Services are available on 1, 24, and 72-hour bases as well as on 7 days to a one-month basis. The *Toronto Star* is the largest English-language newspaper in Canada with 2.2 million readers.

The *Globe and Mail: Canada's Heritage from 1844* is the second-largest newspaper to be digitized in Canada. It runs from an earlier period in Canada's history, 1844 (20+ years prior to the confederation of Canada's four largest provinces) and goes to 2001.[5] It is now made available on a subscription basis through Micromedia ProQuest, which allows the product to reach the more lucrative Canadian Studies market in the United States and other countries. An added feature of this product is the ability to view the results in thumbnail format as well as full-page pdf's with the highlighted search word.

Micromedia has made available another option for both products; namely, perpetual access whereby, subject to license agreements, on a non-exclusive, non-transferable basis, subscribers may download one electronic copy of the database for storage on their internal system. For access (as of 2004) a site would pay a one-time fee of four times their current site license price or $10,000 (U.S.) whichever is greater. A site can choose to discontinue subscriptions and keep the file (in the case of *Globe and Mail*, perpetual access covers 1844 to 1950) and if they were to continue their subscription, the annual cost would be 65% of what they would have paid if they had not opted for perpetual access. It is also available for both the unlimited access and simultaneous user options and has been made available to consortia subscribers.[6]

Non-Commercial Web Sites

In a recent media release, the Bibliothèque nationale du Québec announced an intention to add to its web site more than three million pages of Quebec newspapers from the 19th century up to 1950 as well as cultural reviews from 1900 to 1950.[7] These materials will be available free-of-charge. Société canadienne du microfilm, inc. a company that has filmed a large number of historical French-language newspapers in Canada, has been under negotiations with *La presse* and other French-language newspapers as well as Olive Software to look at digitization of some of the historic pages.

Another Olive Software product available through the University of Alberta Libraries is a digitization of three Franco-Albertan newspapers, *La survivance, Le franco-albertain* and *Le franco* from 1928 to 1967. This is part of a larger Alberta Heritage Digitization Project which is an ongoing project to digitize historical information which is otherwise difficult to access including Alberta folklore; art; aerial photographs; maps; early Alberta newspapers; Alberta's retrospective bills, statutes, and gazettes; and local histories. This project has made use of collections from the University of Calgary, the Provincial Archives of Alberta, the Glenbow and Nickle Arts Museums, the Historical Society of Alberta, and the Universities of Alberta and Calgary and is funded by Canada's Digital Collections Initiative

5 Ibid.

6 Message November 22, 2004 posted on concan-l on behalf of John Durno. The *Perpetual Access Addendum* is available at: http://www.micromedia.ca/products_services/Perpetual_access.htm

7 *La tribune.* Sherbrooke, Quebec, February 18, 2005 p. D3 D'ici peu s'ajouteront plus de trois millions de pages de journaux québécois du XIXe siècle jusqu'en 1950 ainsi que plusieurs revues culturelles des années 1900 à 1950.

at Industry Canada, the Millennium Bureau of Canada, Alberta Historical Resources Foundation, the Alberta Knowledge Network, the Alberta Library, the University of Calgary, the Alberta Law Foundation, the Calgary Foundation, and the Calgary Community Lottery Board.[8]

The HALINET (the HALton Information NETwork) is a partnership of public libraries, the school boards and Sheridan College – all located in the Regional Municipality of Halton in Ontario. The project includes a unified Halton County set of local newspaper indexes from a variety of sources with the added feature of being able to search more than 65,000 newspaper images in black and white and in colour (the colour images are produced directly from the print edition; the black and white from microfilm editions). HALINET employs Lizard Tech's MrSID (Multi Resolution Seamless Image Database) for better delivery of the images over the Internet for purposes of printing. The image files of the newspapers are processed through MrSID and patrons are able to zoom in on the picture or article in which they are interested, and print just that. Alternatively, they are able to shrink the image of an individual page of a newspaper and print that.[9]

The University of Alberta Library and the Manitoba Library Consortium are collaborating on *Manitoba: Life and Times*, a digitization project that will include community newspapers and make them available free-of-charge in a full-text searchable online interface.[10]

The growth of digital newspaper and newspaper indexing pages that feature Canadian newspapers and Canadian newspaper indexes is almost unmanageable. In addition to the snapshot approach that Library and Archives hope to take of this area, we also maintain a list of newspaper web pages, indexes and non-Canadian pages which feature Canadian news sites at News Sites – Internet / Sites d'informations sur l'Internet at: http://www.collectionscanada.ca/8/16/r16-211-e.html and http://www.collectionscanada.ca/8/16/r16-211-f.html

Issues and Concerns

There are quite a few reasons why Canada, and perhaps many other countries have been slow to adopt either whole-scale funding or support for full-text newspaper digitization on a grand scale. The following are the difficulties and challenges that almost any institution has faced at one time or another concerning not only newspaper digitization and access but, in general, access to newspapers in any format as often the same frustrations apply.

Unlike other types of information, newspapers tend to be a conglomerate of styles, fonts, media, presentations and content. While handwritten documents tend to be the most challenging types of documents to scan and index, especially those with a variety of authors, newspapers can be equally challenging. The type of OCR required to not only interpret different kinds and size of print but also photographic images must be quite sophisticated and sophistication means higher cost

---

8 More information on this project is available at: http://www.ourfutureourpast.ca/about.htm
9 Information has been taken from the HALINET description on CIDL (Canadian Inventory of Digital Initiatives at: http://www.collectionscanada.ca/initiatives/; specifically at: http://www.hhpl.on.ca/halinet/demo_home.htm and from HALINET's information page at: http://www.hhpl.on.ca/halinet/demo_home.htm
10 Web announcement Tuesday, March 1, 2005, Email sent on behalf of the School of Library & Information Studies, University of Alberta to slis-everyone@mailman.svr.ualberta.ca on the subject of a Research Seminar, *Manitoba Metadata: Digitizing Manitoba's Cultural Heritage* presented by Bess Sadler, to be held Monday, March 7, 2005 at the School of Library and Information Studies, University of Alberta, Edmonton, Alberta

The digitized product is only as good as the source. All of the inherent problems with microfilm are magnified with the digital product. These include poor quality of the filming, missing microfilm masters, incomplete editions, removal of certain parts of the newspaper from the microfilm product and huge storage costs (although these are decreasing). As well, the cleanup; i.e. removing speckling, scratches, straightening images, and removing borders around pages, is usually dependent upon a proprietary software program.

The bottom line for newspapers is profit; the bottom line for publicly-supported libraries and archives is making information available free of charge to users while preserving original content. The goals of public and private sectors can be mutually exclusive. Most libraries must support digitization in conjunction with some preservation of the original, usually through the recognized standards that apply to preservation microfilming. Most newspapers are not particularly interested in microfilm other than as a revenue-generating part of their business. As libraries opt for digital products, they tend to decrease their subscriptions to print and microfilm editions of newspapers in exchange for the more accessible CD-ROM or online product and most libraries do not have the luxury of subscribing to both versions except perhaps for their local newspaper.

In Canada, most microfilming of newspapers is commercial yet less than 1/10th of the newspapers filmed in Canada are filmed in four or more copies. Thus, in Canada, 9/10th of newspapers filmed are not required to be sent on legal deposit to Library and Archives Canada. Without subscribers, filming decreases and even fewer libraries or local archives or historical societies maintain large print collections. Although Library and Archives Canada does maintain a large print newspaper collection, these papers are in bound volumes and would require refilming to be used in any major wholesale digitization project.

Digitization of coloured pages still requires the use of originals and supplements to print newspapers are often not included in subscription prices. Copyright protection for newspapers is rarely available for the whole newspaper and any subscriber to online systems can relate the frustration of finding whole or parts of stories removed as copyright permission was not obtainable or the copyright for a part of a paper is not available on that particular system. In addition to the copyright as it applies to newspapers as a whole, copyright varies widely as it applies to photographs, republished material, bylines, cartoons, letters to the editor, editorials to name a few.

Newspapers are still searching for a profitable business model for the web version of their product. They have tried putting up their newspaper archives for less than a year or requiring that subscribers to the Net version must be print subscribers. There has been a recent flurry of activity by some of the larger publishers to invest in wholly Net-based products whose audiences primarily access their information on line. In Canada with relatively few independent daily newspapers, the newspaper chains dictate the same digitization and indexing practices and, by and large, they have not marketed parts of their product as a Web source to any particular audience; e.g. their birth, marriage and death notices to genealogists.

For libraries and archives charged with preserving Canada's heritage, digitization poses an interesting dilemma. Most institutions have long given up the idea that they can or should preserve everything centrally but the attitude toward digitization as replacement technology still remains fairly strong especially at the management level or the government level deciding on budgets. Planning for long-term preservation needs to receive more attention. There are no proven standards for digital preservation except for migration of content to other formats and the Association of Research Libraries endorses digitization as an accepted preservation reformatting option. However, many institutions that digitized material and did not keep the originals are finding that they now must produce a microfilm edition from the digital product and some have even reproduced printed copies of digital documents in order to save the content. However, reproduction from the digital content means the loss of the original audio files and digital videos from the born-digital versions.[11]

Conclusion

The newspaper, as we know it, is changing. It flashes, it beeps, it interacts with other media, and it disappears to reappear in another version and reinvents itself several times a day. It is, as one standards expert puts it, a «moving target».[12] In planning digitization projects, we need a digital strategy and some tough decision making as to what can be preserved and in what format and perhaps most importantly, who is responsible and who will take responsibility in the long term.

At a recent Symposium on Web Archiving held at Library and Archives Canada February 3, 2005, Ingrid Mason stressed the need for institutions to demonstrate the integrity of what they do in building a digital archive.[13] In order to arrive at a common goal, it is difficult to meld the aims of institutions, which promote preservation and free access with those of the news business that is constantly experimenting to stay ahead commercially. Future Canadian digitization projects must reflect clear thinking and a common goal to preserve a part of Canada's heritage that is rapidly disappearing. Without a strategy or leaders to convince legislators and funding agencies and a mandate to facilitate access, large-scale co-operative projects will not be successful.

---

11 Digital dark ages: drastic action needed to preserve computerized photos and other files. By Sarah McGinnis, *Telegraph-Journal*, December 11, 2004 *New Brunswick Telegraph-Journal*. p. A1/A8 «Preserving digital files may mean avoiding computers altogether. The provincial archives is putting the most vital information back on microfilm, which avoids the problem of ‹CD rot› and disintegrating data. They are also reverting back to paper by printing copies of digital documents.»

12 NML: the News Business Gets Serious about Content. By Barry Schaeffer *Newspapers and Technology Magazine*, June 4, 1999. (Reprinted at: http://www.xsystems.com/nml.htm)

13 Ingrid Mason. Presentation on New Zealand Digital Web Archiving at Symposium on Web Archiving, February 3, 2005, Ottawa, Canada.

THE CALIFORNIA NEWSPAPER PROJECT: CANVASSING, CATALOGING, PRESERVATION, DIGITIZATION

Henry Snyder

Center for Bibliographical Studies and Research
University of California, Riverside, USA

The California Newspaper Project is a component of the United States Newspaper Project (USNP), a massive effort to record the surviving issues of newspapers published in the United States and ensure their preservation for future generations. In its first years the National Endowment of the Humanities (NEH) invited major humanities scholarly organizations to suggest large-scale projects it might sponsor. The Organization of American Historians responded, Save «America's newspapers». The USNP was the result. Initially the NEH selected ten major repositories to inventory their collections, thus creating a base file. The records were loaded into CONSER, the national serials data base maintained by OCLC. Now, two decades later, projects have been sponsored in all states and territories and the District of Columbia. I believe all are finished except for New York, Pennsylvania and California.

California is the third largest (after New York and Illinois) in terms of total number of titles recovered and second (after Texas) in terms of geographical area. As of the first of this year we had created or edited 8,772 records for California titles and 5,565 for out-of-state titles held in California repositories. Our working file which includes entries not yet verified, some for which no copy survives, and some dupilctes, totals 18,510. We have verified a total of 42,171 holdings records to date. We have visited over 1,400 institutions, some many times. This has meant a great deal of time on the road. If any of you know the Los Angeles area you will know that leaving the Riverside and driving anywhere in the center or west side of Los Angeles County can take up to two to three hours in traffic, each way. Unfortunately our location means that we almost always have to buck the traffic. It is somewhat better from Berkeley or Sacramento but then the distances to travel are longer. I personally visited all the libraries in the mountain counties, traveling from Modoc near the northern border to Mariposa in the South. This has been a formidable undertaking. The sheer size of the state dictated multiple canvass teams. We created three, one based in Sacramento to cover the Central Valley and Sierras; a second based in Berkeley to cover the coast as far south as Ventura County; and a third based in Riverside to cover the state south of the Tehachapis. The Sacramento office, based at the State Library, was the first to finish and was then closed down. The other two offices continue and have undertaken additional duties germane to the project. The full-time assistant director is based at the University of California, Berkeley. The main office of the Center for Bibliographical Studies and Research (CBSR), which houses the project, is located at the University of California, Riverside. In addition to the CNP the Center manages the English Short Title Catalog (ESTC) in North America, CCILA, a union catalog of Latin American imprints to 1851, and the Burney Newspaper Digitization Project, conducted in partnership with the British Library. The ESTC is a joint venture with the British Library and the American Antiquarian Society.

Unlike many states there is no one predominant collection of U.S. or California newspapers in the state. The largest collection is in the Bancroft Library at the University of California,

Berkeley (UCB), which is why we located one of the offices there. UCB has approximately 5,000 titles. The second largest collection is at the State Library, approximately 2,000 titles with another 800 or so sample issues. The State Library undertook an initial survey to determine the scope of the project but declined responsibility for its management. UCB also refused. As a native Californian, and recognizing the importance of the project, I agreed to accept responsibility for it at the Center. We applied for funding in 1990 and received our first award in 1991. To date we have received over $8,000,000 in funding from the NEH. In addition we were able to secure appropriations from the State of California which have generated $1,380,000 to date.

I will not go into detail into the canvassing and cataloging phase. Initially I thought we would do the two phases seriatim, inventorying and cataloging first, preservation, i.e., microfilming second. I was concerned about unnecessary duplication. And because of the existence of several large collections, two I have mentioned, we could not be sure that when we completed the canvass of a county we would have the complete picture. What we did do at the beginning was to key in the holdings of the major commercial microfilm distributors. The most important is Bay Microimaging in the Bay Area with an estimated 65,000 one hundred foot reels. Rivaling it is ProQuest, which has swallowed up the archives of a number of firms over the years. They were two other substantial though smaller firms in the state, Data in Burbank with 1,800 one thousand foot cans and Custom in Riverside with approximately 1,000 one thousand foot cans of California titles, plus another 8 to 900 one thousand foot cans of out-of-state and foreign titles. The latter two were both in Southern California. Once all their catalogs or lists were keyed in we had a fairly complete picture. In the case of the Data film we went and made a physical inventory of their archive as their list was not complete. In addition to its own inventory, BMI also housed some 800 one thousand foot cans filmed for the State Library, mainly of its own holdings.

Aside from concern about duplication, we were also concerned about coverage. As I have indicated California is a large state, over 800 miles from North to South, over 250 miles from East to West. I wanted to be sure we had as complete geographical as well as chronological coverage as possible. I hired a graduate student to make a study for us, listing all the incorporated cities over 100,000 population. I also had her include a least one community for every county. In some of the mountain counties there are very few inhabitants. In at least one county there is no incorporated town, not even the county seat. In the absence of an incorporated town we included the county seat. After identifying the communities according to these guidelines we created a chart showing the coverage by newspapers, dailies or in the absence of dailies weeklies. Then we identified what had been filmed. On this basis we could begin to identify titles for filming. We decided to begin the filming in advance of the completion of the survey, satisfied we had sufficient data to avoid duplication and to fill in the gaps on geographic or chronological coverage. We based the filming operation at the Berkeley office. We obtained some emergency money from the State Library to film titles and runs in danger. But this was only stopgap. NEH required major matching funding for the preservation phase. Given the size of our task I was skeptical of finding foundation funding. My first several efforts were unsuccessful. I went therefore to the State Library and asked if they could include a sum in their budget request for matching funding for us. The Librarian was reluctant, given the cutbacks the Library had already experienced in a time of budget crunches. He did introduce me to a state senator whose family had owned the principal newspaper in Santa Cruz. He had served as publisher but had subsequently sold the newspaper. He responded positively and agreed to enter a bill. I am pleased to say the bill passed through two committees in each House and the Houses themselves without dissent. The Governor subsequently vetoed the bill but wrote the Senator that it was not necessary to have a separate bill. It was such a good project he would find money in the State budget and did so. So far as I am aware we are the only project of more than fifty than has been able to obtain an individual state appropriation.

We began filming in 1999. As we visited publishers' offices, historical societies, libraries, and other repositories we often saw runs in poor condition and vulnerable. We picked them up on the spot, when allowed, and these became the priority titles. We were also interested in filling in gaps in existing runs and re-filming titles that had been poorly filmed. Fortunately so much had been filmed that we have been able to film pretty much anything we have identified of interest.

The most interesting development in the CNP, which leads directly to prospects for digitization, is our acquisition of extensive film stocks. Again, so far as we are aware, this is unprecedented in the USNP. And it was serendipitous. It began when we read a story in the Los Angeles Times of a suburban newspaper publisher that had gone bankrupt. Its effects were sold at auction. They included, according to the story, steel cabinets of microfilm which were sold for $10.00 a piece, that is the cabinet with the film! It took me the better part of a year to track down the purchaser. The auctioneer would not release the name but forwarded our inquiry. The effects were purchased by another suburban publisher, with a string of titles, largely for the names. For another year I tried in vain to gain access to the films. Finally a long-time employee put me in touch with the publisher. He agreed to give me the negatives together with permission to reproduce them. When we went to collect them my colleague saw 563 bound volumes of newspapers, none of which were filmed. On inquiry she found they were about to be pulped. They were given to her and returned to us with the film. In all we obtained about 1,600 hundred foot reels. In many cases we were unaware of any positive. I subsequently made another trip to the publisher's office with another long-time employee who was anxious to see the film saved. We went through the office and retrieved another 200 plus reels. We were just in time. As we searched the office we overhead a heated argument in the board room. The publisher resigned that day at the end of the meeting! We had arrived just in time.

We are not set up to maintain a permanent archive, let alone a film archive. Ours is a term project. Consequently any film we order or acquire is deposited at one of the two University of California library storage facilities that serve the whole system. One is in the North at Berkeley, the other in the South at Los Angeles. The film is deposited in the name of either the UC Riverside or the UC Berkeley libraries.

The Wave film (that was the name of the publisher) was only a taste of what was to come. I have long been concerned about the longevity of film held by commercial filmers or publishers. The history of newspapers in California and elsewhere is one of frequent closures, consolidations, and absorptions. In the process back runs as well as films are not infrequently discarded. But this is also true of commercial filmers. I had heard that Custom Microfilms in Riverside, the third largest in the state insofar as newspapers were concerned, was in financial difficulty. They had a substantial archive. I paid a call on them and offered to relieve them of responsibility for the archive, when they told me they were going to cease microfilming newspapers. I tried several times to make contact again without avail. Suddenly the place shut down and the contents of the building disappeared, including pallets of newspapers awaiting filmed. I later learned the newspapers were all dumped. I had alerted both the State Library and the California Newspaper Publishers Association of the pending closure but neither felt empowered to step in. A year later I received a phone call from a jobber in the high desert, sixty miles north of Riverside. He informed me he had purchased the film archive and had found my name in some correspondence. He asked me if I was interested in acquiring the films. I responded yes and paid him an immediate visit. I asked him how much he wanted for the stock, which he estimated at the equivalent of 10,000 one hundred foot reels. When he would not name a figure I named one and he accepted. The next day I sent a truck up and the film was ours. For the next several weeks he kept turning up more boxes and bags of film which he turned over to us at no additional charge. We ended up with approximately 18,000 reels. After disposing of out-of-state, serial and foreign titles we were left with about 10,000 reels. We have spent several years sorting it out, trying to identify the owners, and then negotiating to keep the films to ensure their retention. In most cases we have been successful. We now had 12,000 reels between the two acquisitions.

Given this history I approached the second largest filmer, Data in Burbank, and offered to take back runs off their hands for which they received little or no orders. They agreed to consider the offer. Several months later they responded they would turn over some of the older material to us. They were moving to a new location and this would reduce the need for storage capacity. When we drove over to pick the film up we found they had already moved. A staff member remained behind to give us the film. They decided to give us almost the entire archive, even some titles still being filmed and published, in all approximately 1,500 one thousand foot cans! We are still finishing the processing of the Custom stock and now have another huge batch on our hands to sort out, inventory, catalog, test for condition, replace where necessary and send to the UC storage facility. And I am negotiating with still another commercial filmer with the prospect of another 5,000 to 10,000 reels.[1] Moreover, the State Library is about ready to turn over its film to us to deposit at UC, another 7,000 to 8,000 reels, to save storage charges. In sum, we now own some 27,000 one hundred foot reels and have the possibility of acquiring another 12,000 to 18,000 reels. We are now the owners of a major film archive! Now we are ready to talk digitization.

Our first foray into digitization began nearly five years ago. The Center for Bibliographical Studies at the University of California, Riverside, in conjunction with the British Library, is currently involved a major project to create digitized and text-searchable versions of the Burney Collection of eighteenth-century English newspapers in the newspapers. The Burney Collection is the largest and most important of its kind in existence. But it is not easily available to scholars. The collection has been withdrawn from circulation because of its fragility. It is accessible to readers only through a single deteriorating service copy of a microfilm made three decades ago. The master negative itself, acetate based, is also deteriorating. A commercial version had been modified by additions and subtractions so did not provide full access to the collection. In 1999 the head of early printed collections at the BL approached me for assistance in obtaining funding to digitize the film. I learned that the National Science Foundation might be interested and applied for funding. We received two successive awards, totalling $703,000. It was the assumption at the British Library that the then current software available could not distill the film because of the unevenness of hand set type, broken letters, inequality in inking, print through, and other problems. As we began to explore the issues involved we learned of the development of a new software in Israel, Olive, that could make this possible with a sufficient degree of accuracy by a combination of fuzzy logic programs.

There was considerable discussion about the various technical requirements which should be specified. After much consultation it was decided to employ bi-tonal rather than gray scale. The reasons were several: the nature of the filmed originals themselves; The much greater cost and storage capacity required for grey scale; the advice of the owner and devel-

---

1   That agreement is now concluded. We expect to receive 14,400 one hundred foot reels.

oper of Olive, Yonni Stern. He advised that the results for the majority of the images would be as good in bitonal as in grey scale; that of the remaining frames half would be better in bitonal, half would be better in grey. After considering factors of economy and file size a DPI rate of 300 was decided. As a result the Center in 2001 applied to the National Science Foundation for funding and received two successive grants of $400,000 and $303,000 respectively to digitize and then distill the film. As part of the digitization proposal there were also detailed specifications for indexing: by title, date, volume and issue number, reel and item number, and the shelfmark of the original. One result has been that for the first time the BL has an accurate record of what the Burney Collection contains! RFPs were issued for the two phases. Three bids were received. Micro-Methods in Yorkshire, England was chosen for the digitization and the contract was signed in the spring of 2002. The digitization was successfully completed late in 2002. Examples of the digitized images can be examined on our webpage, at cbsr.ucr.edu. In the process it was discovered that the estimate of the BL of 650,000 frames was far too low. The final number of frames was 987,000. As a consequence there were not sufficient funds remaining to complete the second phase.

After learning that the number of frames was 50% larger, it was decided to re-issue the RFP for the distillation. Again three responses were received. In the meantime the BL had applied for a received funding from the Joint Information Systems Committee (JISC) in the United Kingdom to digitize and distill two million frames of nineteenth-century British newspapers. The BL suggested that economies could be achieved by employing the same vendor. For example, only one search engine would have to be created. Moreover, scholars would be better served by having significant runs of British newspapers searchable through a single command from Restoration England to the end of the Victorian era.

It is our intent to mount the images in both the United Kingdom and North America and provide free access. We expect the results will transform research into British history from the late seventeenth century to the end of the eighteenth century. The time period spanned by the collections encompasses the development of the English newspaper in Great Britain and Ireland. There are even runs from North America. The frequency, the physical size, the type size, the organization, the contents all developed from inauspicious beginnings until by 1800 the newspapers produced and sold were similar in format, size and content to what we are familiar with today. They include news, commentary, columnists, advertisements, reviews, advice to the lovelorn, obituaries, to mention just a few topics. Now finally with text-searchable, digitized versions available on the desktop or laptop computer of the research in his or her office or home this vast corpus of material will finally be unveiled. Even the Burney Collection is not complete. Some runs are incomplete, many titles are omitted. Because of the digital nature of the file it will be possible to obtain titles and issues to fill in the gaps and them to the online collection for seamless, boolean searching. It is an unparalleled, landmark achievement.

Our next project was a California one. Two years ago the State Library approached us about digitizing the earliest California newspaper, the Alta California, and its immediate successors, the most important title for the third quarter of the nineteenth century. They also contacted the head of preservation at the UC Berkeley library. Now a third party is involved, a consortium of libraries on the peninsula south of San Francisco. Identical sample rolls of second generation negatives of the San Francisco Daily Alta California and related titles were sent to 10 digital services companies. They were asked to scan and OCR all the issues on the film and create a test database and web site and provide cost estimates. We didn't give the vendors specifications since we wanted to see what they would all come up with as their best product. Project evaluators then viewed the various websites to compare the quality of the images, searchability of the text, and the various features for browsing and searching. Because the vendors chose the issues they wanted to scan (we intentionally included some very bad images) and there were no common pages on all the sites, we couldn't compare search results. But, the evaluators were able to rate features as essential, important or not important and also rate the implementation of these features at the various sites. The results can be seen on the web at //cpc.stanford.edu/cndp/. We have applied for funding to the State Library. [2]

Mark Sweeney has told you about the major, twenty year initiative to be funded by NEH, if Congress appropriates the funds, and administered by the Library of Congress to digitize a selection of American newspapers in text-searchable versions through the LC webpage. We have applied for one of the initial grants. The awards will be announced in April.[3] For the test period newspapers only for the years 1900-1910 will be included. When the test results are in and LC has decided on the standards to be employed for the full-scale project the covered will be extended from 1828 to 1922. We have submitted a list of potential titles to be scanned. One of the requirements in the guidelines issued by NEH is that the applicant must own the film. Now you can see the importance of the film archive we have acquired. As we already have potential vendors as a result of the Alta California project, with costs and work samples, we hope to move fairly rapidly if we receive an award.

We now face a whole new dimension of the CNP, thanks in part to the film archive we have acquired. With the results of the Alta California test we have a pool of vendors from whom to choose. If we are successful in obtaining funding from NEH from the Test phase and the full phase that follows we should have sufficient funding to digitize a sizeable number of runs, representing the diversity of the state. But there are many variables we must consider before embarking on an extensive digitization project or series of projects. In many cases the issues are the same we encountered when we began a filming program.

Insofar as technical standards are concerned they are or will be well-defined by LC as a result of the test projects. But the technical issues also include the film itself from which the digitized images are created. One variable is the quality of the film. The process by which the film was created, using acetate base or polyester, dioxide or other processes, is less important than the current state. Acetate film can deteriorate rapidly. There is a test tape one can purchase and place in the can that in 24 hours will give one a measurement of the deterioration. We have done this for a large part of our acetate-based films, which comprise some seventy percent of the total. Where the test level falls below a certain figure the films will be reformatted onto polyester. In a few cases the film is so badly warped it my be impossible to restore. Most of it seems to be in satisfactory condition and the storage conditions at the UC facilities will certainly extend its life.

A second issue is the filming itself. Where the originals of unequal paper color? Is their printout through? Are their tears and missing portions? Are the images indistinct and fuzzy? All or any of these factors may inhibit creating text searchable if not digitized versions. If the film is of poor quality but the title itself is a high priority can it be refilmed? Are the originals still available? Fortunately now that our canvass has been completed we should be able to answer the last question quickly. At the same time any new filming requires an analysis of the originals to insure they are suitable for filming.

---

2 We subsequently received funding for the first year of a two-year project to film the entire run plus another title to fill in the gap from the end of the Alta California to 1900 when the NDNP project takes up. We will thus have a complete run of a California newspaper from 1846 to 1910 on the web for public access by the summer of 2007.

3 We subsequently received notice that we were one of six grantees receiving $400,000 for two years to digitize some 100,000 pages.

A third set of issues is the nature of the run itself. Is it complete? If there are missing issues, what percentage are not present? Is there another title available for the same region and period that is complete? One of the great advantages of creating digitized runs is that we can digitize multiple sets of film and then collate the results to create full, more comprehensive runs, instead of a series of overlapping runs, each required to flesh out others. I recall one county library I visited where the two major titles published in the county seat, extending backwards for more than a century had been filmed. But what had been filmed were nine different overlapping sets, none complete in themselves. For two of the reels they were using the negatives as service copies. For the rest service copies and negatives were present, in some cases as many of three of the former. There was no consistency. This can be a wonderful example of the advantage of digitized images that they can be loaded into a single file and the user will have access to a seamless run by title and date.

Technical issues aside the selection of the titles themselves is a more sensitive issue than it has been for filming. As I suggested earlier, we found that a large part of the surviving runs and issues had been filmed, especially of the most important titles. This gave us the luxury of filling in titles with more limited coverage and circulation but which were still required to provide geographic coverage of the state. But digitization is a different matter. It will require careful selection and the percentage of titles digitized will be only a fraction of those filmed. We must state here that many of the major dailies, those for San Francisco, Los Angeles, San Jose and San Diego were filmed by the publishers who hold title to the negatives. These are in turn being digitized by commercial firms. So far as we can determine at the moment only Sacramento newspapers are not the object of a digitization project. And the city, though not the largest, is important as the seat of state government. Therefore, its contents are likely to be of special interest. I remind you that we own an archive of some 27,000 one hundred foot reels[4]. We estimate that UC Berkeley and the State Library together own approximately 15,000 more giving us a total of over 40,000[5] reels either in or possession or which we can access. We are convening a meeting of the three institutions to discuss possible cooperation. One partial run of a title in one institution may be completed by another run elsewhere. We propose therefore to follow much the same rules we employed for filming. We will aggregate the three collections. We will then analyze the total by factors including:

The length of the run

Where multiple titles exist for a specified time span we will identify the more important title, though modified by completeness, length of run, condition of originals, condition of films and related factor. We will group the titles by geographical coverage. Working with a panel of advisors – librarians, historians – and taking into account the major dailies which are being digitized commercially we will create a priority or desiderata list. We will then re-evaluate the priorities in terms of condition, completeness, frequency, etc. My own choice – made prior to the extensive analyses we expect to make is a Sacramento title. We hope to complete this analysis in the next three to six months. Then, if we receive an award from NEH, we will be in a position to move ahead and begin this new phase of the California Newspaper Project. Recognizing that NEH can only be expected to fund a small percentage of the total number of titles on film in our possession we will then explore with the other

---

4 With the fourth acquisition, which should be received by the end of 2005 the number will climb to over 40,000.
5 Now 55,000.

institutions the possibility of making the films available to commercial firms for digitization.

The California Newspaper Project is a term project. Once it is completed, and funding ends, it will close. But we have become aware that the whole enterprise is too vital for preserving the historical record of the state to simply shut down. For one thing, if there is value in inventorying and preserve what survives of the newspapers published in California surely that value extends to the future as well as the past. It is over a decade since we surveyed the first counties. What has transpired since that time? New titles have appeared, others have been terminated. Are the physical copies still in existence? Have they been preserved safely and filmed? There is an urgent need to provide for a continuing presence. There is the management of the film stock. To whom will that responsibility devolve? Our files include details of issue by issue inventories that cannot be entered in the CONSER records. There are all our historical notes, a library of newspaper histories and special issues, and other related material. All are of considerable value to future researchers. How will they be preserved and accessed? It is my hope that a California Newspaper Archive can be created, location yet to be determined, with continued state funding to ensure the maintenance of this invaluable and unique historical resource.

DEVELOPMENTS OF FRENCH
NEWSPAPER PUBLISHING : A GENERAL VIEW

Else Delaunay

Bibliothèque nationale de France

Abstract

At present the French Newspaper Publishing finds itself in a situation of stagnation and even regression. For the last years most daily newspapers have regressed with regard to circulation, sales and advertising incomings. This decline is due to several reasons : competition of other information media (free newspapers, television, Internet). Means and remedies to fight against the decline and take up the challenge are developed by the author : better editorial quality, better information control and analyzing of the information, new ways to captivate young readers, industrial investors and the risk for press freedom, etc. French press is still hesitating as to which way to go but most newspaper undertakings are reflecting on the problem knowing they have to act very quickly now in order to reverse the present evolution

Introduction

Indeed, it is not easy to give a clear and precise picture of what is going on at the moment. Surely the situation of the French press is difficult as for newspapers in many other countries. However, the reasons of the present stagnation in France may not always be the same as in those countries. I shall try here to introduce you shortly to the present situation, in particular to the daily press and its weekly supplements.

France has a long press tradition. The first French newspaper *La Gazette* by Théophraste Renaudot dates back to 1631. In 1836, when launching his daily newspaper *La Presse* which quickly became a great success, Emile de Girardin cut down the issue price 50 % with regard to other rivaling newspapers as he understood it was neccessary to lower the price in order to multiply the number of readers and, consequently, be more attractive to advertisers who would then pay a part of the newspaper. *The modern newspaper publishing was born.*

Since then, the French press has been living on a double easy theorem: lower sales prices mean better sales; the newspaper sales and the advertising finance the undertaking. But today this model is compromised, both economically and as to the contents of the newspaper. It seems to be the end of an historical cycle. The press must look to new ideas, new settings of presentation and content, in other words a redynamisation is necessary so as to win back lost readership, to captivate new readers, especially the youth, and to find new advertisers. A real challenge for the next years…

In most newspapers there is not yet special contents for young readers. Generally the items which concern young people are to be found in supplements and inserts published weekly by the daily newspapers (ex. *Le Monde 2* which is highly illustrated; *Le Figaro Grandes écoles* and *Les Echos Sup* both meant for students). It is indeed time to reexamine the situation so as to understand young people's new tastes and priorities.

Regulation of French Newspaper Publishing

The Freedom of the press was conceded in 1881, a 100 years after the Human Rights Declaration and the French Revolution ! It was the beginning of a real «gold age» for the French press. Daily and weekly newspapers flourished all over the country and this period lasted until 1914. Even after the First World war the press was still very active.

After the Second World war the French press was totally reorganised but the principle of freedom of expression remained. This freedom is eroded today as newspapers are more and more dependent on funding... and big financial groups do own most of the papers. Under such circumstancies it is indeed difficult for the journalists to remain free to express opinons and ideas or to critisize actions or official statements.

Right now, as the freedom of the press recently has been attacked several times, an association of journalists called «Droit à l 'Info» (which means «Right to Inform») tries to formulate an amendment to the bill in order to defend journalists' rights and freedom and to guarantee their duties.

Reasons of the present stagnation

The economic degradation due to fall of incomings is of course the most serious problem. When funding is cut down, developing possibilities of the newspaper will shrink.

Since 1990, the regional newspapers have lost 660 000 copies; paid circulation concerned 5.6 million copies for 18 million users which means an average reduction of 1.2 % per year.

After the Second World War 175 regional dailies were published in France and 82 dailies in Paris; today 63 regional newspapers are issued every day. In Paris there are only 16 daily newspapers, the same amount as in 1828, at the very beginning of the industrial newspaper publishing !

Sales incomings

Prices seem too high as information has become very cheap at present through audiovisual media (television, Internet) and free newspapers. Readers do not want to spend money on newspapers if they do not get more here than in the free papers or on Internet. Single copy price of a national daily varies from 0,80 euro (*L'Equipe*) to 1,20 euro (*Libération, Les Echos*) and of a regional daily from 0,70 euro (*Ouest-France*) to 0,90 euro (*L'Est républicain*).

The eroding of the single copy sales is also due to the fact that the youth (aged 15 to 25) is not interested in daily newspaper reading as it does not find its marks in the contents of the papers. It is a question of subjects dealt with and the way they are developed but also of accuracy of informations and to what extend one can rely on them. The phenomenon is not limited to France. The sales of the American daily *International Herald Tribune* were reduced by 4.16 % in 2003, in the UK sales of the *Financial Times* regressed by 6.06 % during the same year. Subscriptions represent a small part of the national newspapers sales (23 %) while they are very well off for regional and local newspapers (52 %). In fact, many local readers prefer subscription to daily purchase of a newspaper as selling places may be quite far away, especially for readers outside the towns.

Advertising incomings

At present, newspapers spend an important amount of money on advertising on television but their advertising incomings have lowered very much, especially because of the classified advertising. Only a few national newspapers as *Le Figaro, Aujourd'hui Le Parisien, La*

Croix ... and quite a number of regional newspapers such as *Ouest France, Les Dernières Nouvelles d'Alsace, La Montagne*... have a good deal of classified advertising. Moreover, free newspapers such as *Métro, 20 Minutes, A nous Paris , Paru-vendu* ... have taken over a great part of advertising as the publishing of these papers only depend on advertising incomings. Some national and regional newspapers have now invested in free newspapers.

As to the audience *20 Minutes* touches already an average of 2 million readers per day, while the daily *Le Parisien* (including 11 local editions around Paris) only touches 1.7 million; *Métro* has 1.6 million readers a day and reaches a great number of towns in France. It is true that editorial quality has improved recently in some of the free newspapers.

On the whole *sales incomings* represented 50.4 % in 2003 and *advertising incomings* 49.6 % of which classified advertising represented only 17.9 %. That means a general reduction of 2.2 % with regard to 2002.

Closing down of selling places

France has round 32 400 sales spots of which ca 875 were closed in 2004, especially booths in Paris. It is a hard job to be distributor of newspapers as the French law requires that all newspapers received must be on display, whether they are very much sold or not. It is Bichet's bill of 1947 which forbids all discrimination of distribution among the titles, even if 20 % generate 80 % of the turnover. It is a principle of displaying all trends of the press. A distributor generally manage from 1000 to 3000 titles and has to run big stocks of non sold copies. He also sells other items than newspapers. But he is quite badly paid, in general from 13 to 18 % of the sales price, while his British colleagues obtain 25 % of the sales price. The closing down of selling places is a real problem. The young readership that almost never takes a subscription of a newspaper, is particularly concerned by the reduction of sales spots. The most efficient spots are the «Maisons de la presse» and «Relay».

Circulation

The circulation of daily newspapers in 2003 represented 2,350,609,336 copies a year. That means a fall of 1.88 % with regard to 2002. There is a regular fall in circulation of daily newspapers. Today France only ranks 31st worldwide with regard to the number of circulated dailies per 1000 inhabitants. Weekly and monthly newspapers or magazines are better off. In general they deal with subjects meant for a specific regular audience but it is also necessary for them to modernize presentation and developing of the subjects. In Germany circulation of daily newspapers have regressed by 7 % during the last five years, in Denmark by 9.5 %, in Austria by 9.9 % and in Belgium by 6.9 %. Even Japanese newspapers which show the highest circulation worldwide have regressed by 2.2 %. In the European Union, during the last eight years, the paid daily newspaper circulation had a fall of 7 million copies. Worldwide the paid circulation of newspapers has a yearly average fall of 2 %. Many daily newspapers companies had to reduce their staff in 2004 (ex. *Le Monde*). After negotiations with the trade-unions a two-yearly plan of voluntary retirement is generally proposed and adopted . In the United States, from 2000 to 2004, the written press industry cut down more than 2000 jobs, that means 4 % of the staffs.

Decline due to lower information and editorial quality

As a matter of fact the decline touches all reference press now. A real modernizing of editorial methods is necessary. If the press seems dull to many people, it is probably because of its information sources and the lack of control and analyzing of informations. Most newspapers are informed by AFP (the French News Agency) so you find the same events and news in them and very often dealt with in the same way. Therefore you get a uniformed and flat presentation in many newspapers; photos too are often the same. Why should you then buy a daily newspaper ? You get the same information in the free papers and, of course, on the web. Besides, most papers have now a web site showing a compact version of the paper. And the television too provides with informations.

The rivals (television, free newspapers, news magazines, websites, newspapers on line) are there to supersede the press and they are cheap. In fact, the worst rival is Internet. In 2004, during the first three month, 4.7 million new web sites were created. Today there are some 70 million web sites worldwide and round 700 million web users ! In many countries people abandon newspaper reading – and even the television – preferring the computer screen. The ADSL has particularly changed the situation. The monthly subscription price of the quick Internet line varies from 10 to 30 euros. In France 5.5 million families have ADSL access to the press on line, texts, photos, music, television, radio, films, etc. 79 % of the world press have editions on line. The «blogs» phenomenon must also be considered. It is caracteristic for the web culture; it has exploded during the last six month of 2004. You find here a mixture of private writings, information, opinions, rumors …with no control. The «bloggers» are subjective and partial. The connection of Internet to the mobile telephone which can do everything will certainly speed up developing. Information becomes still more movable and nomadic. At any time it is possible to know what is going on in the world. The SMS (Short Message Service) is a technology that makes it possible to communicate in a quick, short and cheap way.>BR> Result : all information sectors, except Internet, loose audience; the competition between the medias has become merciless.

A special French phenomenon : Subscription It is true that French readers, especially in Paris and other big towns, prefer to buy the newspaper they want, when they want (may be just once or twice a week) and where they want. It is an old tradition corresponding with a certain taste for individual freedom: to be free to choose and to buy when it suits you. But it is not a very comfortable situation for the newspapers that cannot count on a rather precise amount of regular readers. As to *Newspapers of the 7th day (Sunday)* there is not really a tradition for newspaper reading on Sunday in France, except sport news published in *Le Journal de Dimanche* and in *L'Equipe Dimanche*, as well as in some regional Sunday editions which are more like a supplement than a real newspaper.

But how to fight against stagnation and take up the challenge ?

Means

Financial concentrations

How independent is the French press ? Two big defence groups, Dassault and Lagardère, and two luxury-goods groups, Moët Hennessy Louis Vuitton (LVMH) and Pinault Printemps Redoute (PPR), already control a big chunk of the French newspaper business, and this chunk is now even bigger: the banker Edouard de Rothschild just got the control of 37 % of the capital of *Libération* ! The purchase of *Socpresse* (in April 2004) by the defence group Dassault providing the army with fighter aircrafts on state contracts raised objections about the independence of the press from political interference. According to the legislation such concentrations are possible but is it reasonable ? Journalism may then be muzzled or at least be single coloured.

Right now Socpresse is on the point to sell three local newspapers in Western France to the big regional paper *Ouest France* which has the highest circulation in the country : round

800 000 copies a day (while *Le Monde*, for instance, only has a daily circulation of 470 000 copies). *Ouest France* has some 40 local editions ! The second defence industrial Lagardère owns the Group *Hachette Filipacchi Medias*, the biggest publisher worldwide of magazines: 245 titles in 36 countries ! with 47 magazines in France as *Elle, Paris Match*…and daily regional or local newspapers as *La Provence, Nice-Matin, Corse-Presse*. If the newspaper circulation continues to shrink, the written independent press may gradually be submitted to a few industrials' control who multiply alliances between them and therefore threaten the very important pluralism of the press. Of course, all the industrial investors (except Serge Dassault) have promised not to interfere with the opinions expressed by the journalists but is it realistic ? The amalgamating of business, politics and newspaper publishing does not guarantee the freedom of expression and the pluralism of the press. In fact, financial concentrations and amalgamating touched all medias in 2004 and this will probably continue in 2005 and further on. The goodwill journalism is dominating while the critisizing journalism steps back. One may even wonder if at the time of globalisation and media megagroups, the concept of press freedom is not on the point to disappear. Commercial obsession and information ethics are contradictory.

The case of Le Monde

The principal independent group of the written press *La Vie-Le Monde* had severe deficits in 2002, 2003 and 2004. Because of the central role *Le Monde* plays in French intellectual life, one must hope it will remain sheltered from the predators who desire it, and that the new stage which is starting right now will not only bring out a new setting but rather «the search for accuracy» allowing readers to «find a reference, a reply, a validation», briefly «a newspaper where competence surpasses all complicities» (cf. Jean-Marie Colombani, head of *Le Monde* in his article published on 16 December, 2004). But it is also necessary to look for new shareholders in order to recapitalize up to an amount of 50 million euros and seek for new advertising contracts. A complete reorganisation is going on. The real change, however, will be the new presentation of the paper in a few months, the form and the substance ! New and some previous headings and items must balance if *Le Monde* will keep its present readership and develop a new and younger one.

Remedies

Supplements

Most national and regional dailies publish one or several supplements or inserts, every week, of more specific content (fashion, sport, TV programmes…), joining sometimes a DVD or a CD. However, the price of the issue may then be as high as 6 or 7 euros (ex. *Le Monde* and *Le Figaro* join a DVD to some Saturday issues). In spite of the price these issues are quite successful. *Le Figaro* has just started to join an Encyclopedia: 18 volumes in a small format; one volume published every Tuesday; the price is then 11,90 euros + 1 euro for the paper, and it seems to work !

The Tabloid Format

In France this format has not yet been adopted by the daily newspapers, so much more as some of them are already published in a rather small format such as *Le Monde, Libération, Le Parisien, Les Dernières Nouvelles d'Alsace* …The newspaper publishers are still hesitating to publish a tabloid edition. In the UK the tabloid format seems to be successful (ex. *The Independent, The Times* have improved sales significantly since they started publishing an tabloid edition; 16.3 % for *The Independent* and 4.6 % for *The Times*). But the consumer press is regressing in spite of the tabloid format. 4 titles were launched in Germany in 2004: *20 Cent, Welt Kompakt, News* and *Direkt*. Two kinds of publishing are used: the tabloid edition has the same contents as the large size edition but with a more compact setting, or the tabloid edition is rewritten (with a proper editorial staff) using some contents of the large size edition, developing some specific items (Wall Street Stock Exchange news, local news, cultural events …), adopting more or less a magazine feature (ex. *Welt Kompakt, Direkt*). Single copy price: 0,50 euro, half the price of the large size edition. The new tabloid editions seem to be the younger readers' favourite. They aim readers aged 20 to 39 years. The Alexander Springer Group considers to launch tabloid dailies in 2006 in various European countries (East Europe but perhaps also France). In Poland the tabloid *Fakt* launched in 2003 is very successful.

Journalist Schools in France

In this field there is certainly a good deal to be done, especially as to a new organisation and new methods taking into account the present shortcomings of the journalism as well as new developments which already work in other countries. Teaching will have to fit new conditions of the press.

Conclusion

To conclude I would like to quote the *Financial Times* (December 2004): at present the three biggest French national dailies find themselves in a gale which «reflects a paralysing entirety of structural and cyclic problems : high printing costs», antediluvian «trade-unions, closing down of booths and other selling places, a weak and ageing readership, a too slow progress in advertising incomings, the proliferation of free papers and information sources on line … making up an economically indigestible cocktail». I am afraid the *Financial Times* does summarize very well the present situation of the French press.

Newspaper publishing in France still seems to hesitate how to reverse the present stagnation and yet new approaches are starting off. I do not want to finish with a too pessimistic view of the future of the French press. Many efforts are going on right now to take up the challenge: improve editorial contents, not betray the readers' confidence, remain independent, defend freedom of the press... I think journalists do understand how much information is not reliable today and know the quality of the citizen debate depends on the quality of information.

As Hubert Beuve-Méry, founder of *Le Monde* always recalled: *«Facts are sacred, the opinion is free»*.

French newspapers on the web :

www.europresse.com

www.portail-presse.com

www.spqr.fr/lu.asp

www.afp.fr/francais/links/?pid=links

Audit & Statistics on the web :

www.ddm.gouv.fr

www.ojd.com

www.observatoire-medias.info

SELECTION OF NEWSPAPERS FOR DIGITIZATION AND PRESERVATION: A USER PERSPECTIVE

Ross Harvey

Professor of Library and Information Management,
Charles Sturt University's School of Information Studies, Australia

Abstract

Users of newspapers in library collections, or to which access is provided by libraries, are increasingly provided with choices of versions for use. Each choice carries its own implications for usability: using the original paper copy is likely to restrict the user to a physical location; microfilms are notoriously user-unfriendly, but they are portable; and web-delivered digitized versions can be accessed from anywhere potentially and, in some cases, allow text to be searched, but there may be bandwidth and other technological issues. The increasing digitization of newspapers raises many issues that libraries need to address. These include:

- *Whether digitizing can be considered as a preservation mechanism, or only as a way to improve access*

- *The suitability of traditional selection criteria when applied to selecting newspapers to be digitized*

- *The extent to which user needs are incorporated into selection decision-making*

- *The extent to which user needs are accommodated in the provision of digitized versions.*

This paper addresses these issues from a user perspective, focusing on Australian and New Zealand experience. It describes recent research into a New Zealand newspaper, the Inangahua Times (Reefton) of which both the microfilm and the online digitized version was used. It notes some of the issues surrounding the use and usability of newspapers in hard copy, microfilm and digital forms. It provides examples from library practice and from user experience.

Introduction: traditional selection practices

This paper addresses some of the issues in making decisions about which newspapers libraries select to digitize and/or preserve. It provides a perspective from the point of view of the user, and focuses primarily on Australian and New Zealand practice.

The selection of materials for preservation in heritage collections is traditionally made on the basis of certain characteristics of the materials. Much traditional preservation decision-making is driven by the physical condition of artifacts (Gertz 2000: 98). We can characterize the approach traditionally taken by libraries to selecting material for preservation as being based largely on preservation of items (or artifacts) in their original formats. Selection of items is based on key criteria, usually stated as age, evidential value, aesthetic value, scarcity, associational value, market value, and exhibition value, as in the U.S. CLIR (Council on Library and Information Resources) statement about the value of artifacts for research purposes:

1. Evidential value – as evidenced by originality or fixity
2. Aesthetic value – as evidenced by technique and artistry of physical form
3. Market value – as evidenced by age, scarcity, significance
4. Associational value – as evidenced by originality or fixity
5. Exhibition value – which can be strongly correlated with evidential value and aesthetic value (CLIR 2001: 9-11).

Additional criteria are often applied, although these are not consistently recognized by all commentators as valid: physical condition, resources available, use, capital value, and an ill-defined, but nonetheless well-represented, category of social significance (‹is the item held in community esteem›?).

To these criteria we need to add user demand. This is noted in Harris's comprehensive summary of selection for preservation in the library context (Harris 2000: 206-224). She suggests the criterion ‹Has the item been heavily used?›, given that current use is posited as an indicator, albeit imperfect, of future use.

These criteria apply to ‹traditional› (that is, paper-based) materials, of which newspapers are, of course, an example. They need to be redefined (or, at least, refined) in an increasingly digital environment, an environment that includes newspapers, more and more of which are also available in digital form. This paper looks at some of the reasons why they need to be re-defined. Its perspective is that of a user of newspapers – in my case, as a researcher into the history of New Zealand and Australian newspapers. Consequently I present a view untrammelled by resource considerations or by any of the numerous and difficult political, financial, and other administrative issues faced by those who manage newspaper collections.

User expectations: how researchers use newspapers

Let me describe my most recent uses of newspapers for research purposes. I recently completed an article for a collection about the relationship between newspapers published in the British colonies and the British Empire's centre in London. In my contribution I examined, in detail, aspects of the New Zealand Press Association's dealings with the proprietor of the *Inangahua Times*. This newspaper was published in the remote mining town of Reefton, in the north-west of the South Island of New Zealand, and about as far away from London as one can get. This research required that I examine copies of the *Inangahua Times* from the late 1880s and the 1890s.

I examined these copies, not from New Zealand, but from my current home base in Wagga Wagga, about three hours drive from Canberra. This was feasible for two reasons. The first was that a digital version of this newspaper is available from the National Library of New Zealand's web site Papers Past which provides 750,000 page images from New Zealand serials. The second is that I have in my possession microfilm of this newspaper produced by the National Library of New Zealand. It should be noted that, even if I was in New Zealand, it is doubtful whether I could get access to paper copies of this newspaper. The *Inangahua Times* cannot be considered to be a major newspaper, even in its brief heyday, and copies of it are rare. The set that was used to produce the microfilm and, later, the digital page images, was the only set approaching anywhere near completeness, and came from the Blacks Point Museum, located in a tiny settlement outside remote Reefton. When I saw them in 1986 these newspapers were housed in inadequate storage conditions and would have deteriorated under such conditions. (They are now in the custody of the National Library of New Zealand and, therefore, in high quality storage.)

Using the digital page images as well as the microfilms of the *Inangahua Times* provided me with the opportunity to reflect on the advantages and disadvantages of both formats for users, and to these I have added comments based on previous experience in the use of fragile paper copies of New Zealand newspapers from the 1890s.

Format	In Favour	Against
Paper copies	Ease of scanning (reading quickly) (if in good physical condition).	Considerable care required if in poor physical condition; Accessibility limited to one location; Difficult/expensive to copy.
Digital page images	Accessible from desktop; Can quickly access specific dates, pages; Can instantly print out, at a choice of magnifications.	Needs access to computer with high-bandwidth Internet connection; Difficult to scan (read quickly).
Microfilm	Can print out easily if equipment is available; Portability (for mailing etc.) .	Microfilm readers often not user friendly ; Access limited to those institutions which hold microfilm ; Slow to access specific dates and pages.

This list could, of course, be extended considerably; none of the above comments is likely to surprise members of this audience, or researchers who use newspapers in their investigations. However, a new factor has entered the equation, one that was not available until recently but with significant implications for the selection of formats for preservation and access of historical newspapers. I refer to the possibility of full-text searching of the text of newspapers.

Increasingly, users of historical materials are being provided with the ability to carry out searches on the contents of these materials, with the possibility of doing this from their desktop. For newspapers the bar has been raised by offerings such as The Times Digital Archive and ProQuest's Historical Newspapers. These provide page images *plus* the ability to search the text. The Times Digital Archive can be searched in various ways: a keyword search (on words in the text, including advertising, and the metadata), a relevance search (a keyword search which weights the words according to their frequency), Boolean searching, and browsing by data (Readings & Holland 2003: 40-41; http://www.galegroup.com/Times/). ProQuest Historical Newspapers provides the ability to search the full text of selected U.S.-published newspapers by keyword, Boolean operators, and advanced search features (http://www.proquest.com/products/pd-product-HistNews.shtml). Software such as OCLC's Olive software is making it possible, for those institutions that can afford it, to provide searchable full text more readily.

While I was preparing this paper I came across the most recent issue of *RLG DigiNews* [Feb 2005 issue]. It contains a detailed description of a project to digitize a significant Alaskan newspaper, the *Tundra Times*. The authors suggest that the approach described make it ‹both technically and economically feasible for smaller organizations to undertake› digitization of historical newspapers. If I read this article correctly, they have made the full text of seventeen years of the paper (27,000 pages) and Internet-accessible for the sum of US$150,000 (Terpstra et al 2005). While this is still a large amount of money for many organizations, it does perhaps suggest that the costs of and techniques for digitizing and providing full-text access are now within the means and capability of many organizations, not just the large national and state libraries. Margie Barram's presentation about the *Nambour Chronicle* at this conference certainly indicates the feasibility for small libraries.

What are the implications of all of this for selecting of newspapers for preservation? We have already seen that user demand is one factor in the selection of ‹traditional› materials for preservation, and I suggest that user preferences will assume greater significance when we consider digitizing. And not only is it user *preferences*: user *expectations* will also drive the process.

We are increasingly seeing how one-search, instant-result actions in information seeking are raising the expectations users have of information systems – a phenomenon which could perhaps be labelled ‹the Google-isation of society›. I have written elsewhere that

> The Internet is rapidly becoming the first port of call (and for some, the only port of call) for subject searches. A new verb has entered our vocabulary: to *google* ... A *google-ised* search interface is one that is simple to use and produces relevant hits (Harvey & Hider 2005: 167)

People increasingly expect Internet access to their information sources, with easy-to-use search capabilities. Consider this quote:

> Today's younger generation of readers and researchers increasingly assume that electronic access to the sum of the world's knowledge will be available – and if it isn't, it is too tiresome to retrieve, or it probably doesn't exist at all. To many it comes as a surprise that it is only since the mid-1980s that newspapers have been composed electronically (Readings & Holland 2003: 38).

We should not expect newspaper users to be any different. We need, therefore, to address the question of the extent to which user expectations should be accommodated in the selection of newspapers for digitization and preservation.

Managers of newspaper collections have, then, a new set of issues to consider when thinking about selection. There are more and more choices to be made.

1. Is providing paper copy sufficient (with restrictions to a single physical location, and issues of wear and tear)?

2. Is providing microfilm sufficient (with issues of user-unfriendliness, but significant long-term preservation advantages)?

3. Is a digital page image sufficient (with the potential for access from any location, but with technical and social issues associated with its access, and uncertainty about our ability to maintain it long term)?

4. Must the newspaper be available over the Web? And must full-text searchability of digital versions now be provided?

Each of these questions is examined in more detail.

1. Can digitizing be considered as a preservation mechanism, or is it only as a way to improve access?

This is a complex question that has been heavily debated, so far without a universally accepted outcome. However, my recent study of digital preservation has led me to conclude that we now have sufficient experience of preserving digital materials to consider digitization of newspapers as a viable preservation option. This is also the conclusion reached by the Association of Research Libraries (Arthur et al 2004). There is, perhaps, an analogy with preservation microfilming. If certain standards are met and maintained (file format and metadata standards, for instance), if storage conditions meet specified requirements (through trusted digital repositories), and so on, then there is the very strong likelihood that the digitized files will be maintained in usable form into the future. And as with microfilming, it is probably prudent to keep the originals wherever feasible as a safeguard. (I do, of course, appreciate that the extremely poor physical condition of some newspapers means that they may not be in a state worth retaining after they have been handled for digitizing.) It should be noted that I am here not considering whether to digitize newspapers directly from the originals, or from high quality microfilm.

I am not a subscriber to the Nicholson Baker school of thought and do not believe that the preservation of newspapers in their original paper copies is a realistic long-term option. The only realistic choices currently available for the long-term preservation of newspapers are microfilming to preservation standards, and digitizing. I have not looked at any comparisons of the costs of microfilming and digitizing for newspapers (if indeed any exist). Such a costing would need to encompass not only the production costs, but the long-term costs of storage, for example, of master negatives in cold stores, of digital materials in trusted repositories, and many other factors besides. Deegan and Steinvel suggested in 2002 that ‹the cost-effective creation of usable and searchable digital content that offers users a realistic experience of the richness of newspapers is perhaps closer than we have hitherto thought› (Deegan & Steinvel 2002). At present all we can do is to assume that the costs are similar, or will become similar in the near future. Accepting this assumption, then, we can act on the basis of another: that user expectations will play an increasingly large part in preservation decision-making. For newspapers, this means that we need to provide digital versions with searchable text.

2. Do traditional selection criteria apply to selecting newspapers to be digitized?

I want to step out of the role of user for a moment to note some of the technical and resource issues that we have to consider when thinking about selecting newspaper to digitize. Most of the published literature about selecting digital materials is about the selection of analog material to digitize, with the primary reason of improving access to that material. Digitizing programs are usually access-driven, with preservation as a by-product (Gertz 1999). The criteria identified for selecting materials for digitizing can, despite their emphasis on access, provide useful advice for selection criteria for preservation. Many of the traditional selection criteria apply, although the emphasis is different. For example, greater prominence is given to user demand and intellectual property rights (Gertz 2000: 98-99). Gertz has identified the criteria most frequently cited as:

- Does the item or collection have sufficient value to and demand from a current audience to justify digitization?

- Do we have the legal right to create a digital version?

- Do we have the legal right to disseminate it?

- Can the materials be digitized successfully?

- Do we have the infrastructure to carry out a digital project?

- Does or can digitization add something beyond simply creating a copy?

- Is the cost appropriate? (Gertz 2000: 104).

We can add further to this by looking at other statements that articulate additional criteria. One is found in the Cedars Project Team report (Cedars Project Team 2002) which suggests that selection decisions for digital preservation must ‹be pragmatic› and need to be based on the ‹estimated value of the material, the cost of storage and support mechanisms, and the production of metadata to support the material› (Cedars Project Team 2002: 53). Specific primary criteria are proposed:

- currently high use

- the type of material (typically commercially published scholarly works) that we would expect to preserve if it were published in traditional printed format

- tied to the long-term or cultural interests of the organisation (Cedars Project Team 2002: section 4.5.1).

- legal and IP issues: (for example, ‹legal status – IP rights need to be negotiated for preservation purposes›)

- format issues (for example, ‹some formats harder to preserve than others›)

- technical issues (for example, ‹Technical capacity to preserve may be lacking in a library›; ‹some technical environments may be easier to preserve than others›) (Cedars Project Team 2002: 109-110)

In similar vein, the Digital Preservation Coalition's *Decision Tree for Selection of Digital Materials for Long-term Retention* (Jones & Beagrie 2001: section 4) suggests that we consider selection policy (is there an institutional selection policy? Does the material fit into it? Is the material of significant long term value?), *legal and intellectual property issues* (have acceptable rights been negotiated? Can they be?), technical questions (can you handle the file format, now and in the future? Can the material be transferred to a more manageable format?), and the existence of *documentation and metadata* (has sufficient been supplied?).

It is clear, therefore, that changes are required to the selection procedures developed for non-digital artifacts to accommodate digital materials. To the traditional factors new factors are added. The digital selection frameworks developed to date still place high priority on criteria for determining value, but also strongly emphasise criteria such as the legal and intellectual property rights governing a resource, whether we have the technical ability to preserve it, the costs involved in preserving it, and the presence of appropriate documentation and metadata. The table summarizes these factors.

	Traditional Selection Criteria	Criteria Applied to Selection for Digitizing	CEDARS/DPC *Decision Tree*
Value	Evidential Aesthetic Market Associational Exhibition Informational	Sufficient value to current audience Does it add value?	Significant long-term value?
Physical condition	Threat to object Fragility		
Resources available	Management plan?	Is infrastructure available? Is cost appropriate?	
Use	Heavy use	Current demand	Currently high use
Social significance	Held in community esteem?		Tied to long-term interests of organization
Legal rights	Copyright	Rights to digitize Rights to disseminate	Legal status IP rights
Format issues		Can it be digitized successfully?	Type of material (can it be digitized successfully?)
Technical issues			Technical ability to preserve? Can file format be handled?
Policies			Selection policy?
Documentation			Sufficient available?

Table: Selection criteria

We now need to consider such factors when we make selection decisions about newspapers.

3. To what extent should and can the expectations of users be accommodated as part of the process of selecting newspapers for preservation?

In their broadest sense libraries exist to serve society, so of course users must be kept uppermost in mind in selection process. But it is users present and future who must benefit from these selection decisions and actions, and their requirements, as far as they might be identified, are not necessarily the same. Therefore, the immediate expectations and demands of present users should not be the paramount considerations. An anecdote illustrates some of the difficulties. In a much earlier career as the Newspaper Librarian for the National Library of New Zealand, I had input into the selection of newspapers for its preservation microfilming program. There was very strong lobbying from libraries and interest groups in Christchurch to make the Lyttelton Times, an important daily newspaper published in Christchurch from 1851 to 1929, a top priority for microfilming. Their experience was of this significant historical resource being so heavily used that physical damage was occurring. However, I could not give this newspaper high priority because, in the national scheme of things, it was not rare or endangered; there were are least three complete sets in the country, two of which were in excellent condition. User expectations must not be allowed, as this example suggests, to override all other criteria.

4. To what extent should and can the expectations of users be accommodated in the provision of digitized versions?

The answer to this question is not so clear-cut. There is, I have suggested, an already strong expectation – one that is likely to strengthen further in the future – of the availability of searchable text versions of digitized newspapers. However, the user, if faced with the choice between access to digitized page images and having no digitized versions at all (that is, having access only to a microfilm version in the long term), is probably likely to opt for a ‹no-frills› digitized version.

There is also an increasing expectation that digitized materials should be available over the Internet. Newspapers are no exception. This is an expectation that I see no reasonable arguments for disregarding. It is now within the technical and resource abilities of most institutions to do this.

Conclusion

Users make up society, and societal values and imperatives ultimately determine what value is placed on heritage institutions such as libraries; the needs and expectations of users, therefore, are the basis of support that society is willing to provide to heritage institutions. In a crude sense, if users do not believe that heritage institutions serve their needs, politicians will not fund these institutions adequately. We need to go some way to meeting user expectations.

The challenge is balancing user needs with what professional investigation has informed us are the needs of the materials we seek to preserve. Selection is about the nexus between user needs and material needs. When we select, we need to be aware of shifts in attitude by users on the one hand, and changes in the technologies that we have available on the other. The trick is to balance all of the competing factors so that the greatest number of interests and demands are satisfied. It is impossible to satisfy them all, of course, and the best we can hope for is to satisfy most of the people most of the time.

References

Sections of this paper are based on Harvey 2004 and Harvey 2005, which should be referred to for more detail.

Arthur, Kathleen et al. (2004). *Recognizing Digitization as a Preservation Reformatting Method.* Prepared for the ARL Preservation of Research Library Materials Committee. http://www.arl.org/preserv/digit_final.html, viewed 27 September 2004.

Cedars Project Team (2002). *The Cedars Project Report, April 1998-March 2001.* http://www.leeds.ac.uk/cedars/OurPublications/cedarsrepmar01exec.html

CLIR (Council on Library and Information Resources). Task Force on the Artifact in Library Collections (2001). *The Evidence in Hand: Report of the Task Force on the Artifact in Library Collections.* Washington, D.C.: CLIR.

Deegan, Marilyn & Steinvel, Emil (2002). Digitizing Historic Newspapers: Progress and Prospects. *RLG DigiNews* 6(4).

Gertz, J. (1999). Selection Guidelines for Preservation, in *Joint RLG and NPO Preservation Conference: Guidelines for Digital Imaging.* http://www.rlg.org/preserv/joint/gertz.html

Gertz, J. (2000). Selection for Preservation in the Digital Age. *Library Resources & Technical Services* 44, 2: 97-104.

Harris, C. (2000). Selection for Preservation, pp. 206-224 in *Preservation: Issues and Planning* (edited by P.N. Banks and R. Pilette). Chicago: American Library Association.

Harvey, Ross (2004). ‹Preserving Digital Documentary Heritage in Libraries: What Do We Select?›, *Symposium 2003: Preservation of Electronic Records: New Knowledge and Decision-making, Ottawa, Canada, 15-18 September 2003.*

Harvey, Ross (forthcoming 2005). *Preserving Digital Materials: An Australian Case Study.* München, K.G. Saur.

Jones, Maggie & Beagrie, Neil (2001). *Preservation Management of Digital Materials: A Handbook.* London: British Library.

Readings, Reg & Holland, Mark (2003). The Times Digital Archive 1785-1985: ‹The Thunderer› on the Web. *Update* 2(7): 38-41.

Terpstra, Judith A.K., Zarndt, Frederick, Ongley, David & Bodie, Stefan (2005). The Tundra Times Newspaper Digitization Project. *RLG DigiNews* 9(1).

THE NATIONAL DIGITAL NEWSPAPER PROGRAM (NDNP) – AN NEH/LC COLLABORATIVE PROGRAM
Enhancing access to historical newspapers
Release: September 2006

Georgia Higley

Head, Newspaper Section
Serial and Government Publications Division
Library of Congress, USA

NDNP Mission

- Enhance access to all American newspapers
- Improve access to products of United States Newspaper Program (USNP) using current technologies
- Establish standards and «best practices» for newspaper digital reformatting and access
- Use multi-phased approach for research and scaled development
- Develop geographically-diverse program that benefits all US communities

Why Newspapers?

- Newspapers: a unique resource for understanding the fundamentals of history
    - Democracy, free press, diverse geographic viewpoints at the community level
- Enormous corpus of newspapers presents an archival challenge
- Text-intensive layout is labor-intensive to search without reference tools
- Digitization of microfilmed corpus economically feasible

Why a National Effort?

- Voluminous, distributed collections
- No one institution holds the «master collection»
- Broad user-base for newspaper material
- Think nationally, select locally
- Comprehensive chronological coverage, eventually
- Need for leadership to build on past national efforts (USNP)

LC's Historical Newspaper Activities

- 20-year NEH/LC collaboration of USNP
  - Existing national network of cooperative programs
  - Standards established for preservation microfilm
  - Standards established for descriptive metadata/ cataloging
- American Memory's «Stars and Stripes»
  - http://memory.loc.gov/ammem/sgphtml/sashtml/sashome.html
  - Proof-of-concept for historical newspaper format and description

What will NDNP Produce?

- Web access to
  - National directory of US newspaper holdings (what, when, where) – based on USNP legacy data
  - More than 30 million page images of historical newspapers digitized primarily from microfilm, with full-text
  - Historical context of newspaper, printing tech, etc
- Depository of duplicate digitized microfilm at LC

How?

- Multi-partner program
  - NEH: Funds the program («We the People» initiative)
  - LC: Aggregates, preserves and serves
  - Awardees: Selects and converts
- Phase I – FY04-FY06 (Test bed)
  - NEH awardees (up to 10) with existing digital collections infrastructure and master microfilm negatives
  - 100,000 pages each + 100,000 LC pages by 2007 (from 1900-1910)
  - Microfilm reel analysis for research
  - Determine feasibility and potential resource needs for production system and future phases

Phase I Timeline

2004

July – NEH cooperative agreement guidelines issued, LC technical architecture under development

October – Application deadline; 15 applications received

2005

April – NEH Awards announced

May – Award conference held at LC

2006

September – NDNP application publicly available via Web

NDNP, September 2006

- **Web access** – American Chronicle
  - Newspaper Title Directory, 1693-present
  - Full-text of content w/in visual newspaper layout (page-level access)
  - Contextual historical material (Encyclopedia)
- Converted content from all awardees
  - Initial time period covered: 1900-1910

Newspaper Title Directory

- Re-use of CONSER and Newspaper Union List, created under USNP (maintained by OCLC)
- 147,000 newspaper titles
- 900,000 holdings records
- Searchable, Web access to all USNP-collected data, tied to digitized issues when available, as well as external newspaper Web sites

Full Text with Page-level Access

- Preserves integrity of primary historical content, text in context
- Minimal metadata required to achieve reasonable search results
- Economics of large-scale, large-format digitization
- Allows creation of substantial content-base for research and development on additional search strategies and technologies

Digital Asset Specifications

- Page Image – grayscale, 400 dpi, from microfilm
  - TIFF 6.0; JPEG 2000 (.jp2); PDF with Hidden Text
- OCR
  - XML – NDNP/ALTO Schema
  - Page-level, uncorrected, column zones with «bounding box» mapping coordinates

- Metadata
  - XML in METS/MODS for digital objects

Historical Context

An Encyclopedia of Newspaper History
- Brief essays for each title digitized
  - Publisher, geography, significant events covered, audience/community, politics
- History of each participating state and the role of newspapers in its history
- Presentations for technology developments, significant people, places, etc

Future Phases

- Addition of new partners (continuation of Phase I test bed, to represent all 54 states and territories)
- Increased efficiency in workflows, tools, technology, sustainable resources
- Additional access capabilities, improved technology

Aggregate ~ Preserve ~ Serve

For more information, see NDNP Guidelines at http://www.neh.gov/grants/guidelines/ndnp.html. For technical information, contact ndnptech@loc.gov.

YESTERDAY'S NEWS TOMORROW:
PRESERVING MEXICAN NEWSPAPERS, 1807-1929

Adán Benavides

Librarian for Research Programs
Benson Latin American Collection
The University of Texas at Austin Libraries, USA

The University of Texas at Austin has regularly collected Mexican newspapers, especially since the Mexican Revolution that ended in 1917. The purchase of the formidable Genaro García Collection in 1921 brought to the University scores of what were already then, and are especially now, very rare nineteenth- and early twentieth-century newspapers. Other collections acquired by the Nettie Lee Benson Latin American Collection[1] also contained Mexican newspapers. These acquisitions include the Alejandro Prieto Library, purchased in 1941, that is particularly rich in Tamaulipas newspapers, and the Miguel Bolaños Cacho Papers, acquired in 1986, containing newspapers from Oaxaca and Baja California. Several former students and faculty members of the University have contributed newspapers as well.

Benson Collection Microfilming Projects

The report that follows is based on extensive analysis of Mexican newspapers held by the Benson Latin American Collection as well as other United States libraries that participated in two microfilming projects funded in part by the U.S. National Endowment for the Humanities (NEH).

Both projects were conceived and administered by Benson Collection staff. The first project, which was carried out during 2000 through 2002, resulted in a microfilm publication entitled *Revolutionary Mexico in Newspapers, 1900-1929*. The second project is entitled *Independent Mexico in Newspapers, the 19th Century*; it began in 2002 and will terminate in March 2005. These projects were among the first to preserve and catalog foreign newspapers in the United States with National Endowment funding. This paper is a description of the process of preserving certain Mexican newspapers. It is not intended to be a discussion of the subject, content, or publishers of the various newspapers.

The two projects had three basic goals:

* preserving the original paper copies,

* microfilming the papers, and

* cataloging both the paper and microfilm copies of the papers.

In these three areas, best practices and latest standards were employed. All microfilm was produced according to the standards, procedures, and recommended practices specified in the American National Standards for Information and Image Management – Recommended

---

1 See http://www.lib.utexas.edu/benson/about.html for information about the Benson Collection, which is a specialized research library focusing on materials from and about Latin America, and on materials relating to Latinos in the United States. Today, it has about 900,000 books, periodicals, and pamphlets as well as extensive research materials in all other formats.

Practice for Microfilming Printed Newspapers, ANSI/AIIM MS111 – 1994. In addition, the latest versions and updates of all standards (ANSI/AIIM, ANSI/PH, and ANSI/IT) were met in production, testing, and storage of project film. The microfilmer conducted quality checks and maintained records recommended in the *RLG Preservation Microfilming Handbook*.[2]

New cataloging records followed the *Anglo-American Cataloging Rules*, 2nd edition (latest revision) for descriptive cataloging and all relevant CONSER (Cooperative Online Serials Program) standards for serial and microfilm cataloging. Names and subject headings matched authoritative forms found in OCLC Online Authority Files, and all bibliographic records were authenticated full MARC records.

Criteria used to select newspapers for the projects included the following:

1. All Mexican newspapers held by the Benson Collection were considered for the project.

2. Other libraries were asked to lend issues lacking from Benson Collection runs.

3. Other libraries were asked to lend titles based on Steven Charno's *Latin American Newspapers in United States Libraries: A Union List Compiled in the Serial Division, Library of Congress*.[3] Once contacted, the libraries also offered other titles for consideration to be included in the projects.

4. Titles which had already been microfilmed according to contemporary microfilming standards were excluded. Thus some long-running titles like *El Universal* and *El Siglo Diez y Nueve* are not represented in these projects.

5. Titles were included as long as at least one whole issue could be cataloged.

6. Newspaper titles had to conform to a working definition of a newspaper (see appendices 1 and 2). These definitions allowed some flexibility so as to include satirical publications that commented on political events of the day and to include publications that are forerunners to the newspaper format as it developed throughout the nineteenth century.

7. In the first project, issues for newspaper titles that began in the nineteenth-century and that continued into the twentieth-century or those that began after 1900 and continued beyond 1929 were also filmed.

The newspapers were grouped by place of publication – state and city, followed by those published within the federal district – then alphabetically by title thereunder. In preparation for filming, all newspapers were flattened and received minimal preservation cleaning and repair. After filming, all loose newspapers are stored in acid-free folders and archival boxes. Large format items and those composed of especially acidic, brittle paper are stored in a state-of-the-art long-term storage facility. Thereafter, users are encouraged to rely on the microfilm copy, unless there is a compelling research need to see the original.

The microfilm conforms to the most advanced standards for preservation microfilming, consisting of an original negative, a negative print master, and positive service copies as needed. Service copies are available through interlibrary loan and are available for purchase. As of this writing, complete sets of the 345 reels that comprise *Revolutionary Mexico in Newspapers* are available at research libraries in Boston, Chicago, Albuquerque, Mexico

---

2 (Mountain View, CA: Research Libraries Group, 1992)
3 (Austin: Published for the Conference on Latin American History by the University of Texas Press, 1969).

City, and Washington, DC in addition to Austin, Texas. A descriptive catalog of all micro-filmed titles and their issues is available in print and online.[4] A similar catalog will be created for the current nineteenth-century Mexican newspaper project.

The principal reason to undertake these reformatting projects was because time was seriously eroding the usability of many newspapers. This is particularly true of the newspapers published after about 1872, which were published on very acidic paper. Virtually all of the 560 titles in the first project, dated from 1900 through 1929, were printed on acidic paper. In addition, 152 titles (42.6%) of the 356 nineteenth century works which are included in the second microfilming project are on acidic paper. Moreover, improper housing, by today's preservation standards, had weakened bindings and exacerbated chemical changes from glues and cardboard covers.

In the late 1960s a comprehensive list of Latin American newspapers at the University of Texas at Austin was created. That information was incorporated into what became the standard bibliography of Latin American newspapers available in the United States: Steven Charno's *Latin American Newspapers in United States Libraries*. At that time, all University of Texas newspapers were held in a single collection. When the Latin American Collection moved to its present quarters in January 1971, Latin American titles were separated from the general collection and moved to the Benson Collection's new building. Since then, the growth of the Benson Latin American Collection, which more than doubled between 1980 and 2000, demanded that newspapers older than three years be housed off-site. Cataloged newspapers (a small minority of the total number) could be stored in an off-site storage facility with optimum environmental controls, while uncataloged newspapers were housed at another building used for infrequently used library materials. Exceptionally rare cataloged newspapers were retained in the Benson Collection and handled through its Rare Books unit.

By the late 1990s, an assessment of the Benson Collection newspapers revealed the following:

1. Approximately 1,000 Mexican titles existed, over half of which were dated from 1900 to 1929.

2. Approximately 1,000 non-Mexican Latin American titles existed.

3. The vast majority of all titles lacked cataloging

4. The 1960s list of Latin American newspapers was out of date and contained notations that some titles could not be found.

5. Environmental control varied considerably among the three buildings in which they were stored.

6. The materials most at risk were those printed on acidic paper, most dating from about 1872 forward.

A 1999 proposal to the Access and Preservation Program of the National Endowment for the Humanities successfully attained funding to catalog and microfilm approximately 550 Mexican newspapers held by the Benson Collection and whose runs included issues from 1900 to 1929. Thus, some newspapers, those which began in the late 1800s and continued past 1900, could be included in the project. The proposal and associated costs was based

---

4 Adán Benavides and Agnes L. McAlester, comps. and eds., *Revolutionary Mexico in Newspapers, 1900-1929: Guide to the Microfilm Set* (Austin: Nettie Lee Benson Latin American Collection, General Libraries, 2002) and http://www.lib.utexas.edu/benson/revolutionarymexico/.

solely on Benson Collection materials. In the course of the two-year project (2000/02), an attempt was made to borrow as many newspapers as possible, especially to complete runs already held by the Benson Collection. While this proved successful, it also led to unexpected expenses. More newspaper issues meant more original filming. The more libraries that participated, the more service copies of selected reels had to be made and given to the lending libraries. Significant quantities of additional issues and new titles were lent by the Library of Congress (Washington, DC) and the Latin American Library of Tulane University (New Orleans, LA). The Harvard College Library not only lent issues but donated the paper originals to the Benson Collection for long-term storage, this in exchange for the microfilm version. The Boston Public Library also lent materials to the project.

In sum, the first project's success is demonstrated in table 1.

Table 1. *Revolutionary Mexico in Newspapers*, general statistics.

Titles			Pages	Reels
Federal District	**States (60 cities in 28 states)**	**Total**		
326 (58%)	234 (42%)	560 (100%)	227,930	345

Table 2 indicates unique titles contributed by the cooperating libraries and indicates the number of pages borrowed to expand Benson Collection runs.

Table 2. *Revolutionary Mexico in Newspapers*, titles and pages borrowed from participating libraries.

Titles	Benson Collection	Library of Congress	Tulane University	Harvard University	Boston Public Library	Total
Unique	489 (87%)	8	63	0	0	560
Complementary		21	13	1	2	37*
Pages						
Unique	209,959	3,145	3,035	0	0	216,139
Complementary		7,546	1,939	2,160	146	11,791
Page totals	209,959 (92%)	10,691 (5%)	4,974 (2%)	2,160 (1%)	146 (0+%)	227,930 (100%)

*   Number of complementary titles included in total unique titles.

The interest generated in the course of filming the early twentieth-century papers, encouraged the Benson Collection staff to apply for a second grant from the National Endowment to catalog and film Mexican newspapers for the whole of the nineteenth-century. While the number of titles (350) in the Benson Collection was fewer than in the first project, extensive research and planning went into gaining cooperation from other libraries prior to submission of the grant in 2001. In addition to 125,000 pages estimated from its own holdings, Benson Collection staff estimated that at least 20,000 pages would be borrowed from other libraries. Eleven libraries are presently participating in the second project, which will end in March 2005, and have collectively loaned over 70,000 pages.

Table 3. *Independent Mexico in Newspapers*, general statistics.

Titles			Pages	Reels
Federal District	States (60 cities in 28 states)	Total		
284 (49%)	298 (51%)	582 (100%)	192,996	284

Table 4 indicates unique titles contributed by the cooperating libraries and indicates the number of pages borrowed to expand Benson Collection runs.

Table 4. *Independent Mexico in Newspapers*, titles
and pages borrowed from participating libraries.

Titles	Benson Collection	Library of Congress	Yale University (Sterling)	Tulane University	University of Connecticut	Others*	Total
Unique	305 (52%)	91	43	51	52	40	582
Complementary		26	21	17	21	13	98†
Pages							
Unique	119,972	20,043	7,270	1,758	5,672	3,619	158,334
Complementary		10,464	9,185	8,259	3,918	2,836	34,662
Page totals	119,972 (62%)	30,507 (16%)	16,455 (9%)	10,017 (5%)	9,590 (5%)	6,455 (3%)	192,996 (100%)

---

*　Special Collections, University of Texas at Arlington Library; DeGolyer Library, Southern Methodist University; Center for American History, University of Texas at Austin; Harvard College Library, Harvard University; Boston Public Library; New York Historical Society; and Boston Athenæum.
†　Number of complementary titles is included in total unique titles.

Both of these projects resulted in rather impressive gains for the bibliographic universe as electronic bibliographic records were created for both the original paper and its reformatted microfilm copy. Combined statistics from both projects are given in table 5.

Table 5. Mexican newspaper projects, 1807-1929, combined statistics (629 reels).

	Benson Collection	Library of Congress	Yale University (Sterling)	Tulane University	University of Connecticut	Others	Total
Unique titles	794	99	43	114	52	40	1,142
Pages	329,931 (78%)	41,198 (10%)	16,455 (4%)	14,991 (4%)	9,590 (2%)	8,761 (2%)	420,926 (100%)

Additionally, the newspapers were rehoused and received minimal cleaning and preparation prior to cataloging and filming. At the time of cataloging, every attempt was made to flatten them and wrap them in acid-free folders. After filming, Benson Collection papers were boxed in acid-free containers, while borrowed newspapers were returned to their library flattened and in acid-free folders along with a copy of the OCLC record that had been created. After filming, the Benson Collection's large-format papers are generally stored in a state-of-the-art offsite storage facility with optimum environmental control. Most nineteenth-century newspapers, however, remain in the Rare Books unit of the Benson Collection.

Evaluation of the Microfilming Projects

Table 6 demonstrates a significant increase in the number of pages microfilmed as opposed to those projected in the proposals: a 23% increase in the first project (185,000 to 227,930 pages) and a 33% increase in the second project (145,000 to 192,996 pages).

Table 6. Mexican newspaper projects, 1807-1929, projections and outcomes.

	Projected			Completed		
Project	Benson Collection	Others	Total	Benson Collection	Others	Total
20th-Century: Unique Titles	551	?	?	489 (87%)	71 (13%)	560 (100%)
20th-Century: Pages	185,000	?	?	209,959 (92%)	17,971 (8%)	227,930 (100%)
19th-Century: Unique Titles	356	?	?	305 (52%)	277 (48%)	582 (100%)
19th-Century: Pages	125,000	20,000	145,000	119,972 (62%)	73,024 (38%)	192,996 (100%)

The first project, although finished as projected within two years, ran into cost over-runs which were absorbed by the General Libraries. The second project will finish as budgeted, in spite of finishing six months after its two-year projected length. This anomaly can be explained by several factors. First, the proposed budgets were based on the cost of filming one page per frame.

In actuality, many newspapers could be filmed two pages per frame at no extra cost. This point is especially true for early nineteenth-century newspapers, many of which were print-ed in quarto sizes. Thus many thousands of pages beyond those projected in the second project could be added to it without additional cost. The first project, moreover, contained page estimates that were substantially in error. For example, one long-running newspaper was thought to contain eightpages per issue when, in fact, it had sixteen. These kinds of mistakes were eliminated in the second proposal by an actual hands-on review of titles for which the Benson Collection had long runs. But the major factor in cost over-runs in the first project was that no provision had been made to include borrowed newspapers. The addition of nearly 18,000 pages from four libraries added substantially to the cost of the project. The Benson Collection staff, however, argued successfully that the borrowed news-papers would add significantly to the completeness of the project. Tulane University's Latin American Collection greatly enhanced the project with the addition of 63 newspaper titles from southern Mexico (Chiapas, Tabasco, and Yucatán mostly) while the Library of Congress lent many issues to existing Benson runs, especially for Mexico City publications.

Table 6 also demonstrates a significant shift in the number of Benson Collection titles and pages in the nineteenth-century project relative to that of the twentieth-century. This is true whether one looks at titles or pages contributed. Looking at titles, for example, 87% came from the Benson Collection in the first project, while 52% of the titles came from it in the second project. This is logical since a concerted effort was made to borrow more titles and issues from any library known to have newspapers that could be incorporated into the proj-ect.

The drop in projected Benson Collection titles as compared to the number included in the project needs to be explained. Projections for the microfilming proposals were made on serial titles thought to be newspapers using an early newspaper list made in the 1960s. At the time of cataloging, however, some titles were determined not be newspapers as defined for the project. Gazettes, that is, official government publications, were sometimes encoun-tered; these were clearly not newspapers as defined for our purposes. Other publications were cataloged as periodicals, not newspapers. Perhaps more disturbing, however, were the number of unlocated newspapers. Twenty titles could not be located for the first project, and nineteen for the second. Most unlocated papers were single issues or very short runs, although one run was for several years.

The participation of eleven libraries in the second project was gratifying, particularly since it represented a variety of U.S. research libraries. Public and private university libraries and public and private research libraries all contributed. But mention should be made about who did not participate. Some university libraries could not participate because of restrictions in loaning materials for any reason: thus, two of the most significant U.S. libraries for Mexican materials, the Beinecke Library at Yale University and the Bancroft Library at the University of California – Berkeley, were unable to join our efforts. This observation is made to underscore the point that much more needs to be done to locate and preserve Mexican newspapers in U.S. research institutions. Additionally, mistakes were found to exist in the Charno guide. One library noted that they had never had the newspapers in ques-tion. Another library had dispossessed itself of its newspapers without good records of where the papers now existed. Yet another library had transferred all of its Latin American titles to a university library. Fortunately, we were able to trace many of those latter papers to the University of Connecticut whose library then loaned about one-third of the wanted newspapers to the Benson Collection project.[5]

It should also be mentioned that the National Endowment grants could only be used to support the preservation microfilming and cataloging of library materials that existed in and belonged to U.S. libraries. Thus, it is logical to ask how the Benson Collection's projects compare to existing collections in Mexico itself. No doubt, the single most important repository of Mexican newspapers is the Hemeroteca Nacional in Mexico City. Two research trips were undertaken in 2002 and 2004 to compare Benson project newspapers to catalog descriptions available at the Hemeroteca Nacional; no attempt was made to compare the holdings of other institutions in Mexico, however. These comparisons have not been tabulated, but general impressions can be presented at this time.[6] First, there is overlap in holdings in both of the Benson Collection projects. The overlap appears to be more generally true for the nineteenthcentury project than for the twentieth-century one. Nonetheless, the overlap does not exceed fifty percent of the material for either project. Indeed, for papers dated from 1900 to 1929, it probably does not exceed thirty percent. Moreover, little overlap occurs for newspapers published outside of the Federal District in either project. As one would expect, both of the Benson Collection projects reflect the preponderance of Mexico City publications just as do the holdings of the Hemeroteca Nacional. It appears self-evident that collecting materials published outside of Mexico City is more difficult than collecting those from the metropolitan capital. The Hemeroteca Nacional and the Instituto de Investigaciones Bibliográficos of the Universidad Nacional Autónoma de México are to be praised for their continuing efforts to organize and describe Mexican serial publications.[7] Vast numbers of serial titles, including newspapers, have been microfilmed and digitization attempts are being made to make them available via the World Wide Web.[8]

Newspaper collecting, cataloging, and preservation is challenging, demanding, and fraught with frustration. Handling the physical paper object whether by library stack personnel or the user frequently leads to mis-shelving and damaged items. Microfilm, a proven archival reformatting alternative, was the preferred medium for the Benson Collection projects given the exigencies of time and funds beginning as we did in 1999. While digitization of the material was considered in the early stages of the proposals, the expense was prohibitive relative to that of microfilm. Whatever difficulties were encountered in having newspapers sent to Austin, Texas, for processing were well worth their solving given the greater depth and breadth to both of the microfilming projects. But film offers little ease in adding

---

5   Acknowledgement is here made to the Latin American Microform Project at the Center for Research Libraries, Chicago, IL, for having helped underwrite the cost of filming the large number of papers borrowed from the University of Connecticut Library, Storrs, CT.

6   Tabulation of the comparison of holdings will be available after the completion of the nineteenth-century project in March 2005.

7   See, for example, *Publicaciones periódicas mexicanas del siglo XIX, 1822-1855: Fondo Antiguo de la Hemeroteca Nacional y Fondo Reservado de la Biblioteca Ncional de México (Colección Lafragua)* (México: Universidad Nacional Autónoma de México, 2000) and *Publicaciones periódicas mexicanas del siglo XIX, 1856-1876: Fondo Antiguo de la Hemeroteca Nacional de México* (México: Universidad Nacional Autónoma de México, 2003).

8   *Listado general de registros existentes en la base de datos: Inventario de microfilmes ordenados alfabeticamente por título y cada título ordenado cronologicamente* (México: Sala de Lectoras de Microfilmes del Departamento de Servicios de Información de la Hemeroteca Nacional de México, 2001); Gabriela Lorena Gutiérrez Schott, «La Hemeroteca Nacional Digital de México,» paper read at SALALM XLIX, Ann Arbor, MI, 7 June 2004; «Inicia Hemeroteca Nacional Digitalización de su Acervo,» Sistema Nacional e-México, http://www.e-mexico.gob.mx/wb2/eMex/eMex_Hemeroteca# [16 July 2004].

missing issues to existing runs. Digitization and the creation of virtual newspaper runs is the wave of the future, but we must wait for continued technological advances and reduced costs in creating the images and making them widely available to users. The film produced in these two projects, however, is of very high quality and is organized with the potential for digitization at a later time.

It should be underscored that the cataloging of 1,142 newspapers in these projects will help in any attempt to create a union list of Mexican or Latin American newspapers in the United States. This is a goal that has long been wanted since the publication of Charno's guide – after more than three decades, still the definitive holdings list of Latin American newspapers in the United States. The number of newspapers cataloged by the Benson Collection Serials Unit represents nearly twenty percent of all Latin American titles reported by Charno. Even more importantly, these projects have cataloged almost all of the Mexican newspapers published through 1929 listed by Charno. The cataloging of over 1,100 Mexican newspapers resulting from these two projects is a bibliographical tour de force by the Benson Serials Unit.

Laudable as these efforts may be, we are left with a daunting task. How do we locate and preserve disintegrating newspapers, which must surely exist in private and regional collections, in Mexico as well as throughout Latin America? This is the challenge that remains for solution today and tomorrow.

Appendix 1. Definition of a «newspaper,» *Revolutionary Mexico in Newspapers, 1900-1929* (1999 NEH proposal)

In selecting titles to be included in this project, the General Libraries follows the International Organization for Standardization (ISO) definition of a newspaper: a serial publication which contains news on current events of special or general interest, whose parts are listed chronologically or numerically and appear usually at least once a week. Newspapers usually appear without a cover, with a masthead, and are normally larger than approximately 12 by 17 inches in size. For present purposes, the definition is understood to include:

- General interest newspapers mainly reporting events that have occurred with the 24-hour period before going to press.

- Non-daily general interest newspapers (for example, local and neighborhood newspapers) that provide news covering a longer period of time, and also serve their readers as a primary source of general information due to their local origin.

- Newspapers that contain news of special interest, in addition to general information, targeted to clearly identified groups, such as ethnic or racial groups, labor unions, farming community, religious or political groups.

Appendix 2. Definition of a «newspaper,» *Independent Mexico in Newspapers, the 19th-Century* (2001 NEH proposal)

In selecting titles to be included in this project, the General Libraries has followed the precedent set in the Charno guide: «it became evident that the basis of selection should be broadened beyond the somewhat rigid definition originally suggested, in order to provide more comprehensive historical coverage» (p. xi). As a basis, then, the following «rigid definition» follows the International Organization for Standardization (ISO) definition of a newspaper:

A serial publication that contains news on current events of special or general interest, whose parts are listed chronologically or numerically and appear usually at least once a week. Newspapers usually appear without a cover, with a masthead, and are normally larger than approximately 12 x 17 inches in size.

For present purposes, the definition is understood to include:

- General interest newspapers mainly reporting events that have occurred within the 24-hour period before going to press.

- Non-daily general interest newspapers (for example, local and neighborhood newspapers) that provide news covering a longer period of time, and also serve their readers as a primary source of general information due to their local origin.

- Newspapers that contain news of special interest, in addition to general information, targeted to clearly identified groups, such as ethnic or racial groups, labor unions, farming, community, religious or political groups.

- Publications «with the look and feel of newspapers,» that is, printed on newsprint, formatted in a manner similar to dailies, and that comment, sometimes in a satirical way, on contemporaneous events.

- Publications that were forerunners of newspapers and display all the characteristics in the ISO definition save size.

LAS NOTICIAS DE AYER PARA EL MAÑANA: LA PRESERVACIÓN DE LOS PERIÓDICOS MEXICANOS, 1807-1929

Adán Benavides

Bibliotecario para Programas de Investigación
Colección Latinoamericana Benson
Las Bibliotecas de la Universidad de Texas en Austin, USA

La Universidad de Texas en Austin ha recogido de manera regular periódicos mexicanos, especialmente desde la Revolución Mexicana que finalizó en 1917. La compra de la formidable colección Genaro García en 1921 aportó a la Universidad una gran cantidad de lo que ya entonces eran, y especialmente ahora, periódicos muy raros del Siglo XIX y comienzos del XX.

Otras colecciones adquiridas por la Colección Latinoamericana Nettie Lee Benson[1] también tenían periódicos mexicanos. Entre estas adquisiciones se incluyen la Biblioteca Alejandro Prieto, comprada en 1941, que es especialmente rica en periódicos Tamaulipas y los Documentos de Miguel Bolaños Cacho, adquiridos en 1986, que tienen periódicos de Oaxaca y Baja California.

Varios estudiantes y miembros del profesorado antiguos de la Universidad también han aportado periódicos.

Proyectos para la Microfilmación de la Colección Benson

El informe que sigue a continuación se basa en un análisis amplio de los periódicos mexicanos que se encuentran en la Colección Latinoamericana Benson además de en otras bibliotecas de los Estados Unidos que participaron en dos proyectos de microfilmación[1] financiados, en parte, por la Fundación Nacional para las Humanidades (NEH) de Estados Unidos. Ambos proyectos fueron concebidos y realizados por el personal de la Colección Benson. El primer proyecto, que se realizó entre el año 2000 y el 2002, dio como resultado una publicación en microfilm titulada *Revolutionary Mexico in Newspapers, 1900-1929*. El segundo proyecto, que se denomina *Independent Mexico in Newspapers, the 19th Century*, comenzó en el 2002 y finalizará en marzo del 2005. Estos proyectos son de los primeros que se llevan a cabo para preservar y catalogar periódicos extranjeros en los Estados Unidos con la financiación de la Fundación Nacional para las Humanidades. Esta comunicación es una descripción del proceso de preservación de ciertos periódicos mexicanos y no pretende ser un debate sobre el tema, contenido o editores de los diversos periódicos.

---

1   Véase http://www.lib.utexas.edu/benson/about.html para obtener más información sobre la Colección Benson, que es una biblioteca de investigación especializada que se centra en documentos de y sobre Latinoamérica y en documentos relacionados con los Latinos en los Estados Unidos. En la actualidad, tiene unos 900.000 libros, publicaciones periódicas y folletos además de amplios materiales de investigación en otros formatos.

Los dos proyectos tenían tres objetivos básicos:

- Preservar los ejemplares originales en papel
- Microfilmar los documentos
- Catalogar tanto las copias en papel como en microfilm de los documentos.

En estas tres áreas, se emplearon pautas a seguir y las últimas normas. Todos los microfilms se realizaron de acuerdo con las normas, procedimientos y prácticas recomendadas especificadas en las American National Standards for Information and Image Management – Recommended Practice for Microfilming Printed Newspapers, ANSI/AIIM MS111 – 1994. Además, se cumplieron las últimas versiones y actualizaciones de todas las normas (ANSI/AIIM, ANSI/PH y ANSI/IT) en la producción, comprobación y almacenamiento de los microfilms del proyecto. El encargado de la microfilmación realizó comprobaciones de calidad y mantuvo un registro como se recomienda en *RLG Preservation Microfilming Handbook*.[2] Los nuevos registros catalográficos siguieron las *Reglas de Catalogación Anglo-Americanas*, 2ª edición (última revisión) para la catalogación descriptiva y todas las normas principales CONSER (Programa Cooperativo de Publicaciones Seriadas en Línea) para la catalogación de las publicaciones seriadas y en microfilm. Los nombres y los encabezamientos de materia coincidieron con las autoridades de los Ficheros de Autoridades en Línea de la OCLC y todos los registros bibliográficos eran registros MARC totalmente autentificados.

Entre los criterios usados para seleccionar los periódicos para los proyectos se incluyeron los siguientes:

1. Para el proyecto se tuvieron en cuenta todos los periódicos mexicanos de la Colección Benson.

2. Se pidieron en préstamo a otras bibliotecas números que faltaban en la Colección Benson.

3. Se pidieron en préstamo a otras bibliotecas títulos basados en la obra de Steven Charno *Latin American Newspapers in United States Libraries: A Union List Compiled in the Serial Division, Library of Congress*.[3] Una vez establecidos los contactos, las bibliotecas también ofrecieron otros títulos para que se considerase su inclusión en los proyectos.

4. Se excluyeron títulos que ya se habían microfilmado de acuerdo con normas contemporáneas de microfilmación. De este modo, algunos títulos de larga trayectoria como *El Universal* y *El Siglo Diez y Nueve* no están representados en estos proyectos.

5. Se incluyeron títulos en tanto en cuanto al menos se pudiera catalogar un número completo.

6. Los títulos de los periódicos tenían que seguir la definición de trabajo de un periódico (véase apéndices 1 y 2). Estas definiciones permitieron alguna flexibilidad para incluir publicaciones satíricas que comentaban acontecimientos políticos del día y para incluir publicaciones que son precursoras del formato periódico tal y como se desarrolló a lo largo del Siglo XIX.

7. En el primer proyecto también se filmaron los números de títulos de periódicos que comenzaron en el Siglo XIX y continuaron en el Siglo XX o aquellos que comenzaron después de 1900 y continuaron más allá de 1929.

---

2   (Mountain View, CA: Research Libraries Group, 1992)
3   (Austin: Publicado para el Congreso sobre Historia Latinoamericana por University of Texas Press, 1969).

Los periódicos se agruparon por el lugar de publicación – estado y ciudad, seguido por los publicados dentro del distrito federal – y luego alfabéticamente por el título. En la preparación de la filmación, todos los periódicos se aplanaron y se limpiaron y repararon muy superficialmente.

Después de la filmación, todos los periódicos sueltos se guardaron en carpetas de material no ácido y cajas de archivo. Los documentos en formato grande y los compuestos de papel debilitado especialmente ácido se guardaron en una sala de almacenamiento a largo plazo con los últimos avances. Después de eso, se animó a los usuarios a que utilizasen la copia en microfilm, a menos que tuvieran necesidad de ver el original por motivos de investigación.

El microfilm sigue las normas más avanzadas para la preservación mediante la microfilmación, consta de un negativo original, un cliché del negativo y tantas copias positivas como se necesiten. Las copias positivas son accesibles a través del préstamo interbibliotecario y están disponibles para su compra. En este momento, juegos completos de los 345 carretes de los que se compone *Revolutionary Mexico in Newspapers* están disponibles en las bibliotecas de investigación de Boston, Chicago, Albuquerque, Ciudad de México y Washington, DC además de en Austin, Texas. Un catálogo descriptivo de todos los títulos microfilmados y sus números está disponible en formato impreso y electrónico.[4] Se creará un catálogo similar para el proyecto actual de periódicos mexicanos del Siglo XIX.

La razón principal para emprender estos proyectos de cambio de formato fue que el tiempo estaba deteriorando seriamente la usabilidad de muchos periódicos. Esto es especialmente cierto en el caso de los periódicos publicados después de 1872, que se publicaron en papel muy ácido. Casi todos los 560 títulos del primer proyecto, que estaban fechados entre 1900 y 1929, se imprimieron en papel ácido. Además, 152 título (42.6%) de las 356 obras del Siglo XIX que se incluyen en el segundo proyecto de microfilmación están en papel ácido. Además, el almacenamiento incorrecto, según las normas actuales para la preservación, había debilitado las encuadernaciones y agravó los cambios químicos del pegamento y de las cubiertas de cartón.

A finales de la década de 1960, se creó una lista amplia de periódicos latinoamericanos de la Universidad de Texas en Austin. Esta información se incorporó a lo que llegó a ser la bibliografía estándar de periódicos latinoamericanos existentes en los Estados Unidos: *Latin American Newspapers in United States Libraries* de Steven Charno. En ese momento, todos los periódicos de la Universidad de Texas se almacenaron en una única colección. Cuando la Colección Latinoamericana se trasladó a su sede actual en enero de 1971, los títulos latinoamericanos se separaron de la colección general y se trasladaron al nuevo edificio de la Colección Benson. Desde entonces, el crecimiento de la Colección Latinoamericana Benson, que aumentó más del doble entre 1980 y el 2000, demandó que los periódicos con una antigüedad mayor a tres años se almacenaran fuera del edificio. Los periódicos catalogados (una pequeña minoría del total) se pudieron guardar en una sala de almacenamiento fuera del edificio con controles medioambientales óptimos, mientras que los periódicos sin catalogar se almacenaron en otro edificio utilizado para materiales bibliotecarios que rara vez se usan. Los periódicos catalogados excepcionalmente raros se conservaron en la Colección Benson y se trataron a través de su unidad de Libros Raros.

---

4 Adán Benavides y Agnes L. McAlester, comps. y eds., *Revolutionary Mexico in Newspapers, 1900-1929: Guide to the Microfilm Set* (Austin: Nettie Lee Benson Latin American Collection, General Libraries, 2002) y http://www.lib.utexas.edu/benson/revolutionarymexico/.

A finales de la década de 1990, un análisis de los periódicos de la Colección Benson reveló que:

1. Aproximadamente existían 1.000 títulos mexicanos y más de la mitad de los mismos fueron fechados entre 1900 y 1929.

2. Aproximadamente existían 1.000 títulos latinoamericanos no mexicanos.

3. La gran mayoría de los títulos carecían de catalogación

4. La lista de 1960 de periódicos latinoamericanos estaba desfasada y tenía anotaciones de que no se podían encontrar algunos títulos.

5. El control medioambiental varió considerablemente entre los tres edificios en los que estaban almacenados.

6. Los materiales que estaban más en peligro eran los impresos en papel ácido, fechados la mayoría de 1872 en adelante.

Una propuesta de 1999 para el Programa de Acceso y Preservación de la Fundación Nacional para las Humanidades consiguió con éxito financiación para catalogar y microfilmar aproximadamente 550 periódicos mexicanos de la Colección Benson que incluían números de 1900 a 1929. Así pues, se pudieron incluir en el proyecto algunos periódicos, aquellos que comenzaron a finales de 1800 y que continuaron más allá de 1900. La propuesta y los costes asociados se basó únicamente en los documentos de la Colección Benson. En el transcurso del proyecto de dos años (2000/02), se realizó un intento de pedir prestados tantos periódicos como fuera posible, especialmente para completar los números que ya existían en la Colección Benson.

Aunque se tuvo éxito, también conllevó unos gastos inesperados. El tener más ejemplares de periódicos implicó tener que realizar más filmaciones. Al haber más bibliotecas participantes, se tuvieron que hacer más copias de determinados carretes para dárselos a estas bibliotecas. La Biblioteca del Congreso (Washington, DC) y la Biblioteca Latinoamericana de la Universidad de Tulane (Nueva Orleans, LA) prestaron importantes cantidades de números adicionales y nuevos títulos. La Biblioteca Universitaria de Harvard no sólo prestó números sino que donó los originales en papel a la Colección Benson para su almacenamiento a largo plazo, a cambio de la versión en microfilm. La Biblioteca Pública de Boston también prestó materiales para el proyecto.

En suma, el éxito del primer proyecto se demuestra en la tabla 1.

Tabla 1. *Revolutionary Mexico in Newspapers*, estadística general.

Títulos			Páginas	Carretes
Distrito Federal	**Estados (60 ciudades de 28 estados)**	**Total**		
326 (58%)	234 (42%)	560 (100%)	227,930	345

La Tabla 2 indica los títulos únicos aportados por las bibliotecas colaboradoras e indica el número de páginas que se pidieron prestadas para ampliar los números de la Colección Benson.

Tabla 2. *Revolutionary Mexico in Newspapers*, títulos y páginas
que se pidieron prestadas a las bibliotecas participantes.

Títulos	Colección Benson	Biblioteca del Congreso	Universidad de Tulane	Universidad de Harvard	Biblioteca Pública de Boston	Total
Únicos	489 (87%)	8	63	0	0	560
Complementarios		21	13	1	2	37*
Páginas						
Únicas	209,959	3,145	3,035	0	0	216,139
Complementarias		7,546	1,939	2,160	146	11,791
Total de páginas	209,959 (92%)	10,691 (5%)	4,974 (2%)	2,160 (1%)	146 (0+%)	227,930 (100%)

* Número de títulos complementarios incluidos en el total de títulos únicos.

El interés generado en el transcurso de la filmación de los documentos de comienzos del Siglo XX, animó al personal de la Colección Benson a solicitar una segunda subvención a la Fundación Nacional para las Humanidades para catalogar y filmar periódicos mexicanos de todo el Siglo XIX. Aunque el número de títulos (350) de la Colección Benson era menor que en el primer proyecto, se realizó una investigación bastante exhaustiva para conseguir la cooperación de otras bibliotecas antes de solicitar la subvención en el 2001. Además de las 125.000 páginas estimadas de sus propios fondos, el personal de la Colección Benson calculó que al menos se pidieron prestadas 20.000 páginas a otras bibliotecas. Actualmente, once bibliotecas están participando en el segundo proyecto, que finalizará en marzo del 2005, y han prestado conjuntamente más de 70.000 páginas.

Tabla 3. *Independent Mexico in Newspapers*, estadística general.

Títulos			Páginas	Carretes
Distrito Federal	Estados (58 ciudades en 26 estados)	Total		
284 (49%)	298 (51%)	582 (100%)	192,996	284

La Tabla 4 indica los títulos únicos aportados por la bibliotecas colaboradoras y el número de páginas prestadas para ampliar los números de la Coleccción Benson.

Tabla 4. *Independent Mexico in Newspapers*, títulos
y páginas prestadas por las bibliotecas participantes.

Títulos	Colección Benson	Biblioteca del Congreso	Universidad de Yale (Sterling)	Universidad de Tulane	Universidad de Connecticut	Otros*	Total
Únicos	305 (52%)	91	43	51	52	40	582
Complementarios		26	21	17	21	13	98†
Páginas							
Únicas	119,972	20,043	7,270	1,758	5,672	3,619	158,334
Complementarias		10,464	9,185	8,259	3,918	2,836	34,662
Total de páginas	119,972 (62%)	30,507 (16%)	16,455 (9%)	10,017 (5%)	9,590 (5%)	6,455 (3%)	192,996 (100%)

* Colecciones especiales, Biblioteca de la Universidad de Texas en Arlington; Biblioteca DeGolyer,
Universidad Metodista del Sur; Centro para la Historia Americana, Universidad de Texas en Austin;
Biblioteca Universitaria de Harvard, Universidad de Harvard; Biblioteca Pública de Boston; Sociedad
Histórica de Nueva York y Ateneo de Boston.
† El número de títulos complementarios está incluido en el total de títulos únicos.

Estos dos proyectos contribuyeron enormemente al mundo bibliográfico ya que se crearon
registros bibliográficos electrónicos tanto para los originales como para la copia en microfilm. En la tabla 5 se ofrecen estadísticas combinadas de ambos proyectos.

Tabla 5. proyectos de periódicos mexicanos, 1807-1929,
estadística combinada (629 carretes).

	Colección Benson	Biblioteca del Congreso	Universidad de Yale (Sterling)	Universidad de Tulane	Universidad de Connecticut	Otros	Total
Títulos únicos	794	99	43	114	52	40	1,142
Página	329,931 (78%)	41,198 (10%)	16,455 (4%)	14,991 (4%)	9,590 (2%)	8,761 (2%)	420,926 (100%)

Además, los periódicos se volvieron a almacenar y se limpiaron y prepararon superficialmente antes de la catalogación y la filmación. En el momento de la catalogación, se hizo todo lo posible para aplanarlos y guardarlos en carpetas de material no ácido. Después de la filmación, los documentos de la Colección Benson se confinaron en recipientes de material no ácido, mientras que los periódicos prestados se devolvieron a su biblioteca aplanados y en carpetas de material no ácido junto con una copia del registro OCLC que se había creado. Después de la filmación, los documentos de gran formato de la Colección Benson se almacenaron en general en una sala de almacenamiento a largo plazo con los últimos avances y con un control medioambiental óptimo. Sin embargo, la mayoría de los periódicos del Siglo XIX permanecen en la unidad de Libros Raros de la Colección Benson.

Evaluación de los Proyectos de Microfilmación

La Tabla 6 muestra un aumento importante del número de páginas microfilmadas a diferencia de las proyectadas en las propuestas: un aumento del 23% en el primer proyecto (de 185.000 a 227.930 páginas) y un aumento del 33% en el segundo proyecto (de 145.000 a 192.996 páginas).

Tabla 6. proyectos de periódicos mexicanos, 1807-1929, proyección y resultados.

Proyecto	Proyectado			Completado		
	Colección Benson	Otros	Total	Colección Benson	Otros	Total
Títulos Unicos del Siglo XX	551	?	?	489 (87%)	71 (13%)	560 (100%)
Páginas del Siglo XX	185,000	?	?	209,959 (92%)	17,971 (8%)	227,930 (100%)
Títulos Únicos del Siglo XIX	356	?	?	305 (52%)	277 (48%)	582 (100%)
Páginas del Siglo XIX	125,000	20,000	145,000	119,972 (62%)	73,024 (38%)	192,996 (100%)

El primer proyecto, aunque finalizó como se planeó en un plazo de dos años, tuvo unos gastos superiores a los previstos que fueron asumidos por las Bibliotecas Generales. El segundo proyecto finalizará como se presupuestó, a pesar de terminar seis meses después de su duración proyectada de dos años. Esta anomalía se puede explicar por varios factores. En primer lugar, los presupuestos propuestos se basaron en el coste de la filmación de una página por fotograma. En realidad en muchos periódicos se pudieron filmar dos páginas por fotograma sin coste adicional alguno. Este punto es especialmente cierto para los periódicos de comienzos del Siglo XIX, muchos de los cuales se imprimieron en tamaños de cuarto. Así pues, muchos miles de páginas por encima de las proyectadas en el segundo proyecto se pudieron incluir sin coste adicional alguno. Además, el primer proyecto tenía una estimación errónea de las páginas. Por ejemplo, se pensó que un periódico de larga trayectoria tenía ocho páginas por número cuando, de hecho, tenía dieciséis. No se cometieron estos errores en la segunda propuesta mediante un análisis de los títulos de los que la Colección Benson tenía muchos números. Aunque el factor principal de los costes adicionales del primer proyecto fue que no se había tenido en cuenta incluir los periódicos prestados. La inclusión de casi 18.000 páginas de cuatro bibliotecas aumentó sustancialmente el coste del proyecto. Sin embargo, el personal de la Colección Benson pensaba que los periódicos prestados aumentaría significativamente la envergadura del proyecto. La Colección Latinoamericana de la Universidad de Tulane mejoró en gran medida el proyecto con la inclusión de 63 títulos de periódicos del sur de México (en su mayoría de Chiapas, Tabasco y Yucatán) mientras que la Biblioteca del Congreso prestó muchos números de los periódicos existentes en la colección Benson, especialmente de publicaciones de la Ciudad de México.

La Tabla 6 también demuestra un cambio importante en el número de títulos y páginas de la Colección Benson del proyecto del Siglo XIX en relación con el del Siglo XX. Esto es cierto si uno mira los títulos o páginas aportadas. Al mirar los títulos, por ejemplo, 87% procedían de la Colección Benson en el primer proyecto, mientras que el 52% de los títulos procedían de aquí en el segundo proyecto. Esto es lógico ya que se realizó un esfuerzo común para pedir prestados más títulos y números de cualquier biblioteca con periódicos que se podieran incluir en el proyecto.

Es necesario explicar la disminución de los títulos proyectados de la Colección Benson en comparación con el total incluido en el proyecto. Las previsiones para las propuestas de microfilmación se hicieron sobre los títulos de las publicaciones seriadas que se pensaba que eran periódicos usando una lista de periódicos antiguos realizada en la década de 1960. Sin embargo, en el momento de la catalogación se decidió que algunos títulos no eran periódicos tal y como se definían para el proyecto. A veces se encontraron gacetas, es decir, publicaciones gubernamentales oficiales que no se consideraron periódicos tal y como se definieron para nuestros objetivos. Otras publicaciones se catalogaron como publicaciones periódicas, no como periódicos. Sin embargo, quizás lo más preocupante fue el número de periódicos no localizados.

No se pudieron localizar veinte títulos para el primer proyecto y diecinueve para el segundo. La mayoría de los documentos no localizados eran números únicos o tiradas muy cortas, aunque una tirada era de varios años.

La participación de once bibliotecas en el segundo proyecto fue gratificante, especialmente ya que representaban una variedad de bibliotecas de investigación norteamericanas. Contribuyeron tanto bibliotecas universitarias públicas y privadas como bibliotecas de investigación públicas y privadas. Aunque se debería mencionar quién no participó. Algunas bibliotecas universitarias no pudieron participar debido a las restricciones por alguna razón en el préstamo de los documentos: por esto, dos de las bibliotecas norteamericanas más importantes de documentos mexicanos, la Biblioteca Beinecke en la Universidad de Yale y la Biblioteca Bancroft en la Universidad de California – Berkeley, no se pudieron unir a nuestro proyecto. Se hace esta observación para poner de manifiesto que todavía queda mucho por hacer para localizar y preservar los periódicos mexicanos en las instituciones de investigación norteamericanas. Además, se encontraron errores en la guía Charno. Una biblioteca indicó que nunca había tenido periódicos de los que estamos hablando. Otra biblioteca se había deshecho de sus periódicos sin mantener un buen control de dónde estaban ahora. Sin embargo, otra biblioteca había transferido todos sus títulos latinoamericanos a una biblioteca universitaria.

Afortunadamente, pudimos encontrar muchos de estos últimos documentos en la Universidad de Connecticut cuya biblioteca después prestó sobre un tercio de los periódicos que se querían para el proyecto de la Colección Benson.[5]

También se debería mencionar que las subvenciones de la Fundación Nacional para las Humanidades sólo se pudieron usar para apoyar la microfilmación dirigida a la preservación y la catalogación de materiales bibliotecarios que existían en y pertenecían a bibliotecas estadounidenses. Por lo tanto, es lógico preguntarse cómo se comparan los proyectos de la Colección Benson con las colecciones existentes en el propio México. Sin duda, el depósito más importante de periódicos mexicanos es la Hemeroteca Nacional de la Ciudad de México. En el 2002 y en el 2004 se realizaron dos visitas por razones de investigación para comparar los periódicos del proyecto Benson con las descripciones del catálogo disponible en la Hemeroteca Nacional; sin embargo, no se intentó comparar los fondos bibliográficos de otras instituciones de México. Estas comparaciones no se han tabulado, aunque en este momento se pueden presentar impresiones generales.[6] En primer lugar, hay una coincidencia en los fondos bibliográficos de los proyectos de la Colección Benson. El solapamiento parece ser más evidente en líneas generales para el proyecto del Siglo XIX que para el del XX, aunque no excede el cincuenta por ciento del material en ninguno de los proyecto. De hecho, para los documentos fechados entre 1900 y 1929, probablemente no exceda el treinta por ciento. Además, hay un pequeño solapamiento en los periódicos publicados fuera del Distrito Federal en ambos proyectos. Como uno esperaría, los dos proyectos de la Colección Benson reflejan la preponderancia de publicaciones de la Ciudad de México del mismo modo que los fondos bibliográficos de la Hemeroteca Nacional. Parece evidente por sí mismo que recoger materiales publicados fuerra de la Ciudad de México es más difícil que recogerlos de la capital metropolitana. La Hemeroteca Nacional y el Instituto de Investigaciones Bibliográficas de la Universidad Nacional Autónoma de México son dignos de elogio por sus contínuos esfuerzos por organizar y describir las publicaciones seriadas mexicanas.[7] Se han microfilmado un gran número de títulos de publicaciones seriadas, incluidos periódicos, y se han realizado intentos de digitalización para hacerlos accesibles a través de Internet.[8]

La recogida, catalogación y preservación de periódicos es desafiante, exigente y llena de frustración. El manejo del documento en papel, ya sea por el personal responsable de los estantes de la biblioteca o por el usuario, con frecuencia ocasiona que los documentos estén mal colocados en los estantes y se deterioren. El microfilm, una alternativa demostrada para el cambio de formato con vistas a su almacenamiento, fue el soporte preferido por los proyectos de la Colección Benson dadas las exigencias de tiempo y dinero ya que comenzamos en 1999.

---

5   Aquí hacemos un reconocimiento al Proyecto de Microformas Latinoamericano del Center for Research Libraries, Chicago, IL, por haber ayudado a financiar los costes de la filmación de un gran número de documentos prestados por la University of Connecticut Library, Storrs, CT.

6   La tabulación de la comparación de los fondos bibliográficos estará disponible después de la finalización del proyecto del Siglo XIX en marzo del 2005.

7   Véase, por ejemplo, *Publicaciones periódicas mexicanas del siglo XIX, 1822-1855: Fondo Antiguo de la Hemeroteca Nacional y Fondo Reservado de la Biblioteca Ncional de México (Colección Lafragua)* (México: Universidad Nacional Autónoma de México, 2000) y *Publicaciones periódicas mexicanas del siglo XIX, 1856-1876: Fondo Antiguo de la Hemeroteca Nacional de México* (México: Universidad Nacional Autónoma de México, 2003).

8   *Listado general de registros existentes en la base de datos: Inventario de microfilmes ordenados alfabeticamente por título y cada título ordenado cronologicamente* (México: Sala de Lectoras de Microfilmes del Departamento de Servicios de Información de la Hemeroteca Nacional de México, 2001); Gabriela Lorena Gutiérrez Schott, «La Hemeroteca Nacional Digital de México,» paper read at SALALM XLIX, Ann Arbor, MI, 7 June 2004; «Inicia Hemeroteca Nacional Digitalización de su Acervo,» Sistema Nacional e-México, http://www.emexico. gob.mx/wb2/eMex/eMex_Hemeroteca# [16 de julio de 2004].

Aunque la digitalización de los materiales se consideró en las primeras etapas de las propuestas, el gasto era prohibitivo en relación con el del microfilm. No importa qué dificultades se encontraron al tener que enviar periódicos a Austin, Texas, para su procesamiento ya que mereció la pena solucionarlos dada la gran exhaustividad y cobertura de los dos proyectos de microfilmación. Pero el microfilm ofrece poca facilidad para añadir números que faltan a las colecciones existentes. La digitalización y la creación de colecciones de periódicos virtuales es el futuro, aunque debemos esperar avances tecnológicos continuados y costes reducidos en la creación de imágenes y en su puesta a disposición de los usuarios. Sin embargo, el microfilm producido en estos dos proyectos es de muy buena calidad y está organizado con objeto de que se pueda digitalizar posteriormente.

Se debería subrayar que la catalogación de 1.142 periódicos en estos proyectos ayudará en cualquier intento de crear un catálogo colectivo de periódicos mexicanos o latinoamericanos en los Estados Unidos. Este es un objetivo que se ha tenido durante mucho tiempo desde la publicación de la guía de Charno – después de más de tres décadas, todavía el listado definitivo de fondos bibliográficos de periódicos latinoamericanos en los Estados Unidos. El número de periódicos catalogados por la Unidad de Publicaciones Seriadas de la Colección Benson representa casi el veinte por ciento de todos los títulos latinoamericanos citados por Charno.

Incluso lo que es más importante, estos proyectos han catalogados casi todos los periódicos mexicanos publicados hasta 1929 listados por Charno. La catalogación de más de 1.100 periódicos mexicanos resultantes de estos dos proyectos es una proeza bibliográfica de la Unidad de Publicaciones Seriadas de Benson.

Aunque estos esfuerzos puedan ser loables, nos queda una tarea muy ardua. ¿Cómo localizamos y preservamos los periódicos que se están deteriorando, que sin duda deben existir en colecciones privadas y regionales tanto en México como en todo Latinoamérica? Este es el reto que queda pendiente de solucionar hoy y mañana.

Apéndice 1. Definición de un «periódico,» *Revolutionary Mexico in Newspapers, 1900-1929* (propuesta 1999 NEH)

En la selección de los títulos que se incluyeron en este proyecto, las Bibliotecas Generales siguieron la definición de un periódico de la Organización Internacional de Normalización (ISO): una publicación seriada que contiene noticias sobre acontecimientos actuales de interés especial o general, cuyas partes se enumeran cronológicamente o numéricamente y normalmente aparece al menos una vez a la semana. Los periódicos generalmente aparecen sin una cubierta, con una cabecera y suelen tener un tamaño aproximado de 12 por 17 pulgadas. Para los objetivos que aquí presentamos, se entiende que la definición incluye:

- Periódicos de interés general que informan principalmente de acontecimientos que han tenido lugar dentro de las 24 horas anteriores a que se empiece a imprimir.

- Periódicos de interés general no diarios (por ejemplo, periódicos locales y de barrio) que ofrecen noticias que abarcan un periodo de tiempo mayor y que también sirven a sus lectores como fuentes primarias de información general debido a su origen local.

- Periódicos que contienen noticias de interés especial, además de información general, dirigidos a grupos claramente identificados como, por ejemplo, grupos étnicos o raciales, sindicatos, comunidad agrícola, grupos religiosos o políticos.

Apéndice 2. Definición de un «periódico,» *Independent Mexico in Newspapers, the 19th-Century* **(propuesta 2001 NEH)**

En la selección de los títulos que se incluyeron en este proyecto, las Biliotecas Generales han seguido el precedente de la guía Charno: «era evidente que la razón de la selección debería ampliarse más allá de la definición un tanto rígida que se había sugerido originariamente, para ofrecer una cubertura histórica más general » (p. xi). Como criterio, pues, la siguiente «definición rígida » sigue la definición de un periódico de la Organización Internacional de Normalización (ISO):

Una publicación seriada que contiene noticias sobre acontecimientos actuales de interés especial o general, cuyas partes se enumeran cronológicamente o numéricamente y normalmente aparece al menos una vez a la semana. Los periódicos generalmente aparecen sin una cubierta, con una cabecera y suelen tener un tamaño aproximado de 12 por 17 pulgadas.

Para los objetivos que aquí presentamos, se entiende que la definición incluye:

- Periódicos de interés general que informan principalmente de acontecimientos que han tenido lugar dentro de las 24 horas anteriores a que se empiece a imprimir.

- Periódicos de interés general no diarios (por ejemplo, periódicos locales y de barrio) que ofrecen noticias que abarcan un periodo de tiempo mayor y que también sirven a sus lectores como fuentes primarias de información general debido a su origen local.

- Periódicos que contienen noticias de interés especial, además de información general, dirigidos a grupos claramente identificados como, por ejemplo, grupos étnicos o raciales, sindicatos, comunidad agrícola, grupos religiosos o políticos.

- Publicaciones «con el aspecto de periódicos,» es decir, impresos en papel de periódico, con un formato similar al de los diarios y que comentan, algunas veces de forma satírica, los acontecimientos contemporáneos.

- Publicaciones que fueron precursoras de periódicos y muestran todas las características de la definición ISO excepto por el tamaño.

PROJECT: DIGITIZATION OF THE 19TH CENTURY LATIN AMERICAN PRESS
(Digitization of the Great Colombia Press: 1820-1830)
Final report, May 30th, 2004

Alfonso Quintero

ABINIA Executive Secretariat, Caracas, Venezuela

1. Background

At the beginning of the nineties, after researching collections in various Latin American national libraries, the conclusion was drawn that a great part of nineteenth century Latin American press ran the risk of suffering irreparable damage or even disappearance due to the instability of its medium and to the existing limited preservation capabilities. For this reason its inventory and preservation and the spreading of the valuable information these publications contain became a priority for all member countries of the Latin American National Libraries Association (ABINIA,) as well as for UNESCO, which included «Memory of Latin America» as one of its World Memory Pilot Projects. This situation was address through the «Nineteenth Century Press Rescue» project, set up by the National Library of Venezuela and later approved by ABINIA. Three phases were established for its development, the last of which gave rise to the present project.

Phases of the «Nineteenth Century Press Rescue» project:

1. Creation of a catalogue collecting existing information on nineteenth century press in Latin American national libraries so as to create a data base for researchers to use.

2. Training on a regional level in microfilming in order to assure the reproduction of the nineteenth century press and the preservation of library collections in this form.

3. Indexing and digitization of the most representative newspapers and the editing of a CD-ROM in order to facilitate access to available information for researchers from other countries. The first two phases were completed successfully. An inventory of nineteenth century press existing in Latin American libraries was made, in which the evaluation of the state of conservation of the newspaper collections were emphasized, as well as the computerized cataloguing processes and microfilming. As a result, a computerized collective catalogue of nineteenth century newspapers was developed and can be found on microfilm in the national libraries and other Latin American institutions; and, amongst other training activities, the Venezuela National Library set up in 1996 a microfilm workshop for national library staff in six Latin American countries.

With UNESCO contributions, the CD-ROM «Nineteenth Century Latin American Press» was edited, which contains a data base with 8,990 bibliographic entries. This data base facilitates the retrieval of titles from any of the national libraries or other institutions within the fourteen participant countries. This same CD-ROM gives access to the first digitized images corresponding to a period of one year's circulation- of the most important newspaper from each of the fourteen countries. This CD-ROM became the first product of the project.

2. Description

2.1. Objective:

To digitize the most important nineteenth century Latin American newspapers so as to facilitate access for the research community to their content by means of a CD-ROM or on-line through the Internet. Initially, (just as the Andrew W. Mellon Foundation agreed in 1997) it was decided to edit the «Grandcolombian Press, 1820-1830» CD-ROM, which contains the images from one representative newspaper from each of the countries (Venezuela, Colombia, Ecuador, Panama, Peru and Bolivia) which participated in the political integration or confederation of the Latin American countries experience.

2.2. Expected results:

The edition of a CD-ROM which includes digital images of the newspapers, a revision of each title, exhaustive name, geographic and subject indexes to facilitate the retrieval of the information.

2.3. Institutional Coordinator:

Aurelio Álvarez Juan, Director of Library Technical Services, the National Library of Venezuela.

2.4. Technical Coordinator:

Pía Rodríguez, Director of the National Paper Conservation Center of the Venezuela National Library.

2.5. External Financing Institutions:

Andrew W. Mellon Foundation.

2.6. Approval Date:

December 1996.

2.7. Donation:

Andrew W. Mellon Foundation: Bs.(Bolivian currency) 95,150,000,00 ($US 200,000) received on February 26th 1997 by the National Library of Venezuela.

3. Developments

3.1.Acquisition of equipment and software:

Digitization Unit: In 1997, the Computing Division of the Venezuela National Library (SAIBIN) identified and selected the equipment and software required for digitization by direct microfilm scanning. The company «RAM-ROM Computer» was chosen, representative for «Houston Fearless» in Venezuela, to supply a scanner for 16 and 35mm microfilms, «MEKEL M500 (SACN MASTER)», adapted to a computer with a «SCANNER SEAPORT model 1D20»; «Paint Pro Shop and Imaging» software for image manipulation and a «CD-Recorder». This equipment arrived in September 1997.

The setting up of the scanner took more than a year. The problems that this equipment had were not resolved by the company RAM-ROM, who implemented the recommendations supplied by «Houston Fearless». Thanks to the direct help from the «MEKEL Engineering» technical representative and the expertise of our digitization operator, the adequate running of this equipment was achieved in January 1999. All the Venezuelan press digitized up until that date had to be repeated.

Workstations: In 1999 two additional workstations were acquired in order to populate the data base, control the quality of existing data and to clean the images; a «JAZZ (2GB)» unit, to back up the images; and «SCAV 2.5» software, for the creation of the data base and the production of the CD-ROM and «Adobe Photoshop».

In October 2002 a decision was made to buy an additional computer to make easier the processes of entering these records, image manipulation and quality control in order to meet the Andrew W. Mellon Foundation requisite of completing the project by the end of April 2003.

Nevertheless, this purchase was delayed until September 2003 due to the commercial suppliers giving very short term estimates making it difficult to follow through the acquisition processes. And although at that time the official exchange rate was 1,600 Bs(Venezuelan currency) to the U.S.$, importers complained that that was not competitive enough for them and that they had to pay for transactions at the unofficial and fluctuating rate existing in the market which was much higher than the official one.

3.2. Training and hiring of human resources

Training. In 1997, staff from the field of information science were trained by a «Houston Fearless» systems engineer. The tasks relating to the digitization process (configuration, testing) were completed in advance by an operator from the National Center for Paper Conservation, Micrograph Division, who, together with six other civil servants, was trained in using the equipment by computing division staff (SAIBIN).

In September and November !999, The Director of Library Technical Services attended two digitization meetings in the United States which allowed the revision of the structural organization and the activities carried out within the framework of the project: the first from 21st to 23rd September, *Preservation Options in the Digital World: microfilming and scanning*, presented by the Northeast Document Conservation Center in Nebraska and the second, from 2nd to 3rd November, *Digital Images for Libraries and Archives*, given by the University of Cornell, New York.

At the same time, from the 5th to 12th December 1999, the person in charge of the digitization process from the National Center for Paper Conservation carried out a study at the National Center for Editing Compact Discs (CENEDIC) at the University of Colima, Mexico, to observe the complete process: from digitization to the edition of a CD-ROM.

Hiring of human resources. In 1999 two historians were hired in order to compile the subject, name and geographic indexes. This job involved reviewing page by page each of the selected titles. Between June and November 1999 a transcriber was hired using project resources and who later became part of the permanent staff of Library's Digitization Unit until June 2001. In the year 2000 we could count on a graphic designer who dealt with the images in order to maximize their quality.

Due to the high turnover of staff (historians who worked independently and workers who were looking for permanent posts,) in the year 2000 three new civil servants for the National Library were authorized to work on the final stages of the projects activities: a historian for the indexing process of the remaining titles and two civil servants for the creating and quality control of the indexes.

3.3. Digitization and Indexing

At the suggestion of each country's National Library, the most representative Grandcolombian newspapers were selected and due to the limitations imposed by the CD-ROM capacity only five titles we chosen (see table no. 1) represented in 3,542 images.

Comprehensive indexing

The first decision, recommended by Mr. Hans Rutimann, adviser for the Mellon Foundation, was not to apply Optical Character Recognition (OCR) because none of the experimented software gave good results, due to the fact that the types used in Latin America at that time were very irregular. For this reason a decision was made to comprehensively index all the information contained in the five selected newspapers in order to achieve a retrieval of pertinent and complete information by means of name, geographic and subject indexes. This indexing process was carried out by historians specialized in that period and involved a meticulous reading of each page in order to extract the necessary information to complete 26 different fields in each record. This fact, together with the lack of sufficient historians specialized in this period, and their reduced availability to work continuously on the project – most of the time there were only two historians and for long periods only one – meant that this work was not completed until January 2003.

The indexing data entry into the data base was completed in March 2003 and the quality control of each record was finished in May. The quality control of the whole data base concluded in August 2003, due to the loss of information at the moment when records created at different workstations were merged in a single data base.

During the quality control process of scanned images the non-existence of some and the repetition of others was discovered. The subsequent substitution or inclusion of images was done after the repairing of the scanner in April 2003 (it had been damaged since April 2002 due to various technical problems.)

By-product

Without doubt, the indexing process was much slower than the digitization. Therefore, the microfilmed press continued to be scanned and at present we have 63 titles, 12,335 images, corresponding to the period 1820-1830. For this simultaneous task the indexing process was simplified – by country, title, number and page – in order to facilitate retrieval of these titles. To this date the indexing of these titles has been completed. Also, the process of loading the records onto a server in order to allow access on line has been started.

Table No.1 Digitization of the Grandcolombian press (1820-1830).

Country	Title	Digitized Images	Indexed Images	Records Inserted
Bolivia	El Cóndor de Bolivia (1825-1828)	646	100%	100%
Colombia-Panamá	Gazeta de Colombia (1821-1826)	1,208	100%	100%
Ecuador	El Colombiano de Guayas (1828-1830) El Colombiano (1830)	278 138	100% 100%	100% 100%
Perú	La Abeja Republicana (1822-1823)	753	100%	100%
Venezuela	Correo del Orinoco (1818-1822)	519	100%	100%
	Total	3,542	100%	100%

3.4 Creation of the Grandcolombian Press (1820-1830) CD-ROM

In June 1999, the company Semi Crom, C.A., together with the Directors of Information Technology (SAIBIN) from the National Library, made a ‹demo› with the digitized images from *El venezolano*, so as to evaluate the SCAV software.

Since the year 2000, various prototypes made by the company Archicentro,S.A., who developed SCAV software, were tested. The prototype includes the information from the data base corresponding to the Grandcolombian newspapers.

The last prototype was received in September 2003, without including the final corrections in the data base.

4. New Developments

At the time of the arrival of the new CD prototype (September 2003), the institution coordinator, as well as the project's technical coordinator and the person responsible for digitization at the National Library, for different reasons, had ceased working at the Venezuela National Library. Apart from this the National Center for Paper Conservation was beginning its move to a new site, within the new National Library Headquarters. Both of these situations brought with them new delays in the project. On the other hand, ABINIA´s Executive Secretariat , complying with their designation as an entity sponsoring this project and conscious of the need to achieve its definitive completion, assumed a much tighter and more direct supervision of the project. With this in mind, we hired the new Director of the National Center for Paper Conservation at the National Library at the beginning of 2004 and we met with her and the technical staff who had worked on the project. We were able to establish, through common agreement, a work time schedule, which defined the pending activities along with their respective people in charge and finalization dates, up until the end of the project; that is to say, the edition of 1,000 copies of the CD-ROM containing the five previously selected and indexed titles of the Grandcolombian press- 1820-1830 and its free of charge distribution to prime academic libraries in the United States, Latin American National Libraries and other libraries, museums and archives in Latin America and the Caribbean.

Technical Developments.- As a result of moving the scanner it was thrown off balance and a specialist had to be hired to get it working again. This was achieved by the middle of February 2004 with the support of ABINIA. At the same time the technical operator from the digitization team was able to continue his work. However, the most significant was to get a very competent professional in technical processes from the National Library to be in charge of revising the record indexing and, in most cases, to practically make new indexes.

Operational Developments.- Working with the company responsible for producing the CDROM we were able to maintain similar conditions to those established in 2003, for the technical revision of the prototype, edition and production of 1,000 copies of the CD.

Administrative Developments.- Support from new authorities at the Venezuela National Library and, in particular, from the Director of the National Center for Paper Conservation, as well as the careful following-up of pending developments by ABINIA´s Executive Secretariat.

5. Limitations

5.1. Research Material and Contents:

Scarce availability of microforms in the Gandcolombian Countries.- From the beginning, with the help of Venezuelan historians and librarians from the national libraries of each country, the most important newspapers from the participant countries in the project were identified. However, few newspapers were already microfilmed. At the Venezuela National Library the microfilming was done from facsimile editions or duplicated rolls of microfilm positives that

5.2. Human Resources:

Handling new technologies.- This project was, the first of its kind, developed in Venezuela and became a learning process, as it developed, for all those involved. In fact, it served as a trial and error process for the RAM-ROM Computer company and for the computer science science and conservation technicians from the National Library.

Highly specialized historians.- It became very difficult to find qualified staff to index 19th century newspapers. This type of information requires historians with a wide capacity to research historical figures from the time and achieve their correct identification. Generally speaking, these experts – so as to obtain enough income – work autonomously for many different institutions at the same time and constantly look out for new projects. For this reason they do not undertake anything for a long period of time. At the best of times we could count on two historians working simultaneously on the project, but for the majority of the time there was only one.

5.3. Techniques:

As it happens with all new techniques, at first we are faced with the obvious problem of selecting and training adequate staff. Moreover, the microfilm scanner failed to work properly for long periods of time, the network configuration did not work (September 1997-January 1999, April 2002-April 2003), and both the supplier in Venezuela and the dealer took a long time to identify the causes and provide the technical support required.

5.4. Management:

At the beginning, the lack of experience in handling the new technology, the lack of knowledge concerning conditions in other National Libraries and the naïve academic aspiration to carry out exhaustive indexing (26 fields in each record) did not reflect reality and were the reason for the delay in carrying out the activities within the predicted terms and also in establishing the time scale for different activities.

5.5. Administrative:

The program was considered an external project (ABINIA), which made it difficult to obtain support from all of the technical and administrative departments of the National Library. Executive Secretariat, ABINIA, Caracas, June 2004.

PROYECTO: «DIGITALIZACIÓN DE LA PRENSA LATINOAMERICANA DEL SIGLO XIX»
(Digitalización de la prensa de la Gran Colombia: 1820 a 1830)
Informe Final, 30 de mayo de 2004

Alfonso Quintero

Secretaria Ejecutiva de ABINIA, Caracas, Venezuela

1. Antecedentes

A comienzos de los años 90, después de realizar diagnósticos en las colecciones de varias bibliotecas nacionales de América Latina, se pudo constatar que buena parte de la prensa latinoamericana del siglo XIX, corría el riesgo de sufrir daños irreparables o desaparecer, debido a la inestabilidad propia de su soporte y a lo limitado de sus condiciones de preservación. Por esto su inventario y preservación, y la diseminación de la valiosa información que estas publicaciones contienen, pasaron a ser una prioridad para todos los países miembros de la Asociación de Bibliotecas Nacionales de Iberoamérica (ABINIA), al igual que para la UNESCO, que incluyó *Memoria de Iberoamérica* entre los proyectos piloto del Programa Memoria del Mundo. A esta situación se le respondió mediante el proyecto «Rescate de la Prensa del siglo XIX», formulado por la Biblioteca Nacional de Venezuela, el cual fue, posteriormente aprobado por ABINIA. Para su desarrollo se establecieron tres fases, la última de las cuales da origen al presente proyecto.

Fases del proyecto «Rescate de la Prensa del Siglo XIX»:

1. Creación de un catálogo colectivo de la información existente en las bibliotecas nacionales de América Latina sobre sus existencias de prensa del siglo XIX a fin de crear una base de datos para el uso de los investigadores.

2. Capacitación de recursos humanos, a nivel regional, en el área de microfilmación a fin de asegurar la reproducción de la prensa del siglo XIX y la preservación de las colecciones de las bibliotecas en este soporte.

3. Indización y digitalización de los periódicos más representativos y la edición de un CD-ROM para favorecer el acceso de los investigadores de otros países a la información disponible.

Las dos primeras fases fueron concluidas con éxito. Se realizó un Inventario de la prensa del siglo XIX existente en las Bibliotecas Nacionales de Iberoamérica, donde destacaba la evaluación del estado de conservación de las colecciones hemerográficas y de los procesos de catalogación automatizada y microfilmación. Como resultado, se desarrolló un catálogo colectivo automatizado de los periódicos del siglo XIX que se encontraban microfilmados en las bibliotecas nacionales y otras instituciones de Iberoamérica; y, entre otras actividades en materia de capacitación, la Biblioteca Nacional de Venezuela dictó en 1996 un taller de microfilmación para el personal de las bibliotecas nacionales de seis países latinoamericanos. Con aportes de la UNESCO, se editó el CD-ROM «Prensa Iberoamericana del Siglo XIX», el cual contiene una base de datos con 8.990 registros bibliográficos. Esta base de datos permite localizar los títulos en cualquiera de las bibliotecas nacionales u otras instituciones de los catorce países participantes. A través de este mismo CD-ROM, se tiene acceso a las primeras imágenes digitalizadas -correspondientes a un período de un año de circulación- del periódico más importante de cada uno de los catorce países. Este CD-ROM constituyó el primer producto del proyecto.

2. Description

2.1. Objetivo:

Digitalizar los periódicos latinoamericanos más importantes del siglo XIX a fin de facilitar el acceso a la comunidad de investigadores a la información contenida en ellos a través de un CD-ROM o en línea, a través de Internet. Inicialmente (tal como lo aprobó la Fundación Andrew W. Mellon en diciembre de 1997), se acordó editar el CD-ROM «Prensa Grancolombiana, 1820-1830», el cual contiene las imágenes de un periódico de cada uno de los países (Venezuela, Colombia, Ecuador, Panamá, Perú y Bolivia) que participaron en la experiencia de integración política o confederación de países latinoamericanos.

2.2. Resultados esperados:

Edición de un CD-ROM, que incluya las imágenes digitales de los periódicos, una revisión de cada título, índices exhaustivos onomástico, geográfico y de materias para facilitar la recuperación de la información.

2.3. Coordinador institucional:

Aurelio Álvarez Juan, Director de Servicios Técnicos Bibliotecarios de la Biblioteca Nacional de Venezuela.

2.4. Coordinador Técnico:

Pía Rodríguez, Directora del Centro Nacional de Conservación de Papel de la BN de Venezuela

2.5. Instituciones de financiamiento externas:

Fundación Andrew W. Mellon

2.6 Fecha de aprobación:

Diciembre de 1996

2.7 Donación:

Fundación Andrew W. Mellon: Bs. 95.150.000.00 (US$ 200,000), recibida el 26 de febrero de 1997 por la Biblioteca Nacional de Venezuela.

3. Desarollo

3.1 Adquisición de equipos y software

Unidad de digitalización: En 1997, la Dirección de Informática de la BN de Venezuela (SAIBIN) identificó y seleccionó los equipos y «softwares» requeridos para la digitalización por escaneo directo de microfilme. Se escogió la empresa «RAM-ROM Computer», representante de «Houston Fearless» en Venezuela, para el suministro de un escáner de microfilmes 16 y 35 mm,« MEKEL M500 (SACN MASTER)», acoplado a una computadora, con un controlador «SCANNER SEAPORT mod. 1D20»; «software» «Paint Pro Shop and Imaging» para manipulación de imágenes y un «CD-Recorder». Estos equipos ingresaron en septiembre de 1997. La instalación y puesta a punto del escáner tomó más de un año. Las fallas presentadas por este equipo no fueron resueltas por los técnicos de la empresa «RAM-ROM», quienes implementaban las recomendaciones de «Houston Fearless». Gracias a la asesoría directa del representante técnico de «MEKEL Engineering» y la calibración de nuestro operador de digitalización, se logró en enero de 1999 el adecuado funcionamiento de este equipo. Toda la prensa venezolana digitalizada como prueba hasta esa fecha tuvo que ser digitalizada nuevamente.

Estaciones de trabajo: En 1999 se adquirieron dos estaciones de trabajo computarizadas adicionales para el ingreso de los registros a la base de datos, control de calidad de la data existente y depuración de las imágenes; una unidad «JAZZ (2 GB)», para respaldo de las imágenes; y los «softwares» «SCAV 2.5», para la creación de la base de datos y la producción del CD-ROM y «Adobe Photoshop». En octubre de 2002 se decidió comprar una computadora adicional para hacer más efectivo el proceso de creación de registros, manejo de imágenes y control de calidad para cumplir con lo acordado con la Fundación Andrew W. Mellon de concluir el proyecto para finales de abril de 2003. No obstante, esta compra se retrasó hasta septiembre de 2003, ello debido a que los proveedores comerciales emiten cotizaciones con una validez muy corta que impide concretar los procesos de adquisición. Si bien, para ese entonces, exisía una tasa oficial de cambio de Bs. 1.600 por dólar, los importadores aludían que su acceso era muy restringido, lo cual implicaba efectuar sus transacciones a la tasa paralela no oficial, y fluctuante, existente en el mercado, muy superior a la oficial.

3.2 Capacitación y contratación de recursos humanos

Capacitación. En 1997, personal del área de informática fue entrenado por un ingeniero de sistemas de «Houston Fearless». Las tareas propias del proceso de digitalización (fijación de parámetros, realización de pruebas) fueron adelantadas por un operador del Centro Nacional de Conservación de Papel, División de Micrografía, quien, además de otros 6 funcionarios, fue capacitado en la operación del equipo por personal del área de informática (SAIBIN). En septiembre y noviembre de 1999, el Director de Servicios Técnicos Bibliotecarios asistió a dos eventos de digitalización en los Estados Unidos, que permitieron revisar la organización estructural y las actividades desarrolladas en el marco de este proyecto: el primero, del 21 al 23 de septiembre, *Opciones de preservación en el mundo digital: microfilmar o escanear*, presentado por el Northeast Document Conservation Center en Nebraska, y el segundo, del 2 al 4 de noviembre, *Imágenes digitales para bibliotecas y archivos*, dictado por la Universidad de Cornell, en Nueva York. Asimismo, del 5 al 12 de diciembre de 1999, el encargado del proceso de digitalización del Centro Nacional de Conservación de Papel realizó una pasantía en el Centro Nacional Editor de Discos Compactos (CENEDIC) en la Universidad de Colima, México, a fin de observar el proceso completo: desde la digitalización hasta la edición de un CD-ROM.

Contratación de recursos humanos. En 1999 se contrataron dos historiadores para realizar los índices temático, onomástico y geográfico. Esta tarea conlleva la revisión página por página de cada uno de los títulos seleccionados. Entre junio y noviembre de 1999 estuvo contratado un transcriptor con recursos del proyecto, que luego pasó a formar parte del personal fijo de la Biblioteca adscrito a la Unidad de Digitalización, hasta junio de 2001. En el año 2000 se logró contar con un diseñador gráfico que realizó la manipulación de las imágenes para optimizar la calidad de las mismas. Debido a la alta rotación del personal (historiadores que trabajaban en forma independiente y empleados que buscaban trabajo fijo), en el año 2002 se autorizó la incorporación de tres nuevos funcionarios de la Biblioteca Nacional para trabajar en la culminación de las actividades del proyecto: un historiador para el proceso de indización del título faltante y dos funcionarios para la creación y control de calidad de los registros.

3.3 Digitalización e indización

A sugerencia de la Biblioteca Nacional de cada país, se seleccionaron los periódicos grancolombianos más representativos, y considerando la capacidad de memoria del CD-ROM, se escogieron solamente cinco títulos (ver Cuadro No. 1) representados en 3.542 imágenes.

Indización exhaustiva. La primera decisión, por recomendación del Sr. Hans Rutimann, asesor de la Fundación Mellon, fue no aplicar OCR porque ninguno de los softwares probados producía buenos resultados, debido a que los tipos usados en América Latina durante ese período eran muy irregulares. Por esta razón, se decidió indizar exhaustivamente toda la información contenida en los 5 periódicos seleccionados, para lograr una recuperación de información pertinente y completa mediante índices onomástico, geográfico y temático. Este proceso de indización fue realizado por historiadores especializados en la época, e implicó una minuciosa revisión página por página para completar 26 campos diferentes. Este aspecto, aunado a la insuficiencia de historiadores especializados en esa época, y su poca disponibilidad para trabajar continuamente en el proyecto – la mayor parte del tiempo hubo sólo dos historiadores, y por períodos largos, sólo uno –, lo que significó que esta actividad lograra concluirse en enero de 2003.

El ingreso de los datos de la indización a la base de datos (es decir, la creación de registros a partir de formatos de indización) finalizó en marzo de 2003 y el control de calidad de cada registro fue completado en mayo. El control de calidad de la base de datos completa concluyó en agosto de 2003, debido a la pérdida de información al momento de integrar en una sola base de datos los registros creados en estaciones de trabajo distintas. Durante el proceso de control de calidad de las imágenes escaneadas, se evidenció la inexistencia de algunas imágenes y la repetición de otras. La sustitución o inclusión de las imágenes faltantes luego de su digitalización se efectuó después de la reparación del escáner en abril de 2003 (estuvo dañado desde abril de 2002 a causa de diversos problemas técnicos).

Sub-producto: Indudablemente, el proceso de indización fue más lento que la digitalización. Por lo tanto, se continuó escaneando la prensa microfilmada y se cuenta actualmente con 63 títulos, 12.335 imágenes, correspondientes al período 1820-1830. Para este trabajo simultáneo, se simplificó el proceso de indización – por país, título, fecha, número y página – a fin procurar el acceso a estos títulos. Hasta ahora se ha completado la indización de todos estos títulos. Adicionalmente, se ha procedido a cargar los registros en un servidor para permitir su acceso en línea.

Cuadro No. 1 Digitalización de la prensa grancolombiana (1820-1830)

País	Título	Imágenes digitalizadas	Imágenes indizadas	Registros ingresados
Bolivia	El Cóndor de Bolivia (1825-1828)	646	100%	100%
Colombia-Panamá	Gazeta de Colombia (1821-1826)	1,208	100%	100%
Ecuador	El Colombiano de Guayas (1828-1830) El Colombiano (1830)	278 138	100% 100%	100% 100%
Perú	La Abeja Republicana (1822-1823)	753	100%	100%
Venezuela	Correo del Orinoco (1818-1822)	519	100%	100%
	Total	3,542	100%	100%

3.4 Creación del CD-ROM de la prensa de la Gran Colombia (1820-1830)

En junio de 1999, la empresa Semi Crom, C.A., conjuntamente con la Dirección del Informática (SAIBIN) de la Biblioteca Nacional, elaboró un «demo» con las imágenes digitalizadas de *El Venezolano*, a fin de evaluar el software SCAV. Desde el año 2000, se evaluaron varios prototipos elaborados por la empresa Archicentro, S.A., quienes desarrollaron el software SCAV. El prototipo incluye la información de la base de datos correspondiente a los periódicos de la Gran Colombia. El último prototipo fue recibido en septiembre de 2003, sin incluir las últimas correcciones a la base de datos.

4. Nuevas Acciones

Para la fecha de recepción del nuevo prototipo del CD (Septiembre de 2003), el coordinador institucional , como la coordinadora técnica del proyecto y el responsable de digitalización de la BN, por distintas razones, habían dejado de trabajar en la BN de Venezuela. Además, se iniciaba la mudanza del Centro Nacional de Conservación de Papel, a un nuevo local, ubicado en la Nueva Sede de la Biblioteca Nacional. Ambas situaciones trajeron consigo nuevos retrasos en el proyecto. Por otra parte, la Secretaría Ejecutiva de ABINIA, en cumplimiento de sus atribuciones de ente que auspicia este proyecto y consciente de la necesidad de lograr su definitiva culminación, asumimos una supervisión mucho más estrecha y directa del mismo. En tal sentido, a comienzos del 2004, contactamos a la nueva directora del Centro Nacional de Conservación del Papel de la BN y nos reunimos con ella y el personal técnico que había trabajado en el proyecto. Se logró establecer, de común acuerdo, un cronograma de trabajo, en el cual se definieron actividades pendientes por realizar, con sus respectivos responsables y fechas de culminación, hasta la finalización del proyecto, es decir: la edición de 1.000 copias del CD-ROM, contentivo de los 5 títulos previamente seleccionados e indizados de la prensa de la Gran Colombia – 1820/1830 y su distribución gratuita entre las principales bibliotecas académicas de los Estados Unidos, las bibliotecas nacionales iberoamericanas y demás bibliotecas, museos y archivos de América Latina y el Caribe.

Acciones Técnicas.- Producto de la mudanza el escáner se desniveló, siendo necesario la ubicación y contratación de un especialista que lo nivelará y pusiera a funcionar nuevamente. Esto se logró a mediados de Febrero de 2004 con el apoyo de ABINIA. Por otra parte, se logró asimismo que el operador técnico del equipo de digitalización continuara en sus funciones. Pero, lo más significativo, fue lograr que, una muy competente profesional de procesos técnicos de la BN, se encargara de la revisión de la indización de los registros y, en algunos casos, prácticamente, de efectuar nuevas indizaciones.

Acciones Operativas.- Se logró, con la empresa responsable de la producción del CD-ROM, el mantenimiento de condiciones similares a las establecidas en el 2003, para la revisión técnica del prototipo, edición y producción las 1.000 copias del CD.

Acciones Administrativas.- Apoyo de las nuevas autoridades de la BN de Venezuela y, en particular, de la Directora del Centro Nacional de Conservación del Papel, además del cuidadoso seguimiento de las acciones pendientes por parte de la Secretaría Ejecutiva de ABINIA.

5. Limitaciones

5.1. Material y contenidos de investigación:

Escasa disponibilidad de microformas en los países de la Gran Colombia.- En un primer momento, se identificaron, con la ayuda de historiadores venezolanos y bibliotecarios de las bibliotecas nacionales de cada país, los periódicos más importantes de los países participantes en el proyecto. Sin embargo, pocos periódicos se encontraban ya microfilmados. En la Biblioteca Nacional de Venezuela se realizó la microfilmación a partir de ediciones facsimilares o rollos duplicados de positivos de microfilme que las bibliotecas participantes enviaron.

5.2. Recursos humanos:

Manejo de nuevas tecnologías.- Este proyecto fue, el primero en su tipo, desarrollado en Venezuela, y constituyó un proceso de aprendizaje, sobre la marcha, para todos los involucrados en él. De hecho, significó un proceso de ensayo y error para la empresa RAM ROM Computer, y para los técnicos de informática y conservación de la Biblioteca Nacional.

Historiadores altamente especializados.- Resultó muy difícil encontrar personal capacitado para la indización de los periódicos del siglo XIX. Este tipo de información requiere historiadores, con una amplia capacidad para investigar sobre personalidades históricas de la época y lograr la correcta identificación de las mismas. Generalmente, estos expertos – a fin de tener suficientes ingresos – trabajan en forma independiente para diversas instituciones al mismo tiempo y, constantemente, buscan nuevos proyectos. Por lo tanto, no se comprometen por tiempo prolongado. En el mejor de los casos, se pudo contar con dos historiados trabajando a la vez en el proyecto, pero la mayor parte del tiempo, sólo había uno.

5.3. Técnicas:

Inicialmente, como ocurre con toda tecnología nueva, enfrentamos el problema obvio de seleccionar y capacitar al personal adecuado. Además, el escáner de microfilme presentó fallas durante largos períodos, la configuración de la red no funcionó (septiembre 1997-

enero 1999, abril 2002-abril 2003), y tanto el proveedor en Venezuela como el distribuidor demoraron en identificar las causas y prestar el soporte técnico requerido.

5.4. Gerenciales:

En un principio, la falta de experiencia en el manejo de la nueva tecnología, el desconocimiento de las condiciones de otras Bibliotecas Nacionales y la ingenua aspiración académica de hacer una indización exhaustiva (26 campos) no reflejaban la realidad y fueron causa de retrasos en la ejecución de las actividades dentro de los términos previstos y también en el establecimiento del cronograma para la realización de las distintas actividades.

5.5. Administrativas:

El programa fue considerado un proyecto externo (ABINIA), lo cual dificultó lograr el respaldo de todas las unidades técnicas y administrativas de la Biblioteca Nacional. Secretaría Ejecutiva de ABINIA, Caracas junio de 2004.

COLOMBIAN JOURNALISM BEFORE 1900: COLLECTIONS, MICROFILMING AND DIGITIZATION

Jorge Orlando Melo

Luis Ángel Arango Library, Bogota, Colombia

Colombian journalism in the 19th century

The first Colombian newspaper appeared in 1785, during the Spanish rule period: a simple information sheet informing of an earthquake, of which 3 copies were published. *La Gaceta de Santafé*, published the same year, could not maintain regularity either. El *Papel Periódico de la ciudad de Santafé de Bogatá*, which appeared in 1791 and was in circulation until 1796, was the first regular periodical publication in the present territory of Colombia. Between the time it closed down and the independence of the country, in 1810, another 6 newspapers were published, bringing the total of publications during Spanish domination to 9 titles. To determine how many titles were published between 1810 and 1900 is more difficult, as will be seen in the following notes. On the one hand, republican life was accompanied by an eagerness to publish news and opinions that many considered excessive. Journalism became an essential element of public life and politics fed itself on the controversies of the newspapers. In 1836 journalistic fervor was such that it was decided appropriate and viable to establish a newspaper paper factory in Bogotá, a city with less than 30,000 inhabitants. In general, the press enjoyed reasonable freedom of speech, although it was subject to some pressure from the government and judicial procedures to avoid any possible excesses. It was only between 1886 and 1900, however, that censorship and repression held back the opposition press with some amount of efficiency.

On the other hand, newspapers emerged from many cities and small towns, printed on manual presses and with local distribution. Many of these newspapers have disappeared or their collections are very incomplete. Numerous newspapers died out without getting past the first edition, which creates a confusing category for existing catalogues of 19thC newspapers in which loose pages and other short-lived printed sheets get mixed up with periodical publications in the strict sense.

Newspaper distribution was very irregular and editions rarely got past a few hundred copies. The first daily was the *Diario Oficial*, which since 1864 served as a an official acts register. The first private and commercial daily was *El Telegrama* which began its existence in 1886.

Newspaper collections

The National Library collections: A public library has existed in Bogotá since 1777. Its Director at the end of the 18thC was, in fact, the founder and editor of *Papel Periódico*. Although the library never made very active efforts to collect newspapers published in the country, the editors themselves usually sent their publications to the library. From 1832 onwards, a law established the obligation to legal deposit. This law was more closely complied with in the case of publications made in Bogotá, while provincial newspapers complied much more irregularly.

The National Libraries newspaper collections from the first half of the 19thC seem to be owed just as much, if not more, to the legal deposit laws as to the initiatives of some collectors. The most important of all was Colonel Anselmo Pineda, who since 1810 dedicated himself obsessively to collecting all publications from the country and many from Latin America and in 1852 he handed his collections over to the National Library. The catalogue of material given in that year, which included works up to 1850, was printed in 1872 and a second catalogue from 1873 added the contents of a second donation: the colonel had continued to collect all possible publications from 1850 until this date.

Other private collections were later added to the previously mentioned: that belonging to José María Quijano Otero, who had been Director of the Library, was bought in 1894. At the beginning of the 20thC, the collection of another director was added, that of José Vergara y Velasco. After this date the arrival of new titles corresponding to the 19thC has been minimal. At present the number of records of 19thC newspapers is approximately 2,200.

The National Libraries newspaper collections have been described in various catalogues. The first was published in 1855 and then the *Pineda Collection* (1872 and 1873) and some partial catalogues published in the *Public Instruction* magazine. In the 20thC the Pineda collection catalogue was reprinted (1936) and general lists of newspapers were published (1935). A catalogue of 19thC newspapers from 1995 is the most complete to date.

Luis Ángel Arango Library collections: This library was opened in 1958 and for this reason, its collection of 19thC newspapers is mostly the result of purchasing private collections. The most important was that of Laureano García Ortiz, a historian who collected from the end of the 19thC until the 1930's, a rich collection about Colombia. Purchased in 1945, it constitutes the base of this libraries collection of patrimonial value. At present the number of records in this collection is approximately 1,200. Most of these records duplicate those in the National Library, although they also often complement incomplete series. There may be about 25 titles which are not in the National Library. The majority of newspaper collections and libraries acquired have been obtained in Bogotá, with occasional regional contributions, meaning that they do not offer much variation from the National Library. Most of the new titles correspond, as is to be expected, to the last third of the 19thC when the García Ortiz collection was formed.

In 1980 this library put a catalogue into circulation containing approximately 900 titles from the 19thC[1]. In spite of the fact that all the records can be found on the electronic catalogue, it is not easy to obtain a comprehensive, precise list due to the limitations of the present OPAC search systems which generate a large number of additional records or references that do not refer to single titles.

The University of Antioquia Collections: This university's library has a similar collection in size to that of the Luis Ángel Arango Library. According to its printed catalogue it has 1,194 records of newspapers between 1828 and 1900, which shows that the total number of records for last century could be about 1,250[2].

Although it has fewer complete series of newspapers from the independence period, the collection is surprising for its large quantity of records which are not found in either of the other two big libraries. On going over the titles it can be seen that those who collected them were capable of bringing together newspapers from very remote geographical regions of the

1   (Banco de la República, Hemeroteca Luis López de Mesa, *Catálogo general, volume 1*, Bogará, Graphic workshops at Banco de la República. s. f.)

2   Uribe de Hincapie, María Teresa and Jesús María Álvarez, *Cien anos de prensa en Colombia, 1840-1940*: indexed catalogue of the existing press in the newspaper room at the Central Library of the University of Antioquia, 2ª. Ed, Medellín: Editorial Universidad de Antioquia, 2002.

country and they preserved material that for some reason have not been preserved in Bogotá. Of course this is especially true of newspapers from the end of the 19thC. An initial revision reveals that at least 300 titles mentioned are not found in the National Library which makes this collection a critical element in any preservation program.

There is no adequate document explaining the way in which this collection was made. An important part of it undoubtedly comes from the public library opened in Medellín in 1881 and which was directed by the doctor and liberal historian Manuel Uribe Ángel. The collection was received by the Library of Zea, then considered very rich, from the writer and editor Juan José Molina and probably grew through the management of its first directors. In 1916 a guide from the city of Medellín said that the library had a rich newspaper collection, including *El Semanario del Nuevo Reino de Granada*, Francisco José de Caldas' scientific journal[3]. However, during the first half of the 20thC both the collection and the library appear to have come to a standstill and in 1951 were handed over to the University of Antioquia. Despite this university being founded in 1867, its library seems to have been almost non-existent until the mid-19thC: in 1935 it had only 35 titles and 4 journal titles[4].

Other collections: Without doubt, the examination of other smaller collections would bring new findings of periodical publications not known up to now, or which we find mentions of but not copies. There does not really exist any library other than these three that is making an organized effort to search for, record, conserve and catalogue Colombian newspapers. However, the university libraries and the historical research centers have received private collections that might be very important for their contributing of regional titles.

Collections with the highest probability of contributing new copies to known titles or new titles are:

1. The Colombian Academy for History Library: Its collections are especially rich in the end period of the century and they have received gift collections from some of their members.

2. The National University of Colombia Library.

3. The University of El Valle Library.

4. The Pedagogical and Technological University of Tunja Library. Indispensable to complete the records of publications from the Boyacá region, since it manages the Boyacense Academy for History Library.

5. The University of Nariño Library.

6. The History Archives of Cauca.

7. Private collections. Some private collections are very rich in regional newspapers. The most noteworthy is without doubt that of Alfonso Harker Villamizar, which has various newspapers from the Santander region.

8. Convents and Seminaries. They would help to complete the record of ecclesiastical publications.

9. Pilot Public Library of Medellín.

10. Luis Eduardo Nieto Arteta de Barranquilla Library.

11. History Archives of Cartagena.

---

3 Juan Peyrat, *Guía de Medellín*, Medillín, 1916.
4 La Biblioteca de la Universidad de Antioquia: más de un siglo de historia. *Interamericana de Bibliotecología Magazine*. (Medellín). Vol. 16, no. 2 (July/Dec. 1993) – p. 65-84.

Conservation, microfilming and digitization

When the stock of these three libraries is compared with the total number of 19thC publications the level of loss is considerable. The most prestigious documents, high impact newspapers have been practically preserved in their entirety There are series of *Papel Periódico de Santa Fe* from 1791 or of the *Semanario* from Caldas, of the *Neogranadino* or *El Porvenir* at the National Library or the Luis Ángel Arango Library, although there are some tragic exceptions since there does not appear to exist any complete collection of such an important newspaper as *El Espectador*. However, the loss of provincial newspapers or marginal Bogotá newspapers was very high: there are hundreds which only have a few sample copies and there are surely many titles which do not have a copy in the collections[5].

This loss was produced mostly in the 19thC. We can assume that many minor newspapers, that were not sent to the National Library, were not collected by their readers. The capacity of the three heroic collectors mentioned in these notes (Pineda, García Ortiz, Molina) was limited and many titles almost definitely escaped them. Without doubt, many collections outlived their editors and printers but we know that families in general do not value these collections, which are bulky, difficult to keep and practically unmarketable[6]. Some of them were probably recycled into cardboard or simply thrown into the rubbish bin.

Preservation in Colombian heritage libraries is on the whole adequate. Climatic conditions in Bogotá greatly favor the conservation of paper, so we can be sure that what was deposited in the National Library and the Luis Ángel Arango Library is still there. I am certainly ignoring some anomalies: climate effects in places like Cartagena or Tumaco, inadequate weeding, of which there are more or less founded rumors or researchers stealing or careless handling. Pineda himself and some National Library directors admitted that their collection had suffered losses through careless handling at the library but until we have a comparison and quantity study of titles, I tend to think that they were not too great. Neither can we ignore the contribution made many times by the pious descendents of the heroes to the disappearance of national history, systematically cutting out all mentions of their deeds from library newspapers. In other cases, relatives worried about their honor cut out and removed, for example, everything they could find about the sentimental activities of Nicolasa Ibáñez and her sisters.

Let us hope that these things are of the past. Today, originals are reasonably well kept and their transfer to an alternative format, which will reduce the use of originals and offer an almost total back-up of the newspapers' contents, is the greatest necessity.

Since 1985 the microfilming effort has been great. At the outset, through Lina Espitaleta's initiative, director of the Luis Ángel Arango Library at the time and current director of the National Library, a joint microfilming program was developed between the two main Bogotá libraries. The collections were put together into one in order to obtain a more complete series and the majority of 19thC newspapers were systematically microfilmed. In 1990 the National Library decided to suspend the program when about 1,450 rolls had been processed (which covered 19thC newspapers and some important 20thC newspapers) the

---

5   As far as I know, no attempt has been made to list disappeared newspapers: those that appear mentioned in other media and newspapers, but which do not figure in known collections. My statement comes from arbitrary pointers: there are small cities from where tens of newspapers have been preserved /Honda, Socorro) whilst other places of equal intellectual development do not have any record (Salamina, Santa Rosa de Osos, Armenia.)

6   In foreign Archives and Libraries some new titles can be found. Some private Colombian collections found their way into university libraries in the United States, like Texas or Berkeley.

master copies of which can be found at the Luis Arango Library. From that moment the two institutions continued microfilming independently and with different strategies. Whilst the Luis Arango contracts microfilming with external companies, the National Library has preferred to do it on its own for which it set up a modern microfilming laboratory in 1995. However, because of resource limitations progress has been slow. Since then a few rolls of 19thC newspapers have been microfilmed. As far as the Luis Ángel Arango Library is concerned, it is about to complete the microfilming of its own 19thC newspaper collection and now has more than 7000 rolls of newspapers microfilmed.

At the present moment, the National and Luis Ángel Arango libraries are in agreement to again develop a joint program. This program may complete the microfilming of all pre-1900 Colombian newspapers existing in their collections in a short period of time (before the end of 2005). The ideal thing would be to be able to coordinate the microfilming of titles that do not exist in Bogotá collections with the University of Antioquia.

To this day, the libraries have considered it right to continue using microfilming. However, some digitization programs of periodical collections are being developed. The Luis Arango is beginning the digitization of the most important cultural magazines from the 19thC. These magazines have a small format, usually smaller than A4 size, and can be processed on simple digitization equipment. The files will be kept on servers with access to researchers and in some cases will be put onto the net on the Luis Ángel Arango virtual website (www. lablaa. org). *El Mosaico* and the *Papel Periódico Ilustrado* will be the first two magazines to receive this treatment. It is worth mentioning that the main objective of this job is not conservation as the two publications I have mentioned have previously been microfilmed. Also, the Public Pilot Library, in cooperation with the University of Antioquia, will digitize some magazines from that region, for the Antioquia Virtual Library.

Catalogues and control lists: The three printed catalogues make up an interesting set. In all of them a real effort has been made to include the newspaper titles in the collections, but the design of the indexes is such that search results are useless or difficult to handle.

The Luis Ángel Arango catalogue is chronological. For this reason it includes an alphabetical index of the recorded titles. Surprisingly, the alphabetical index has been divided into two large groups, worked out from the way in which the newspapers are bound in the Library. The titles grouped into a series called *Periódicos Varios* are indexed separately from the rest. In this way, the user has to look for each title in two different places. Meanwhile, an index by place of publication was not done, which is obviously useful for readers. The index cards include the editor or director's names, as well as the number of copies in existence. Newspapers are also recorded under every year they appeared, which makes it very difficult to define which are unique titles and makes it necessary, in order to find out the number of copies of a newspaper, to look sometimes at scores of years. (To this of course is added the real problem of frequent changes of titles which undergo unexpected metamorphosis, to the cataloguer's despair: when there are very few copies and many are missing, it is not always possible to know if a similar title is a simple change or a new title.

The National Library catalogue was edited without any apparent order: it follows an approximately alphabetical order, but not systematic. Because of this they have had to publish a separate volume of records: alphabetical, chronological and geographical, referring the user to the the detailed index cards. At least one of these indexes could have been avoided if the publication had followed one of these orders. The indexes are very complete: they often include the editors and they have a record of copies in existence. They also indicate whether there is a microfilm of the newspaper, but they do not say which of the master rolls are in the Library or which are at the Luis Ángel Arango. Although, sometimes they say that the microfilm is more complete than the actual collection, they never specify where the copies are that were used to complete the rolls: the most probable likelihood, although there may be exceptions, is that they are also from the Luis Ángel Arango.

The University of Antioquia's catalogue has an extensive introductory study on Colombian newspapers but it does not explain why the few pre-1840 titles were not included (or before 1828, as a few titles between 1828 and 1840 are recorded, which does not seem logical that those are all the collection has). The indexes are very complete and attempt not only to fulfill the librarians wishes but also those of historians and social researchers: they describe the newspaper's character (commercial, cultural, political, etc.,) its political orientation, it shows who they debate with and they provide a very ample list of collaborators. This makes this document a very useful tool. However, no one seems to think about how the records should be: the publication of the indexes is alphabetical and indicates which page to go to to find it in the newspaper. The useful ones are an analytical index of material dealt with in the newspapers, an index of editors and collaborators and an index of mentioned places. Curiously, neither was it considered useful to compile a index by places the newspapers were edited in. These are probably the last catalogues on paper of this kind that will be published. Library catalogues mean you can retrieve information from the files but they have not been developed in a systematic way that would allow integral retrival of 19thC newspapers. For that, the researcher intending to examine newspapers from a city or those that were published in a specific period, needs comprehensive lists that can be consulted and transformed. Of course strict cataloguing rules could be applied that would allow these lists to be obtained from the OPAC but the retrospective effort required to standardize the records is very great. For this reason I see it fitting that a simple list controlling newspapers published in the country during the last century be developed, that can serve eventually as a basis for a wider catalogue. A list that simply records titles of newspapers, place where printed, printer, dates of publication, copies in existence in different libraries, copies on microfilm, editions and facsimiles in existence and full indexes of specific newspapers. To find solutions to ambiguities it would be a good idea to include, for some newspapers, the names of the editors as well as some other additional information.

The three current lists, in the three printed catalogues, produce titles that we could call ghosts because they are just variations of the original title. An inventory of unique titles, initially from the three libraries we have discussed, but that could be gradually extended to others, would give a more precise map of the world of journalism in the 19th century.

As an initial contribution towards this effort, this communication has as an appendage a draft copy of a «Control list of 19th century newspapers and magazines», which includes all existing records of the three main collections in the country, approximately 2,800 titles. This number will get smaller as duplications are eliminated. On finding new titles, titles that had disappeared or that have copies in other libraries or collections, it could also get larger. The future is just as much as full of uncertainties as was the past.

EL PERIODISMO COLOMBIANO ANTES DE 1900: COLECCIONES, MICROFILMACIONES Y DIGITALIZACIONES

Jorge Orlando Melo

Biblioteca Luis Ángel Arango, Bogotá, Colombia

El periodismo colombiano del siglo XIX

El primer periódico colombiano apareció en 1785, durante el período de dominio español: una simple hoja de información acerca de un terremoto, de la cual se publicaron 3 números. *La Gaceta de Santafé*, publicada el mismo año, tampoco pudo mantener regularidad. El *Papel Periódico de la ciudad de Santafé de Bogatá*, que apareció en 1791 y circuló hasta 1796, fue la primera publicación periódica regular en el territorio de la actual Colombia. Entre su cierre y la independencia del país, en 1810, se publicaron otros 6 periódicos, lo cual eleva el número de publicaciones realizadas durante la época de la dominación española a 9 títulos.

Determinar cuantos títulos se publicaron entre 1810 y 1900 es más difícil, como se verá en las notas siguientes. Por una parte, la vida republicana estuvo acompañada de un afán que muchos consideraban desmedido por publicar noticias y opiniones. El periodismo se convierte en elemento esencial de la vida pública y la política se nutre de las polémicas de los periódicos. En 1836 era tal el furor periodístico que se pensó conveniente y rentable establecer una fábrica de papel periódico en Bogotá, una ciudad que tenía menos de 30.000 habitantes. En general, la prensa disfrutó de una razonable libertad de expresión, aunque estuvo sujeta a presiones informales del gobierno y a procedimientos judiciales para combatir sus posibles excesos. Solo entre 1886 y 1900, sin embargo, la censura y la represión frenaron con alguna eficacia la prensa opositora.

Por otra parte, surgieron periódicos en muchas ciudades y pequeños pueblos, realizadas con imprentas manuales, con una circulación local. Muchos de estos periódicos han desaparecido o sus colecciones lson muy incompletas. Son numerosos los periódicos que morían sin pasar de primer número, lo que genera una categoría confusa en la que tienden a mezclarse, en los catálogos existentes de la prensa del siglo XIX, hojas sueltas y otros impresos efímeros con publicaciones periódicas en sentido estricto.

La circulación de la prensa fue muy irregular, y las ediciones raras veces pasaban de unos pocos centenares de ejemplares. El primer diario fue el Diario Oficial, que desde 1864 llena ante todo la función de registro de los actos oficiales. El primer diario privado y comercial fue El Telegrama, que comenzó a existir en 1886.

Las colecciones de prensa

Las colecciones de la Biblioteca Nacional. Desde 1777 existía en Bogotá una biblioteca pública. Su director, a fines del siglo XVIII, fue justamente el fundador y editor del Papel Periódico. Aunque la biblioteca no realizó casi nunca esfuerzos muy activos para reunir la prensa que se publicaba en el país, fue usual el envío de las publicaciones a la biblioteca por parte de sus mismos editores. A partir de 1832, una ley estableció la obligación del depósito legal. Se cumplió con mayor precisión con relación a las publicaciones hechas en Bogotá, mientas que los periódicos de provincia lo hacían en forma más irregular.

Las colecciones de prensa de la primera mitad del siglo XIX de la Biblioteca Nacional parecen deberse, tanto o más que al cumplimiento de las leyes de depósito legal, a la actividad de algunos coleccionistas. El más importante de todos fue el Coronel Anselmo Pineda, quien desde1810 se dedicó obsesivamente a reunir todas las publicaciones del país y muchas de Hispanoamérica, y en 1852 entregó sus colecciones a la Biblioteca Nacional. El catálogo de lo entregado en ese año, y que incluía obras hasta 1850, fue impreso en 1872, y un segundo catálogo, de 1873, añadió los contenidos de una segunda donación: el coronel había seguido reuniendo todas las publicaciones posibles desde 1850 hasta esta fecha.

Otras colecciones privadas se añadieron posteriormente a la anterior: la de José María Quijano Otero, quien había sido director de la Biblioteca, fue comprada en 1894. A comienzos del siglo XX se añadió la colección se otro director de la biblioteca, el general José María Vergara y Velasco. A partir de esta fecha parece que ha sido mínima la llegada de nuevos títulos correspondientes al siglo XIX. En la actualidad el número de registros de prensa del siglo XIX es aproximadamente de 2200.

Las colecciones de prensa de la Biblioteca Nacional han sido descritas en diversos catálogos. El primer fue publicado en 1855, y luego se publicaron los de la Colección Pineda (1872 y 1873), y algunos catálogos parciales publicados en la revista de Instrucción Pública. En el siglo XX se reprodujo el catálogo de la colección Pineda (1936) y se publicaron listas generales de periódicos (1935). De 1995 es un catálogo de prensa del siglo XIX, el más completo publicado hasta hoy.

Las colecciones de la Biblioteca Luis Ángel Arango: Esta biblioteca fue abierta en 1958, y por lo tanto su colección de prensa del siglo XIX es ante todo el resultado de la compra de colecciones privadas. La más importante fue la de Laureano García Ortiz, un historiador que reunió desde finales del siglo XIX hasta la década de 1930 una rica colección sobre Colombia: comprada en 1945, constituye la base de la colección de valor patrimonial de esta biblioteca. En la actualidad el número de registros de esta colección es de aproximadamente 1200. En su gran mayoría, estos registros duplican los de la Biblioteca Nacional, aunque con frecuencia complementan series incompletas. El número de títulos que no están en la Biblioteca Nacional puede acercarse a 25 La mayoría de las colecciones y bibliotecas de prensa adquiridas han sido conformadas en Bogotá, con ocasionales aportes regionales, por lo cual no ofrecen muchas novedades en comparación con la Biblioteca Nacional. La mayoría de títulos nuevos corresponden, como es de esperarlo, al último tercio del siglo XIX, cuando se conformó la colección de García Ortiz.

Esta Biblioteca puso en circulación un catálogo impreso en 1980, que reportaba aproximadamente 900 títulos del siglo XIX[1] Aunque todos los registros se encuentran en el catálogo electrónico, no es fácil obtener un listado integral preciso de sus existencias, por las limitaciones de los sistemas de búsqueda del OPAC actual, que generan un número elevado de registros adicionales o referenciales que no remiten a títulos únicos.

Las colecciones de la Universidad de Antioquia. La biblioteca de la Universidad de Antioquia tiene una colección similar en tamaño a la de la Biblioteca Luis Ángel Arango: según su catálogo impreso tiene 1194 registros de prensa entre 1828 y 1900, lo que indica que el número total de registros para el siglo pasado puede acercarse a 1250[2].

---

1 (Banco de la República, Hemeroteca Luis López de Mesa, *Catálogo general*, volumen 1, Bogotá, Talleres gráficos del banco de la República, s.f.,).

2 Uribe de Hincapie, Maria Teresa y Jesús María Álvarez, *Cien anos de prensa en Colombia, 1840-1940*: catalogo indizado de la prensa existente en la sala de periódicos de La Biblioteca Central de la Universidad de Antioquia, 2a. ED, Medellín: Editorial Universidad de Antioquia, 2002.

Aunque tiene series menos completas de los periódicos de la época de la independencia, la colección es sorprendente por la gran cantidad de registros que no se encuentran en ninguna de las otras dos grandes bibliotecas. Al revisar sus títulos se advierte que quienes la conformaron fueron capaces de recoger prensa de regiones geográficas muy remotas del país y conservaron materiales que por alguna razón no se han conservado en Bogotá. Por supuesto, esto es verdad ante todo con relación a la prensa de finales del siglo XIX. Una revisión inicial revela que al menos 300 de los títulos mencionados no se encuentran en la Biblioteca Nacional: esto convierte esta colección en un elemento crítico de cualquier programa de conservación.

No existe una documentación adecuada sobre la forma como se formó esta colección. Una parte muy importante proviene sin duda de la biblioteca pública abierta en Medellín en 1881, y que fue dirigida por el médico e historiador liberal Manuel Uribe Ángel. La Biblioteca de Zea recibió la colección, considerada entonces muy rica, del escritor y editor Juan José Molina, y probablemente creció por la gestión de sus primeros directores. En 1916 una guía de la ciudad de Medellín decía que la biblioteca tenía una rica colección de prensa, incluyendo el Semanario del Nuevo reino de Granada, la revista científica de Francisco José de Caldas.[3] Sin embargo, durante la primera mitad del siglo XX la colección y la biblioteca parecen haberse estancado, y en 1951 fueron entregadas a la Universidad de Antioquia. Aunque esta universidad fue fundada en 1867, su biblioteca parece haber sido casi inexistente hasta mediados del siglo XIX: en 1935 tenía apenas 35 títulos de revistas[4].

Otras colecciones: Sin ninguna duda, la revisión de otras colecciones menores producirá nuevos hallazgos de publicaciones periódicas hasta ahora desconocidas, o de las cuales se encuentran menciones pero no ejemplares. Prácticamente no existe ninguna biblioteca distinta a estas tres que esté haciendo un esfuerzo ordenado de búsqueda, registro, conservación y catalogación de prensa colombiana. Sin embargo, las bibliotecas universitarias y las de centros de investigación histórica han recibido donaciones de colecciones privadas que pueden ser muy importantes por el aporte de títulos regionales.

Las colecciones con mayores probabilidades de aportar ejemplares nuevos a los títulos conocidos o nuevos títulos son:

1. Biblioteca de la Academia Colombiana de Historia. Sus colecciones son especialmente ricas para fines de siglo, y han recibido bibliotecas de algunos de sus miembros.

2. Biblioteca de la Universidad Nacional de Colombia.

3. Biblioteca de la Universidad del Valle.

4. Biblioteca de la Universidad Pedagógica y Tecnológica de Tunja. Indispensable para completar el registro de publicaciones de la región de Boyacá, pues administra la biblioteca de la Academia Boyacense de Historia.

5. Biblioteca de la Universidad de Nariño.

6. Archivo Histórico del Cauca.

7. Colecciones particulares. Algunas colecciones particulares son muy ricas en prensa regional. La más notable es sin duda la de Alfonso Harker Villamizar, que tiene varios periódicos de la región de Santander.

---

3 Juan Peyrat, *Guía de Medellín*, Medellín, 1916.
4 La biblioteca de la Universidad de Antioquia: más de un siglo de historia. *Revista Interamericana de Bibliotecología* (Medellín). Vol. 16, no.2 (Jul./Dic. 1993). – p. 65-84)

8. Conventos y seminarios. Ayudarán a completar el registro de las publicaciones eclesiásticas.
9. Biblioteca Pública Piloto de Medellín.
10. Biblioteca Luis Eduardo Nieto Arteta de Barranquilla.
11. Archivo Histórico de Cartagena.

Conservación, microfilmación, digitalización

Cuando se comparan las existencias de estas tres bibliotecas con el universo de lo que se publicó en el siglo XIX las pérdidas son elevadas. Los documentos más prestigiosos, los periódicos de mayor impacto se han conservado prácticamente completos (hay series del Papel Periódico de Santa Fe de 1791 o del Semanario de Caldas, del Neogranadino o El Porvenir en la Biblioteca Nacional o la Luis Ángel Arango), aunque hay algunas excepciones trágicas: no parece existir ninguna colección completa de un diario tan importante como El Espectador. Pero la pérdida de periódicos de provincia o de periódicos bogotanos marginales fue muy elevada: hay centenares para los cuales solo existen unos pocos ejemplares de muestra, y seguramente son muchos los títulos que no tienen ningún ejemplar en las colecciones.[5]

Esta pérdida se produjo en buena parte en el siglo XIX: podemos presumir que muchos periódicos menores, que no se remitieron a la Biblioteca Nacional, no fueron coleccionados por sus lectores. La capacidad de los tres coleccionistas heroicos mencionados en estas notas (Pineda, García Ortiz, Molina) era limitada, y seguramente se les escapaban muchos títulos. Algunas colecciones sin duda sobrevivieron a la muerte de los editores e impresores, pero sabemos que las familias en general no valoran estas colecciones, que son engorrosas, difíciles de mantener y que prácticamente son invendibles[6] Algunas de ellas pudieron convertirse en cartón o simplemente se echaron a la basura.

La conservación en las bibliotecas patrimoniales en Colombia es generalmente adecuada. Las condiciones atmosféricas de Bogotá facilitan mucho la conservación del papel, de modo que uno puede confiar en que lo que entró a la Biblioteca Nacional y la Luis Ángel Arango está allí. Estoy ignorando, es cierto, algunas anomalías: el efecto del clima en sitios como Cartagena o Tumaco, descartes inadecuados, de los cuales existen rumores más o menos fundados, o robos por parte de investigadores, o un manejo descuidado. Pineda mismo, y algunos directores de la Biblioteca Nacional, afirmaron que su colección había sufrido pérdidas por un manejo despreocupado por parte de la biblioteca, pero mientras no tengamos una comparación de títulos y existencias tiendo a pensar que no fueron grandes. Y tampoco puede ignorarse la contribución que han hecho muchas veces los piadosos descendientes de los héroes a su desaparición de la historia nacional, recortando sistemáticamente en los periódicos de las bibliotecas todas las menciones de sus hazañas. En otros casos, descendientes inquietos por su honra recortaron y retiraron, por ejemplo, todo lo que

---

5   No se ha hecho, que yo sepa, ningún intento de listar periódicos desaparecidos: aquellos que aparecen mencionados en otros medios y periódicos, pero que no figuran en las colecciones conocidas. Mi afirmación parte de indicios arbitrarios: hay pequeñas ciudades de las que se han conservado decenas de periódicos (Honda, Socorro) mientras que otros sitios de igual desarrollo intelectual no tienen ningún registro (Salamina, Santa Rosa de Osos, Armenia).
6   En Archivos y Bibliotecas del exterior pueden encontrarse algunos títulos nuevos. Algunas colecciones privadas colombianas encontraron el camino a bibliotecas universitarias de los Estados Unidos, como Texas o Berkeley.

pudieron encontrar relativo a las actividades sentimentales de Nicolasa Ibáñez y sus hermanas.

Pero confiemos en que estas cosas son asunto del pasado. Hoy los originales se conservan razonablemente, y la transferencia a un formato alterno, que restrinja el uso de los originales y ofrezca un respaldo casi total al contenido del periódico, es la necesidad mayor.

Desde 1985 el esfuerzo de microfilmación ha sido grande. Al comienzo, por iniciativa de Lina Espitaleta, entonces directora de la Luis Ángel Arango y actual directora de la Biblioteca Nacional, se desarrolló un programa de microfilmación conjunto entre las dos bibliotecas grandes de Bogotá. Las colecciones se unieron, para obtener la serie más completa, y se microfilmaron sistemáticamente la mayoría de los periódicos del siglo XIX. En 1990 la Biblioteca Nacional decidió suspender el programa, cuando se habían procesado unos 1450 rollos (que cubrían prensa del XIX y algunos periódicos importantes del XX) cuyas copias maestras se encuentran en la Luis Ángel Arango. Desde ese momento, la microfilmación la siguieron haciendo en forma independiente las dos instituciones, y con estrategias distintas. Mientras la Luis Ángel Arango contrata la microfilmación con empresas externas, la Biblioteca Nacional ha preferido hacer su microfilmación propia, para la cual montó en 1995 un moderno laboratorio de microfilmación. Sin embargo, por limitaciones de recursos, el ritmo de trabajo ha sido lento: desde entonces se han microfilmado unos pocos rollos de prensa del siglo XIX. Por su parte, la Biblioteca Luis Ángel Arango está a punto de completar la microfilmación de su propia colección del siglo XIX y tiene ahora más de 7000 rollos de prensa microfilmada.

En este momento, la Biblioteca Nacional y la Luis Ángel Arango están de acuerdo para desarrollar nuevamente un programa conjunto. Este programa puede completar en un tiempo breve (antes del fin de 2005) la microfilmación de toda la prensa colombiana anterior a 1900 existente en sus colecciones. Lo ideal sería poder coordinar con la Universidad de Antioquia la microfilmación de los títulos que no existen en las colecciones de Bogotá.

Hasta hoy, las bibliotecas han considerado conveniente continuar usando esta tecnología. Sin embargo, se están desarrollando algunos programas de digitalización de colecciones de publicaciones periódicas. La Luis Ángel Arango está comenzando la digitalización de las revistas culturales más importantes del siglo XIX. Estas revistas tienen formatos reducidos, usualmente inferiores al tamaño A4, y pueden procesarse en equipos sencillos de digitalización. Los archivos se guardarán en servidores con acceso a los investigadores, y en algunos casos se pondrán en la red en la página virtual de la Luis Ángel Arango (www.lablaa.org). El Mosaico y el Papel Periódico Ilustrado serán las dos primeras revistas que recibirán este tratamiento. Vale la pena señalar que el objetivo central de este trabajo no es la conservación, y las dos publicaciones que he mencionado han sido microfilmadas previamente. Por otra parte, la Biblioteca Pública Piloto, en cooperación con la Universidad de Antioquia, hará la digitalización de algunas revistas de la región antioqueña, para la Biblioteca Virtual Antioqueña.

Catálogos y listas de control: Los tres catálogos impresos forman un interesante conjunto. En todos ellos se ha hecho un esfuerzo práctico de incluir los títulos de los periódicos en las colecciones, pero el diseño de los índices despliega una gran imaginación para producir resultados inútiles o de difícil manejo.

El catálogo de la Luis Ángel Arango es cronológico. Por lo tanto, incluye un índice alfabético de los títulos registrados. El índice alfabético, sorprendentemente, se ha dividido entre dos grandes grupos, derivados de la forma como los periódicos están empastados en la Biblioteca: los títulos agrupados en una serie llamada Periódicos Varios se indizan por separado de los demás. De este modo, el usuario debe buscar cada título en dos sitios diferentes. Mientras tanto, no se hizo un índice por sitios de publicación, que es de obvia utilidad para los lectores. Las fichas incluyen los nombres de los redactores o directores, así como los ejemplares existentes. Por otra parte, los periódicos se registran en todos los años en que estaban apareciendo, lo que hace muy engorroso definir cuales son títulos únicos y obliga, para seguir las existencias de un periódico, a mirar a veces decenas de años. (A esto se añade, por supuesto, el problema real de las transformaciones frecuentes de los títulos, que sufren inesperadas metamorfosis, para desespero de los catalogadores: cuando los ejemplares son pocos y con muchos faltantes, no es siempre posible saber si un título similar es una simple transformación o un título nuevo).

El catálogo de la Biblioteca Nacional se editó sin ningún orden aparente: sigue una ordenación aproximadamente alfabética, pero nada sistemática. Por ello, han debido publicar un volumen separado de índices: alfabético, cronológico y de lugar, que remiten a las fichas detalladas Por lo menos uno de estos índices podría haberse evitado si la publicación hubiera seguido alguno de esos órdenes. Las fichas son muy completas: incluyen con frecuencia los editores y tienen un registro de existencias. Señalan además si existe un microfilm del periódico, pero no se indica 67 cuales de los rollos maestros están en la Biblioteca o cuales son de la Luis Ángel Arango. Aunque a veces se indica que el microfilm es más completo que la colección física, nunca se especifica donde existen los ejemplares que se usaron para completar los rollos: lo más probable, pero puede haber excepciones, es que sean también de la Luis Ángel Arango

El catálogo de la Universidad de Antioquia tiene un extenso estudio introductoria sobre la prensa colombiana, pero no dice por qué se excluyeron del catálogo los pocos títulos anteriores a 1840 (o a 1828, pues se registran algunos títulos entre 1828 y 1840, que no parecería lógico fueran todos los que tiene la colección). Las fichas son muy completas, y buscan no solo llenar los deseos de los bibliotecarios sino de historiadores e investigadores sociales: describen el carácter del periódico (comercial, cultural, político, etc), su orientación política, señalan con quienes polemizaron, y dan una lista muy amplia de colaboradores. Esto hace de este documento una herramienta muy útil. Sin embargo, nadie parece pensar en como deben ser los índices: la publicación de las fichas es alfabética, pese a lo cual el libro publica un índice general alfabético que indica la página a la que hay que ir para buscar en periódico. Los que si son útiles son un índice analítico de materias tratadas por los periódicos, un índice de nombres de editores y colaboradores y un índice de lugares mencionados. Curiosamente, tampoco consideraron útil hacer un índice de periódicos por lugares de edición.

Probablemente estos son los últimos catálogos en papel de este tipo que se publicarán. Los catálogos de las bibliotecas permiten obtener la información de las fichas, pero no se han desarrollado en forma sistemática para permitir recuperaciones integrales de prensa del siglo XIX. Por ello, el investigador que va a revisar los periódicos de una ciudad, o los que se publicaron en un período preciso, requiere unos listados integrales que pueda consultar y transformar. Por supuesto, podrían aplicarse reglas estrictas de catalogación que permitieran obtener estos listados de los OPAC, pero el esfuerzo retroactivo de normalización de registros es muy grande. Por ello, considero pertinente que se desarrollo simplemente una lista de control de los periódicos publicados en el país en el siglo pasado, que puede servir eventualmente de núcleo de un catálogo más amplio. Una lista que registre simplemente los títulos de los periódicos, el lugar de edición, la imprenta, las fechas de publicación, las existencias del título en las diversas bibliotecas, las copias en microfilm y las ediciones y facsímiles existentes, y los índices de periódicos concretos desarrollados. Para resolver ambigüedades es conveniente incluir, para algunos periódicos, los nombres de los editores, así como otros datos auxiliares.

Las listas actuales, en los tres catálogos impresos, generan títulos que podríamos llamar fantasmas, pues son simplemente variantes del título original. Un inventario de títulos únicos, inicialmente a partir de las tres bibliotecas que hemos discutido, pero que puede extenderse gradualmente a otras, permitirá tener un mapa más preciso del mundo del periodismo en el siglo XIX.

Como un aporte inicial a este esfuerzo, esta ponencia tiene como anexo un borrador de una «Lista de control de periódicos y revistas del siglo XIX», que incluye todos los registros existentes en las tres colecciones principales del país: son aproximadamente 2800 títulos. Este número esta destinado a disminuir, al eliminar las duplicaciones que se han creado hasta ahora, al encontrar nuevos títulos, desaparecidos o que tengan ejemplares en otras bibliotecas y colecciones, puede también aumentar. El pasado, como el futuro, está lleno de incertidumbres...

INTERNATIONAL NEWSPAPER WORK

Hartmut Walravens

Berlin State Library, Germany

The IFLA Section on Newspapers consists of a small but dedicated group of experts that deal with aspects of newspaper work in libraries and archives and seek the cooperation of publishers and distributors. The major recent event was the IFLA Conference «Newspapers in Central and Eastern Europe».

The IFLA Section on Newspapers has an unwritten tradition to focus its annual programme on the host country of the IFLA General Conferences and reach out to colleagues to foster cooperation and spread information on newspaper work in that area. Berlin seemed particularly attractive for this purpose as after the fall of the Berlin Wall the press not only in East Germany, the German Democratic Republic, but also in all of the former Socialist countries underwent radical changes. The previous government directed, strictly censured newspapers were largely privatised, marketing was needed, competition arose, and freedom of speech and reporting were introduced. The names of some newspapers remained, but in many instances the appearance, the contents, and the management changed, not always immediately but gradually. Many new papers were established and tried to find their share of the market. The business side found repercussions on the side of the libraries and archives. Legal deposit copies did not come in as regularly as before, sometimes not at all. Readers made bold of asking for formerly stowed away or classified material. Frequent use tended to damage originals, especially newspapers, and new preservation programmes had to be considered.

The internet showed up and became popular immediately; newspapers were published on the net and one had to think about proper archiving.

The open borders made it possible for foreign students to use libraries and archives in a never anticipated degree. Historical newspapers that few people had cared for, like German language newspapers in the Baltic collections, were falling apart owing to heavy use. Immediate microfilming or digitising was necessary but often unrealistic for lack of resources. In some cases cooperation programmes were started. The German Bosch Foundation saw to the microfilming of a large number of serials in Polish collections. Helsinki University Library joined forces with their Estonian colleagues to digitise Estonian newspapers.

All this led to the proposal of holding an IFLA-sponsored conference on the Newspapers of Central and Eastern Europe in conjunction with the General Conference in Berlin.

But there was also an other reason, namely the situation of the newspapers in Central Europe proper, especially in Germany.

Newspapers in Germany

Germany is a traditional newspaper country, and in a few years people will celebrate the 400th anniversary of the publication of the first newspaper in the country. German history was, however, not favourable to newspaper collecting – the country, the Holy Roman Empire, consisted of many kingdoms, dukedoms, principalities, cities, and counties with different press regulations. It took till 1871 that legislation was harmonised in a unified country. Attempts at investigating and recording what newspapers were extant were already made by Martin Spahn before WWI but he did not receive enough support. Hans Traub prepared a catalogue finally in 1933[1] but WWII with the destruction of German cities and the subsequent division of the country turned previous newspaper collections into a patchwork of scatters. Many holdings perished or were moved to other places, and Traub's pioneering effort has only historical value today. The urgent need of taking stock of existing serials after WWII – in the interest of research and scholarship – led to a Union Catalogue of Foreign Serials (*Gesamtverzeichnis ausländischer Zeitschriften und Serien*, GAZS) which was combined with a later Union Catalogue of German Serials (Gesamtverzeichnis Deutscher Zeitschriften und Serien, GDZS) and grew into an online database on a cooperative basis – the German Union Catalogue of Serials (*Zeitschriftendatenbank*, ZDB, briefly described in this volume by Bernd Augustin).[2] Newspapers were of the lowest priority to many libraries as their users were interested mainly in scholarly and scientific journals. Nevertheless, a few libraries included their newspapers in ZDB, and then thanks to the generous support of the German Research Association (Deutsche Forschungsgemeinschaft, DFG) several important collections were integrated in it: A small Union File of Foreign Newspapers (*Standortverzeichnis ausländischer Zeitungen und Illustrierten*, SAZI), the holdings of the former Deutsche Staatsbibliothek (the part of the Preußische Staatsbibliothek that remained in East Berlin) and those of the former Institute of Marxism-Leninism (now part of the Federal Archives, Berlin branch). Thus the number of newspapers in ZDB grew to currently 67,000, a number which includes, however, magazines, illustrated papers etc.[3] Nevertheless, this figure is estimated to represent only one third of the papers published in Germany. So what Germany urgently needs is a national programme for the systematic investigation and cataloguing of existing newspapers, their preservation microfilming and subsequent digitisation for the sake of scholars and students who so far are frustrated by the situation and more often than not dispense with using newspapers as source material.

The example of other countries might serve as a model for Germany:

* The Scandinavian countries have practically all their newspapers catalogued and most of them filmed.

* In the UK the Newsplan[4] project provides a nationwide survey of newspaper holdings and see to preservation microfilming. Currently £ 5 mill. from the Heritage Lottery Fund have been devoted to the support of newspaper work.

---

1 Hans Traub: *Standsortskatalog wichtiger Zeitungsbestände in deutschen Bibliotheken*. Leipzig: Hiersemann, 1933. XXXI,254 pp.

2 http://zdb-opac.de

3 An excerpt from the online database, but with a geographical index added, is: H. Walravens [ed.]: *Internationale Zeitungsbestände in deutschen Bibliotheken*. Ein Verzeichnis von 54 000 Zeitungen [...] 3.Ausg. München: K. G. Saur, 2001. XXIV,2287 pp.– A cataloguing handbook is: *Staatsbibliothek zu Berlin: Zeitungen und zeitungsähnliche Periodika – ihre Beschreibung und Erfassung in der Zeitschriftendatenbank*. Bearb. von Marielusie Schillig. München: Saur 1998. 313 pp. See also H. Walravens: Shared preservation: bibliographic information. *Proceedings of the IFLA Symposium Managing the Preservation of Periodicals and Newspapers. Bibliothèque nationale de France, Paris, 21-24 August 2000.* Edited by Jennifer Budd, IFLA-PAC. München: Saur 2002 (IFLA Publications.103), 151-154; Newspaper cataloguing in Germany. In: *Newspapers in international librarianship. Papers presented by the Newspapers Section at IFLA General Conferences.* München: K. G. Saur, 2003. (IFLA Publications.107.), p. 71-75; Zeitungen und die Zeitschriftendatenbank. In: *Zeitungen verzeichnen und nutzen.* Aktuelle Ansätze und Unternehmungen zur bibliographischen und archivalischen Beschreibung und Nutzung deutschsprachiger Zeitungen. Herausgegeben von Hans Bohrmann und Wilbert Ubbens. Berlin: DBI 1998 (Informationsmittel für Bibliotheken. Beiheft. 7.),71-80; Topographie der Zeitungssammlungen. *Bibliotheksdienst* 2000,1293-1296.

4 See http://www.newsplan.co.uk

- In France the *Bibliographie de la presse française*[5] is an impressive descriptive catalogue of the newspaper holdings in each département.

- In the United States so far about $ 60 mill. have been spent, largely by the National Endowment for the Humanities, on a systematic research and cataloguing as well as microfilming of newspapers, state by state. The project is expected to finish by 2007 with the two states with the highest newspaper concentration, California und New York.[6] The records are added to the CONSER file of the Library of Congress while the marketing is managed by OCLC.

- Finland and Sweden conducted a model project for the provision of digitised newspapers on the internet (TIDEN).[7]

- Austria started a digitisation project after having catalogued the extensive newspaper holdings in Vienna.

- Estonia is running a digitisation project.

A number of libraries in Germany started an initiative together with archives to follow the example of the mentioned countries; but alas! the point in time was ill chosen – with the current stictures on public budgets and the heavy demand for support of scientific projects the DFG did not see fit to accept such a not exactly cheap application. Only a regional Bavarian project received funding, and this may serve as a model for further activities which may perhaps be started in other federal states.

So with regard to newspaper work Germany is still a developing country, and the idea of the IFLA Section on Newspapers was to promote professional newspaper activities in Germany and foster cooperation in the whole region by arranging for this international conference.

Work of the Section

The IFLA Newspaper Section existed for many years as a small but active Round Table on Newspapers and was only in 2002 promoted to the rank of a section, as part of a wider restructuring of IFLA (International Federation of Library Associations). Its objectives are:

- Initiating and realising projects within the IFLA Medium Term Programme

- Organising meetings separately from IFLA Conference, such as seminars, colloquiums, workshops, and poster sessions

- Publishing a newsletter.

Among its latest activities are

- a highly successful even if small hands-on workshop on newspaper digitisation, conducted by Helsinki University (Center for Microfilming and Digitisation, located in Mikkeli), in June 2003

- the publication of *Guidelines for Newspaper Preservation Microfilming*. The Hague 1996. (IFLA Professional Report; 49)

---

5 Latest volume: *Bibliographie de la presse française: politique et d'information générale; des originees à 1944.* 64. *Pyrénées-Atlantique (anciennement Basses-Pyrénées),* par Patrice Caillot. Paris: Bibliothèque nationale de France, 2002. 162 pp. Just published: Else Delaunay: 13. *Haute-Loire.* 2003. 64 pp.
6 For the United States Newspaper Program see: http://www.loc.gov/preserv/usnmppr.html and http://neh.gov/projects/usnp.html
7 http:// tiden.kb.se

- the publication of the 2000 Paris conference proceedings: *Managing the Preservation of Periodicals and Newspapers*. Munich: K. G. Saur, 2002. (IFLA Publication; 103)

- and the preparation of a *Guidance for the Best Practice of Digitisation from Preservation Microfilms* (on the Section's website)

- the organisation of a session on Newspapers and Copyright at the IFLA General conference in Berlin, 2003. The recent publication *Newspapers in International Librarianship. Papers presented at IFLA General Conferences, 1990-2002*. Munich: K. G. Saur, 2003. (IFLA Publication; 107) gives an impression of the Section's broad interests and activities.

The Section welcomes both membership and informal cooperation in order to promote awareness of newspaper issues and to foster cooperation in the field worldwide.

Among its current projects and plans are:

- the preparation of a session on the press of Latin America at the forthcoming International Congress on Libraries and Information in Buenos Aires

- a survey of African newspapers

- the preparation of a newspaper handbook

- a listing and evaluation of internet resources for newspaper work

We sincerely hope that our present meeting at the Shanghai tushuguan will encourage Chinese colleagues to cooperate with their international partners in solving the intricate problems connected with newspapers – collection building, cataloguing, access, copyright, electronic versions, preservation and archiving.

NEWSPAPERS IN THE SHANGHAI LIBRARY

Min Wu

Librarian, Reader's Service Center of Shanghai Library, China

Introduction

In the Shanghai Library, newspapers are of great interest to a wide variety users as an indispensable record of all kinds of information on day to day life in a country or world-wide historical, economic, cultural facts or events. Around the world there are many examples of good practice in building newspaper collections and providing library service to newspaper users. As the largest city library and one of the ten largest public libraries in the world, the Shanghai Library also pays extra attention to developing and improving newspaper collections services. This article aims at addressing this issue based on experiences at the Shanghai Library.

Collection of printed materials

According to the publishing years and languages, newspapers in printed form in the Shanghai Library are divided into 4 parts: Domestic newspapers, international newspapers, current newspapers and older newspapers..

At present, newspapers published in mainland China comprise over 2000 titles. The Shanghai Library subscribes to 1,100 of them and is thus one of the libraries with the largest Chinese newspaper collections. How do we select these newspapers? We subscribe on a basis of the following principles: Collect all provincial and municipal newspapers; selectively collect high-quality local, commercially published newspapers. We can say, modern Chinese newspapers in the Shanghai Library cover most provinces and cities in China, with authoritative contents. Multi-cultural service is promoted in the Shanghai Library. As an important part of the multi-cultural collections, more than 90 overseas newspapers are collected in many languages. How do we select them? Wide geographic distribution is most important. We subscribe to newspapers from countries like USA, Britain, Germany, France, Japan, Russia (former the Union Soviet), Korea, Canada, Australia, Philippines, Malaysia, Thailand, Singapore, India, Norway, Vietnam and so on. In the Shanghai Library the valuable collections of newspapers are older newspapers. As Shanghai was the largest economic centre in old China, so a lot of newspapers were published in Shanghai at that time. Now you can see the oldest Chinese language newspaper published in Shanghai in the Shanghai library. That is the *Shanghai Xin Pao*, a business newspaper using high quality paper at that time. It started publication in 1862, during the Qing dynasty, but it could not compete with *Shun Pao*, and ceased in 1872.

The most famous newspaper is the *Shun Pao* in Chinese language. The Newspaper was created in 1872 and ceased in 1949. The *Shun Pao* had been published for 77 years total in 25,600 issues. It is a valuable research source and was collected by many libraries, but only the Shanghai Library holds a complete set. Now it is most frequently used by both Chinese and foreigners. The Shanghai Library has collected about 92 kinds and more than 5200 volumes of old foreign-language newspapers, mainly from China, Japan, France, Britain, USA, Russia, and Italy and in French, German, Russian, Italian, and Japanese. Among these the most famous newspaper is *North China Herald*, started in 1850 and ceased in 1951. It was called The Times in China. This old foreign-language newspaper of which the Shanghai

Library owns a complete run is important source material which reflects important Chinese and international social events that happened during the years 1850-1950, and so it is most popular reading matter.

Collection in digital materials

Digital collections have been growing rapidly during recent years in the Shanghai Library. Both CD-ROMs and web-base databases of newspapers are held.

CD-ROMS

In April 2003, *Xinmin Evening News* and *Wen Hui Daily* DVD-ROMs were acquired. These DVD-ROMs were donated by the Wen Hui Xinmin United Press Group. Xinmin Evening News is one of the early newspapers in China that have enjoyed the longest history; it started publication in September 1929 in Nanjing. The DVD-ROM of *Xinmin Evening News* incorporates all the graphic & text data since its inception - 132,000 pages, with over 510 million words and over 270,000 pictures in total. *Wen Hui Daily* on DVD-ROM contains 108,000 pages of newspaper, more than 0.75 billion Chinese words and 230,000 pictures. The DVD-ROM gives a detailed index to the external characteristics of the articles. You can search date, issue number, headline, column, writer and special issue or column etc.

Web-Based Databases

WiseNews is a database of full-text news articles including more than 260 newspapers issued by mainland China and the Hongkong special district. Among which there are 260 titles of newspapers from the mainland, mainly important newspaper and professional newspaper of all provinces and cities in China; 4 are newspapers of Hongkong district, that is, *Hong Kong Economic Times*, *Chinese Commercial News*, *Wenhui Daily* and *Ta Kung Pao*. The database deals with more than 200,000 items of information every day. Up to now, it has accumulated over 10,000,000 records. The database provides full-text search function and automatically expands the vocabularies correlative or synonymous to the searched words, thus making searching more convenient and quick. The coverage begins with the year 1998.

The China Core Newspaper Database, covers more than 360 titles from every province and region of China. While its archive only dates from 2000, it already has nearly 2,000,000 articles, with thousands added every day via the internet and 1.2 million articles added annually. With the dynamic changes affecting all aspects of life in modern China, this database is destined to become an essential resource for almost anyone interested in this part of the world. CCND is divided into 6 series databases:

- Literature / History / Philosophy
- Politics / Military Affairs / Law
- Economics / Education
- Social Science
- Science / Technology
- Love / Marriage / Family / Health

Ebsco Newspaper Source provides selected full text for 23 national (U.S.) and international newspapers, including *USA Today*, *The Christian Science Monitor*, *The Washington Post*, *The Times* (London), *The Toronto Star*, etc. The database also contains selected full text for more than 200 regional (U.S.) newspapers, including *The Boston Globe*, *The Chicago Tribune*, *The Detroit Free Press*, *The Miami Herald*, *The New York Daily News*, *The San Jose Mercury News*, etc. In addition, full text television & radio news transcripts are provided from CBS News, FOX News, NPR, etc.

Index to Chinese Serials is the most important database on newspapers and periodicals in the Shanghai Library. The Editorial Department of the Index is a department of the Shanghai Library. This database covers more than 8,000 periodicals published in China, including Hong Kong, Macao and Taiwan. It contains almost all the periodicals in the fields of philosophy, social sciences, natural sciences, engineering and technology. There are more than 5.60 million records accumulated in the database since 1857. It is one of the largest databases in China. Each record contains the following items: sequence number, classification number, title, author, serial title, date of publication, named person in title and subject words, etc. It can be linked to the content database, offering a basic description of the serials in the Content Database.

Online newspaper

Internet newspapers have begun to sprout up in China since the end of last century. At present, there are about 500 kinds of web newspapers in China. These web newspapers are still in the phase of development. Many Chinese readers are very interested in them. Therefore, we collect almost all web newspapers and put them together, thus forming a new portal called «Chinese E-Newspaper Navigation» linked to the website of the Shanghai Library. Chinese E-Newspaper Navigation offers readers convenient on-line reading of Chinese newspapers. Many old people who lack computer knowledge learn what Internet is by on-line newspaper reading in the Shanghai Library. Now, they spend more time on e-newspapers than on printed newspapers. If the day is not fine, they will read newspapers on-line at home, and don't have to go to the library everyday as usual. I think Chinese E-newspaper Navigation not only a new way of reading news, but also partly changes their lives.

Service for government and legislature from 1960s

Beginning from the 1960s, the information needs of the city government and the legislature were on the increase. So experienced, professionally trained librarians were called together to respond to questions on any topic. In fact, most librarians working for this task were very excellent industrial experts or social experts. They provided timely and complete responses to all requests. Requests were treated with impartiality, objectivity, and strict confidentiality, although the information resources were just public newspapers and periodicals world-wide. From then on, the Shanghai Library became the most famous institute of special information supply in China.

Today, the information sources and options of the city government and the legislature are stronger and wider, but they still get information from the Shanghai Library. Their interests include feedback from enterprises, monitoring the industry, experiences of developed countries etc. Our librarians offer information assistance by writing special newsletters.

Sorting out of the older newspapers in the 1970s and 1980s

In 1970s, librarians sorted out all old foreign newspapers and prepared a «Catalogue of old foreign newspapers in the Shanghai Library». Now, most of them are retired. At that time, they didn't have such advanced computers and input tools like today's, therefore the catalogue was written mostly by hand. But it is very useful. Until now it is still being used by our readers and young librarians, and we never find mistakes in it. I presented this book many times in training courses for new staff. It is not only a catalogue book to us, but also a good lesson in responsibility.

In the 1980s, another index book of the older Chinese newspapers in the Shanghai Library was compiled. It is also useful today, because the old Chinese newspapers were written in traditional Chinese, but most young people can only read simplified Chinese characters. The index book helps them to find the exact documents from all these old newspapers without difficulty. The index book was published in 2,000 copies and is held by libraries all over the world. We can say the book is now actually a bridge between the older Chinese newspaper collection in the Shanghai Library and people world-wide.

Newspaper conservation and utilization in recent years

In the 1990s, our collections were rapidly growing, the relative services were becoming heavy and complicated. First of all, we put the most frequently used catalogues online, we put the other catalogues in searchable databases, including those of old newspapers. Then, we had to pay attention to the conservation of older collections. We know that generally a newspaper may crumble away after 20 or 30 years, or even less. It is obvious that our older collections are endangered. We microfilmed over 500 old newspapers. The microfilms amount to over 6,000 reels. The oldest Chinese paper *Shanghai Xin Pao* which I mentioned above is also among them.

Third, Press clipping service is provided, it brings great convenience to users who are just interested in certain topics. For example, a lot of Shanghai citizen pay attention to the 2010 expo in Shanghai. It only takes them half an hour a week to read the 2010 expo clipping files.

Newspaper reading areas

The total reading area for newspaper is about 1100m^2 and comprises more than 200 seats. It appears that different newspapers attract different persons and demand different, but we are not very clear about the detail. So a library users survey is undertaken by the Readers Service Department every year. The survey gives users the opportunity to tell us what kind of assistance they need, what they think about our existing library services and how they would like to see them develop in the future. The results provide valuable feedback and are used to help us plan and develop newspaper services. For example, results from previous surveys led to the decision to arrange 4 different reading areas corresponding to the above-mentioned 4 kinds of newspapers. The results also led to the extension of the opening hours of the current Chinese newspapers reading room, in line with user needs. Results have also helped us to carefully plan different programs of staff training and development, to improve upon our staff knowledge, expertise and helpfulness in different reading areas.

The older foreign newspaper reading room

The older foreign newspaper reading room is located in the Bibliotheca Zi-Ka-Wei, a branch of the Shanghai Library. The Bibliotheca Zi-Ka-Wei was renovated on the principle of «renewing the building as it was»; it treasures the largest foreign-language collection in China. It reopened to the public in July 2003. Visitors come from varies countries, they are social science researchers, historians, some old immigrants who lived in Shanghai half a century ago as well as the visitors who are attracted by its reputation. They all enjoy the special cultural feeling there. Librarians working there are required to have a very good foreign language command and a basic knowledge of world-wide historical, economic, cultural facts or events of the past 150 years. These are very important for offering effective assistance to users.

The older Chinese newspaper reading room

The older Chinese newspaper reading room has about 300 m^2. The collection of microfilms including over 500 old newspapers is located in the area. Microfilm readers are also in the reading room. Editors, writers and college students are the majority of users here. Generally they want to find exact information related to their interested topics. Librarians working here should be familiar with various Chinese word styles, title variations, special notes on mergers or other information.

Current foreign newspaper reading room

College students and other young people visit the current foreign newspaper reading room frequently. Most of the time they find what they want by themselves. They are also familiar with database searching.

Current Chinese newspaper reading room

Our current Chinese newspaper reading room provides a comfortable reading environment, it is also the biggest reading area for newspapers in the Shanghai Library. There are about 1000 titles of current Chinese newspapers on open access. The latest 2 years are available in the reading room. Papers older than 2 years are put in the stacks and can be borrowed through Circulation. Some old people come here to browse news stories and stock market news every day. According to the statistics, there were 154,000 readers here in 2003, with an average of more than 400 persons every day. It is one of the most heavily used reading rooms. The reading room is open 12 hours a day, from 8:30 am to 8:30 pm, every day of the year.

Last year, we rebuilt the reading room. We tried to construct it to be a news reading room with multi-media. Some new equipment was added, such as computers and television sets. Now in this reading area, readers can get real time news through newspaper, television, online reading and searches by computer.

Librarians are required to be laborious and patient enough. They do shelf locating frequently, they help readers find the exact papers of which they don't know the titles, they explain the same thing many times a day, they teach old readers how to operate computers for reading online, even including how to open or close a browsing window.

Conclusion

I hope this short presentation of newspaper collections and services in the Shanghai Library has given an impression of what we do and how we do it. Finally, I would like to summarize: First, public libraries hold newspaper collections now in a wider range, and the available news information service is undoubtedly more efficient in public libraries than before. This can be proved by statistics and other strong evidence.

Second, the information needs of the public library users have undoubtedly increased. Newspapers in libraries have more opportunities to be used for varies purposes. It should not be regarded as being beyond doubt that what we are offering today is enough for tomorrow.

NEWSPAPERS IN THE ROYAL LIBRARY, STOCKHOLM

Lars Olsson

Head of the Newspaper Section
The Royal Library National Library of Sweden

The Royal Library is the National Library of Sweden – with legal deposit since 1661. The birth year of the Swedish press is 1645, when Sweden got its first newspaper. Newspapers and legal deposit came into existence approximately at the same time and under the same political conditions. The purpose of the one and only first newspaper was to present a governmental view of things. The purpose of legal deposit was to make it possible for the government to control the printers.

The political conditions have changed many times since then, but an efficient central administration including the system of legal deposit is a heritage from those days, which means that we have no problems with the collecting of imprints. Sweden has a population of about nine million people. There are now about 200 newspapers – 194 to be exact, counted at the end of 2003. These newspapers have 17 editions with a title of its own and 100 other editions. There are also about 500 free papers financed by advertisements.

Some newspapers in Swedish published abroad can be added to these figures. We subscribe to 12 newspapers from Finland, and to four from the United States. About one hundred years ago there were many Swedish newspapers in North America, but the Swedish immigrants have been assimilated and their interest in the few and small remaining newspapers seems to be mostly nostalgic.

The staff of the Royal Library consists of about 275 people. Fourteen of them belong to the newspaper section, where we collect the newspapers, preserve them, microfilm them and describe them in catalogues and bibliographies, and digitise them – to a very small extent so far. The newspapers received as legal deposit are placed in boxes of acid free paper (we don't bind them) and sent to a repository 50 kilometers outside Stockholm. The general idea is that they shall rest out there and never be touched. Instead, microfilm is to be used for reading. We are obliged since 1979 not only to preserve the deposit copies but also to get all the newspapers microfilmed. Furthermore we have to produce microfilm both for our own use and for the university libraries at Gothenburg, Lund, Umeå and Uppsala.

The actual microfilming is carried out by a company at Kalmar in southern Sweden. This company gets a deposit copy of its own for microfilming purposes.The copy will be discarded, when the microfilming is done. The university library at Lund gets a third deposit copy to be kept as the so-called national reserve copy.

The 200 current newspapers in Sweden mean a production of something between 1,800 and 1,900 rolls of microfilm pro year. (We do not microfilm the free papers, although we keep them in the newspaper collection and catalogue them as newspapers.) The microfilm version of the newspapers is complete with all editions and news-bills. The camera negatives are vacuum packed and kept in a climate chamber with a temperature of 12 degrees centigrade and an air humidity of 30%. A duplicate negative is used for producing new copies. The duplicate negative is kept in the library building, while for security reasons the camera negative is stored on other premises. In addition to the free distribution of microfilm to some university libraries, microfilm is sold to a great number of other libraries. Public libraries in various parts of the country generally want to have a complete microfilm set of their local newspaper. For copyright reasons we are free to sell microfilm only to those libraries which already subscribe to the original paper version of the newspaper.

In 1983 we started microfilming old newspapers retrospectively. This retrospective filming is carried out much in the same way as the continuous filming. We use copies from Uppsala University Library, which has ceased to function as an archive library and is getting rid of its newspaper collection. The copies will be discarded after having been microfilmed. Thanks to this arrangement we can handle the copies in a way that is best for the microfilming process regardless of preservation aspects.

Quite a lot of newspaper microfilming was done also before 1979. A private company microfilmed the most important newspapers and sold microfilm copies to libraries and other customers. This company does not exist anymore, but its stock of negatives has been bought by the state and is now managed by the Royal Library.

All our newspapers can be found in the national union catalogue LIBRIS: http://websok.libris.kb.se/websearch/form?type=simple

Every microfilm is provided with a bibliographic target, where editors, printing plant, circulation etc. are recorded. There is also a special bibliography of twentieth and twenty-first century newspapers on the web: http://www.kb.se/nl/nlnav.htm. It continues a printed bibliography of Swedish periodicals covering the years 1645-1899.

We still lack governmental funding for regular digitisation, but we are a part in the Nordic Tiden project (http://tiden.kb.se), where the national libraries of Denmark, Finland, Norway and Sweden have digitised newspapers for the web. So far we have digitised about 25,000 pages of old newspapers from the 17th and up to the beginning of the 19th century.

Legal deposit of websites does not exist but has now been suggested in a report to the government in January this year. In anticipation of such a legislation, however, the Royal Library has been harvesting the web for Swedish websites since 1997. A description of this activity can be found at http://www.kb.se/kw3/ENG/. The harvesting has been done four times a year, which means that we have quite a lot of stored websites, but still only samples, and especially not all issues of the daily newspapers. Last year, however, we started harvesting newspapers daily. Nowadays also traditional newspapers on paper have a digital original. One can imagine a future when we will get a deposit copy of this digital original instead of a paper copy. The above-mentioned government report expects the Royal Library to consider this possibility. In addition to our obligations as a national library we also keep a collection of foreign newspapers. Most remarkable is our unique collection of about 270 seventeenth and eighteenth century foreign newspapers, which were originally sent to the Swedish government by diplomats, who had to report events abroad.

DAILY PRESS IN FRANCE IN 2004
A BRIEF INTRODUCTION

Isabelle Rollet

Head of the Newspaper section
at the French national library (Bibliothèque nationale de France, Paris)

Top ten – titles and circulation

- 1 – R – *Ouest-France* (1944) – 765,000
- 2 – R – *Le Parisien* (1944) – 507,000
- 3 – N – *Le Monde* (1944) – 361,000
- 4 – N – *Le Figaro* (1854) – 345,000
- 5 – N (sports) – *L'Equipe* (1946) – 321,000
- 6 – R – *Sud-Ouest* (1944) – 320,000
- 7 – R – *La Voix du Nord* (1941) – 307,000
- 8 – R – *Le Progrès* (1859) – 254,000
- 9 – R – *Le Dauphiné libéré* (1945) – 252,000
- 10 – R – *La Nouvelle République du Centre-Ouest* (1944) – 238,000

R = regional N = national

Followers – titles and circulation

- 19 – N – *Libération* (1973) – 156,000
- 23 – N (financial) – *Les Echos* (1908) – 117,000
- 26 – N – *La Croix* (1883) – 91,000
- 29 – N (financial) – *La Tribune* (1967) – 80,000
- 31 – N – *France-Soir* (1944) – 77,000
- 41 – N – *L'Humanité* (1904) – 46,000
- 53 – N – *International Herald Tribune* (1887) – 26,000
- ? – N – *Present* (1982) – ?

R = regional N = national

Chinese newspapers

2 dailies are edited in Paris:

- *Renmin Ribao* – Haiwai ban (1985?) – ?
- *Ouzhou Ribao* = Europe journal (1982) – 20,000

Cumulative circulation

2,514,000,000 copies a year (down)

- ageing of the readership
- increase of the cover prices
- closing of selling places
- free papers
- new media (internet publishing)

Revenues

3,560 million euros (down)

- Sales revenues 50,4%
    - Single copy 38,6%
    - Deliveries 11,8%
- Advertising revenues 49,6%
    - Display advertising 31,7%
    - Classified advertising 17,9%

Type of newspaper sales

- National press
    - *Single copy 77 %*
    - *Home & Postal delivery 23 %*
- Regional press
    - *Single copy 48 %*
    - *Home delivery 38%*
    - *Postal delivery 14%*

Retail outlets

- 33,000 sales spots
    - 30,000 bookshops (« maison de la presse »)
    - 2,800 corners in general stores
    - 720 booths
        - 310 booths in Paris

Companies & employment

- 30,000 workers
  - 105 companies of more than 20 workers
  - among them, 21 companies of more then 500 workers (70% CA)
  - average size = 270 workers
    - *Ouest-France* : 1,950 workers
    - *Sud-Ouest* : 1,150 workers
    - *Le Monde* : 750 workers

French newspapers on the web

- Europresse

www.europresse.com

-> AFP [French news agency] – 9 national newspapers, several regional newspapers and weeklies and French Canadian newspapers

- Portail de la presse

www.portail-presse.com

-> 18 national, 59 regional dailies – 240 regional weeklies & round 11,000 French current

magazines

many links towards professional associations & newspaper websites, especially

www.spqr.fr/lu.asp

www.afp.fr/francais/links/?pid=links

Audit & statistics

- Circulation is audited by
  Diffusion contrôle OJD
  www.ojd.com
- Statistics are published by
  Direction du développement des médias
  www.ddm.gouv.fr

FRENCH CURRENT DAILY PRESS

Isabelle Rollet

Head of the Newspaper section
at the French national library (Bibliothèque nationale de France, Paris)

French current daily press

- National press – 12 titles
- Regional presse (with several local editions) – 39 titles – 406 editions
- Local press (single edition) – 23 titles

3 possibilities

- Microfilming by the newspaper itself
- microfilming by the BnF
- no microfilming

National press

- 8 titles : microfilming by the newspaper itself
- 4 titles : no microfilming

National press – microfilming by the newspaper itself

Title	Agency
La Croix	ACRPP
L'Equipe	ACRPP
Le Figaro	Flash Copy
France-Soir	ACRPP
L'Humanité	ACRPP
Libération	ACRPP
Le Monde	Flash Copy
Aujourd'hui (Le Parisien)	ACRPP

8 titles

National press – no microfilm

Les Echos

International Herald Tribune

La Tribune

Présent

4 titles

Regional press

• 17 titles – 248 editions – microfilming by the newspaper itself
• 17 titles – 99 editions – microfilming by the BnF
• 5 titles – 59 editions – no microfilming

Regional press – microfilming by the newspaper itself

Title	Agency
L'Alsace (Mulhouse)	Flash-Copy
Le Courrier picard (Amiens)	Flash-Copy
Le Dauphiné libéré (Grenoble)	DL
Les Dernières nouvelles *d'Alsace* (Strasbourg)	DNA
L'Est républicain (Nancy)	Flash-Copy
La Marseillaise (Marseille)	Flash-Copy
Nice matin (Nice)	Flash-Copy
Nord éclair (Lille)	Flash-Copy
La Nouvelle République du *Centre-Ouest* (Tours)	Flash-Copy
Ouest-France (Rennes)	OF
Le Parisien (Paris)	ACRPP
Le Progrès (Lyon)	Progrès
Le Républicain lorrain (Metz)	Flash-Copy
Sud-Ouest (Bordeaux)	SO
Le Télégramme de Brest (Morlaix)	Flash-Copy
L'Union (Reims)	Flash-Copy
L'Yonne républicaine	Flash-Copy

17 titles – 248 editions

Regional press – microfilming by the BnF

Le Bien public (Dijon)

Le Courrier de l'Ouest (Angers)

La Dépêche du Midi (Toulouse)

L'Echo (du Centre) (Limoges)

L'Echo – La Marseillaise (du Berry) (Châteauroux)

L'Echo républicain (Chartres)

L'Eclair (Nantes)

L'Indépendant (Rivesaltes)

Le Journal de Saône-et-Loire (Chalon-sur-Saône)

La Liberté de l'Est (Epinal)

Le Maine libre (Le Mans)

La Montagne (Clermont-Ferrand)

Paris-Normandie (Rouen)

Le Populaire du Centre (Limoges)

Presse Océan (Nantes)

La République du Centre (Orléans)

Var matin (Nice)

17 titles – 99 editions

Regional press – no microfilm

La Charente libre (Angoulême)

Le Midi libre (Montpellier)

La Provence (Marseille)

Vendée matin (Nantes)

La Voix du Nord (Lille)

5 titles – 59 editions

Local press

• 23 titles : no microfilm

Local press – no microfilm

L'Ardennais (Charleville-Mézières)

Le Berry républicain (Bourges)

Centre presse (Poitiers)

Centre presse (Rodez)

Corse matin (Nice)

La Dordogne libre (Périgueux)

L'Eclair Pyrénées/Pays de l'Adour (Pau)

L'Est éclair (Troyes)

L'Eveil de la Haute-Loire (Le Puy)

Le Havre libre (Le Havre)

Le Havre presse (Le Havre)

Le Journal de la Haute-Marne (Chaumont)

Le Journal du Centre (Nevers)

Libération Champagne (Troyes)

Nord littoral (Calais)

La Nouvelle République des Pyrénées (Tarbes)

Paris Mantes Poissy (Rouen)

Le Petit bleu de Lot-et-Garonne (Agen)

La Presse de la Manche (Cherbourg)

Le Progrès (Le Havre)

La République des Pyrénées (Pau)

23 titles

MAKING KNOWN A NATIONAL COLLECTION
OF NEWS MEDIA IN CANADA

Sandra Burrows

Newspaper Specialist, Library and Archives Canada

In 2002 two very important events occurred to heighten the awareness of newspapers and the news media in Canada. We celebrated the 250th anniversary of the oldest newspaper published in Canada and we held a national consultation on newspapers called *Canadian Newspapers online : a national consultation*. At first, these two events do not seem to be related. However, they both served to heighten Canadian awareness of a valuable print collection and the danger it is in as well as draw attention to the fact that we are in greater danger of not preserving for future generations what will be the news heritage of 2002.

In locating an issue of the *Halifax gazette*, published in Halifax Nova Scotia in 1752, we were very lucky. We had several good verified sources that told us where we could find the issue. We already had both a microfilmed copy and a reprint and through careful negotiations in 2002, we acquired not only the first issue published March 23, 1752 but also an almost complete run of the paper up until 1754. The history of this paper serves as an illustration of how history can take strange twists and turns.

The paper was published by a Bostonian and the early issues were returned to Boston in the 19th century in a folio to the Massachusetts Historical Society where they remained until the late 19th century when a newspaper editor from Yarmouth visited Boston and saw the newspaper. Up to that time, it was thought that the earliest newspaper in Canada was the *Quebec Gazette* published in 1764. In 2002, the Massachusetts Historical Society kindly made it possible for the National Library to acquire the copies from them, including the first issue. This is not an unusual story in the history of newspaper publishing in Canada. Out of the close to 20,000 newspapers published in Canada, the National Library has perhaps ? of these in any print form, usually the first issue or an issue published in the first year and of these, perhaps only ? have been microfilmed in their entirety. This portion of Canada's newspaper heritage is the result of a decision to collect decentrally and to retain a representative portion of the Canadian press.

Canadian newspapers are not required on legal deposit although we do collect 10 representative dailies from across Canada since their original dates and we have over 18,000 volumes of newspapers collected and bound by the Library of Parliament who donated them to the National Library in 1967 when the new building was opened. We also try to collect first, last and special issues of Canadian newspapers as well as all ethnic Canadian titles, all titles published by aboriginal groups and all student newspapers. Our definition of a newspaper is somewhat narrower than many libraries use. Publications which are devoted to a specific subject, industry or interest; e.g. financial, industrial or military or magazine supplements, house organs, reviews, alumni publications and political, labour, religious and community publications printed monthly without news, editorials, features, ads or other matters of current interest are considered to be periodicals and are subject to legal deposit since 1952. As well, we have acquired long and complete runs of the pre-1952 periodicals. Nevertheless, we do rely on a very good network of interlibrary loan and communications as well as our online catalogue AMICUS which includes the updated *Union List of Canadian Newspapers* to allow us to locate newspapers, both in print and on microfilm, that we do not have. We are also different from many national libraries in that we have not had a retrospective or current microfilming program for newspapers. Since 1981, we have relied on a Decentralized Program for Canadian Newspapers whereby the ten provinces and now three territories of Canada are responsible for listing and filming their newspapers and the National Library of Canada then purchases a copy of the microfilm and lists it in the AMICUS. We also provide standards for acquisitions, cataloguing and preservation of newspapers as well as purchase copies of the filmed newspapers as funds permit.

In 2002, when we highlighted the 250th anniversary, we were also increasingly aware of the limitations of collecting only the print and microfilmed newspaper. We extended legal deposit in 1993 to all CD-ROM's and in 1995 to all electronic publications on all types of physical formats. However, we were still missing the newspaper as it appeared in its many electronic versions on the web. In 2002, we decided to hold a national consultation on newspapers to try to answer such questions as what were the trends in e-papers, who was ensuring long-term access to Canadian newspapers in electronic format and what was the industry perspective and what role would it play? Eighty participants including provincial and academic librarians, newspaper publishers and newspaper electronic vendors met at the National Library a few days after the National Librarian and the National Archivist announced a decision to join the two institutions together to become the Library and Archives of Canada. This consultation became part of a movement to articulate a national strategy to strengthen access and preservation of Canadian newspaper and the news in Canada.

As one institution, we would be in even a better position to develop common goals such as good housing for current and future collections in all formats, making known all types of news in our collections ranging from print to broadcast news and from news histories to newspaper photographs and making these collections accessible to all Canadians and to all people interested in Canadian news. There was no one solution as a result of the consultation but there were a number of good issues raised and very strong concerns. Primary of concern was the need for a leader to establish a newspaper centre which could address on a more permanent and high profile basis the strategies developed by the consultation participants, including legislation, standards, and preservation. It would lobby for funds, be a research centre of excellence, and develop digitization toolkits and other resources. The Centre would also promote the value of digital newspapers as a source of information for Canadian education, research and innovation at all levels and monitor newspaper access and preservation initiatives in other countries, including the goals and activities of the American working group on newspapers formed under the OCLC Digital and Preservation Co-op. There were also recommendations for other long-term strategies such as

- ensuring that comprehensive historical coverage was the goal for the preservation of currently-produced online newspaper content and for retrospective digitization of historical Canadian newspapers.

- Respecting the current complementary approach, whereby the private sector digitizes those Canadian dailies for which they see a market, and public-sector-based projects digitize newspapers of more local or limited reach.

- Strengthening the pan-Canadian coverage by developing a strong provincial approach, building upon and extending the scope of the original Decentralized Plan for Canadian Newspapers.

- Creating an inventory of all online newspapers and retrospective digitization projects, including those of libraries, historical societies, genealogical and other associations so that the full extent of gaps in coverage can be better known.

- Preparing an integrated, pan-Canadian strategy to address retrospective newspaper digitization. The focus should be on needs assessment, funding priorities, a business model, coordinated collaborative applications for funding, and a plan for funding the digitization of newspapers of limited or niche-market interest. Such a document would assist in the development of private/public sector partnerships.

- Funding a national strategy by compulsory legal deposit of electronic newspapers

- Preparing a business case for the digitization of Canadian newspapers and seeking government funding.

- Creating national technical standards by inventorying standards employed in current projects.

- Developing a set of recommended practices. For example, digitization projects in Canada should support, as a minimum, full-text keyword searching and the ability to view the original page image.

- Continuing to provide leadership in dialogue/discussions on technical standards, which should be vendor neutral to allow maximum interoperability.

Stakeholders agreed that unless new relationships are established, collections are at risk and a body of valuable Canadian digital content will be lost. The importance of partnerships and of complementary activity between private and public sectors was underlined, and meeting participants affirmed that sustained leadership from the Library and Archives of Canada was required.[1]

In May 2003, the National Librarian and National Archivist announced the creation of a Centre for Newspapers and the News in Canada (provisional title) in order to address the challenges of preserving the newspaper collection and of ensuring improved access to the treasures of information contained therein and the appointment of Mary Jane Starr, former Director General of Communications, to manage and direct the development of the Centre. The vision for the Centre is that it would enhance public access to the content of Canadian news media, as well as public understanding of their impact and influence on Canadian life and that it would make the content of the national collection of news media easily accessible to all Canadians. The mission of the Newspaper Centre manager would be to make recommendations to the Librarian and Archivist of Canada on the organization of the Centre and on the definition of its objectives and appropriate strategies; develop partnerships and synergies within the new institution (genealogy, caricature, news reels, photographs etc.) which will permit the collection both a heightened profile and a better utilization;develop partnerships outside the institution with the industry, the professions, educational community, electronic newspaper sector and others as appropriate and desirable and plan the marketing and the promotion of the collection. In the spring of 2003 in conjunction with Phase 1 of the move to a new institution called the Library and Archives of Canada, a Working Group for the Centre began with the identification of the news media within the one LAC Collection. The identification process focused on significant collections, their provenance, characteristics, access and preservation. With this information in hand the Working Group developed a vision and the plans for the Centre in alignment with the strategic drivers of the new institution. This autumn, the Working Group concentrated on the functional model of the Centre, within the context of the Making Known component. Work involved identifying the core functions, the necessary supports, the crossovers with other areas of the institution, and the initial plans for the Centre's operation as of April 1, 2004. The Working

---

1 The above-listed recommendations are from *Canadian Newspapers Online: a national consultation toward a national strategy to strengthen access to Canadian newspapers online. Library and Archives Canada, Ottawa, October 7-8, 2002* available at: http://www.nlc-bnc.ca/8/3/r3-650-e.html

Group's report to the Making Known component identified seven activities for the period January to March 2004. These seven activities are:

- Developing a content strategy with special emphasis, in the first instance on the news media related to Aboriginal and cultural communities

- Compiling a users' guide to news media at LAC based on an inventory of the collection

- Planning for the collection move to the interim storage facility

- Designing and populating the Web site with direct access to the digital editions of news media

- Consulting with targeted stakeholders and clients

- Developing the interpretation (‹making known›) plan

- Proposing a product line of merchandise

It may seem strange to see newspaper preservation and access articulated in terms of a business plan but in Canada, cultural resources compete for the same taxpayer dollars as any other resource whether it is energy conservation, maintenance of a national sponsored free health programme, funds for defence or employment strategies. Cultural communities such as the Library and Archives Canada have to prove to Canadians that the resources they require will be of benefit to all Canadians. It is not difficult to persuade an academic that it is absolutely necessary to have free full-text access to many Canadian daily newspapers in both official languages but if this access is already provided by the university, it is more difficult to convince the academic that all Canadians should have access to a resource such as this through the newspaper that it would benefit future researchers to be able to look at his or her newspaper at the Library and Archives. It is more difficult to persuade this same publisher to make the paper accessible online currently and retrospectively to all Canadians through the electronic resources of the Library and Archives when this may effectively destroy all sales revenue and the basis of the newspaper's existence. In convincing people that funding is necessary to create adequate storage, preservation and access to print newspapers, electronic newspapers and broadcast news, we need to showcase these collections, provide truly national finding aids to what we have, embrace the digital news media by providing digitization on demand, place ourselves in a leadership role in providing educational programmes on Canadian news media and in the stewardship of news collections and develop navigational tools that match the client's needs for finding information through full-text searching of news media. As institutions that care about our print heritage, it is our responsibility to share our problems and our solutions. We must work together to ensure that we make responsible decisions, that we communicate these decisions effectively and that we encourage participation from our researchers. We need to stop worrying about conserving everything and look at what we can appropriately. Most importantly, we need to become strong voices in the digital age and demand standards that will allow the news of 2003 to be as effectively conserved and accessible as the news of 1752.

NEWSPAPER COLLECTIONS AND SERVICES IN COLLEGE LIBRARIES IN CHINA

大学图书馆报纸资源的收藏与开发

Keqian Xu

Dean of Nanjing Normal University Library, China

I. Newspapers as a Source of Information

The newspaper in China has a long history. According to some scholars, as early as in the Spring-Autumn period (722-461 B.C), a kind of official newspaper served the feudal states then (Ref. 1, p. 10). Of course, it was not printed on paper, but carved on bamboo slips. Modern newspapers were first introduced into China by western missionaries, mainly for the purpose of religion. Since then, newspapers have been playing an important role in Chinese society. The newspaper as a source of information has certain features that make it different from other information sources such as books, periodicals, radio, television and internet. No other source can compete with newspaper in the abundance and variety of information contents. The huge volume of information in newspapers is usually timely and instant, and much more closely related to social reality and people's daily life, which gives newspapers a superiority over books and periodicals. Newspapers have a vast amount of readers, and a huge circulation. Some leading newspapers in China have a circulation of several millions of copies. Actually, the newspaper is still the first information resource for most people in China today. A survey shows that 47.17% people take newspapers as their first source of information, this rate is much higher than TV and radio (Ref. 6, p. 53). Comparatively speaking, the information provided by newspapers is of higher authenticity, and once it is issued, the information is recorded in a stable and unchangeable way, which gives newspaper an advantage over radio, TV and internet.

II. Newspaper Collections in College Libraries in China

Due to those features of newspaper information mentioned above, newspapers have long been an important part of both public and academic library collections that cannot be replaced by other resources. Newspapers are a very valuable resource in college education and academic research, especially to those disciplines such as journalism, sociology, politics, international affairs, law, the current history, education and social works. To the professors and students of certain departments, newspapers are even a more important resource in their study and research than books and journals.

Today, more than 2000 newspapers are currently published in China. However, most college libraries usually subscribe only to about 100-200 of them. As in the case of Nanjing Normal University Library, we subscribe to nearly 150 newspapers, most of which are important and serious newspapers, such as the top national newspapers, important local newspapers, or newspapers with special professional and academic subjects. We do subscribe to some entertainment newspapers such as sports newspapers and weekend papers, but we don't consider them as serious collections, and only keep them on the shelf for one year or few months. We only keep the back issues of about 95 Chinese newspapers.

III. Cooperative-storage Plan for Newspaper Back File Collections among Regional Academic Libraries

The storage and cataloguing of newspaper back issues has always been a headache in college libraries. In the case of Nanjing Normal University Library, we find that newspaper back files occupy more space while serving less readers. Our limited storage spaces do not allow us to keep all the back issues of the newspapers we have subscribed to. Even so, more than 60% of our back issue newspapers were only accessed by less than 10 readers during the past 5 years. However, most of these readers usually seem have a very urgent and important need for the document they want to find, and feel very happy when they find it. In order to release storage spaces, in the later 1980s, four academic libraries in Jiangsu province (Nanjing University Library, Nanjing Normal University Library, Jiangsu CPC School Library and Jiangsu Social Science Academy Library) signed an agreement to share their storage of newspaper back issues. Each library is responsible to keep only certain newspaper back issues, four libraries share their mutually supplemented collections, thus to save each libraries' space. Since then, Nanjing Normal University Library only keeps in stock the back issues of some frequently used leading nationwide newspapers, important local newspapers and the newspapers published in north-east China.

IV. Information Services Provided by College Libraries Based on Newspaper Collections

Most college libraries had a very simple catalog of their newspaper collection. Clients usually use the National Newspapers and Periodicals' Index to find the article or information they need, and then go to the library to find it. But the National Newspapers and Periodicals' Index only covers less than 200 newspapers. It is not an adequate index for college library newspaper collections. Consequently, some librarians compiled their own special subject index for articles published in newspapers. There are always market needs for using newspapers as a resource to provide reference services. Some librarians have been providing a newspaper clipping service for their clients for many years. Other library services based on newspaper collections include writing and compiling special subject digests from newspaper articles, providing background information for current events, copying and delivering newspaper documents, etc.. With computers, scanners, OCR software and e-mail, these jobs become much easier than before. Some university libraries provide this kind of information service not only to the teachers and students in their universities, but to the whole society, and even make it a big business. At the same time, some commercial agents also provide this kind of service. There are more than 300 registered commercial information consulting companies in China, whose main job is collecting information from various kinds of newspapers and offering their services such as market investigation (Ref. 3, p. 83).

V. New development of Chinese newspapers in the past two decades

After the cultural revolution, when China began to open to the outside world, newspapers as the most important and popular information medium, have been growing at an accelerated speed. 1998 statistics show that there were 2149 registered newspapers published in mainland China, while in 1978, there were only 186 registered newspapers (Ref. 6, p. 52). Dramatic increases not only happened in variety and numbers of newspapers, but also in pages of a single newspaper. There were seldom any newspapers of more than 10 pages per issue 20 years ago. But today lots of daily newspapers have 50, 60 or even over hundred pages per issue. China's newspapers today are no longer exclusively «the tongue of the Party and government», but also the «voice of people». In newspaper we can find different opinions, dispute about public affairs, civilians suing the government, disclosure of scandals and official corruption ... all this demonstrates a dynamic and vivid picture of open China, which would have been unimaginable 20 years earlier.

While we witnessed more serious and valuable academic information increasing in all kinds of newspapers, we also watched a simultaneous increase of information rubbish. Market oriented motivation sometimes urge the newspaper editors to give more pages to trash to play to the gallery. Readers are exposed to much irrelevant commercial information. The variety of ways to promote circulation also causes confusion and makes library acquisition more complex.

VI. Electronic newspapers and digitized newspapers databases

Another important trend is digitization and online publishing, which is an even more serious challenge to library newspaper collections and services. New technology advances in the past decade have dramatically changed the way of news publication, and changed the librarians' job as well. Some years ago our library bought some newspaper back issues in microfilm form, but soon this was replaced by CD-ROMs and then full-text newspaper databases.

In 1995, the first electronic version of a Chinese newspaper appeared. Before long, more newspapers went online. Today, many newspapers are available electronically, It is estimated that there are about 300 Chinese newspapers now online. Some leading newspapers also produced their back issue database, such as *People's Daily* database, which provides the contents of *People's Daily* from 1994 till present, and also includes other dozens of newspapers belonging to the People's Daily Group. Similar newspaper databases are the database of *Guangming Daily*, *Economy Daily*, etc. Some leading newspapers also sell their back issues in CD-ROM form. CNKI's The Full Text Database of the Important Newspapers of China is the biggest digitized newspaper database in China today. It is one of the series of products of the «China National Knowledge Infrastructure» project, carried out by the Tsinghua Tongfang company. It claims a collection of 500 «important» newspapers published in China, from June 2000 till present, averagely adding 2500 articles every day. But the criteria for its collection are questionable. Some quite «important» newspapers, such as Shanghai's *Xin Min Evening*, Nanjing's *Yangtze Evening*, are not included in the list. Moreover, not all the articles in every issue are included. (Ref. 4, p. 64).

VII. Advantages for today's newspaper librarianship

Librarians were used to provide newspaper-clipping services for their clients with scissors and paste two decades ago. Now with computer, network and digitized newspaper databases, they are able to fulfil that task only with few mouse clicks. Librarians today can use vaster and more varied resources for their information reference, they can provide more timely and effective service. They can also use multiple ways to deliver their services and communicate with their clients.

VIII. Challenges faced by today's newspaper librarianship

However, new technology and electronic or network publishing also produced new challenges for college libraries' newspaper collections and services. For instance, how to deal with the relations between printed, electronic, and online newspapers? Shall we stop keeping the back issues and just keep the digital form from now on? If we have a collection of a newspaper right from its initial issue, and this newspaper is not frequently used, do we have to spend a lot of money to buy its retrospective database?

In the past decade, college libraries in China have made great endeavours in building combined OPAC for their collections of books and periodicals. But newspaper collections seems be neglected. We need a combined online public access catalog of newspaper collections of different libraries on the regional and even national level. Compared with periodicals and books, newspaper-based information is more difficult to search, so we also need more powerful searching and indexing tools with vast coverage. These jobs can never be done by a single library, we need cooperation and organization, and build standards and regulations. Cataloguing the internet newspapers and integrating newspaper collections of various type and from various sources, are also some jobs that should be done by our librarians. There are many online newspapers, updating everyday, or even updating every hour. It is possible for librarians to catalogue these online newspapers, or build a library guiding website, and build virtual newspaper reading rooms on the net. We also need to integrate printed newspapers, electronic newspapers on CD-ROM, in databases, and online newspapers, all together in a uniform service platform, for our clients' convenience.

Anyway, our tasks are heavy, and we still have a long way to go.

References:

1. 倪延年：中国古代报刊发展史.东南大学出版社，南京，2001.6。
2. 张效赤：中国报纸索引沿革述略。图书馆理论与实践，1995 年4 期，30-34 页。
3. 王振海：从报纸文献的特点谈图书馆报刊资源的开发。国家图书馆学刊，2000 年1 期，82-87 页
4. 王效锋：CNKI 报纸数据库的收录范围质疑.四川图书馆学报，2002 年4 期，63-66 页。
5. 徐云：新技术条件下报纸文献信息的利用开发.国家图书馆学刊，2001 年第 2 期。
6. 顾厚明：馆藏报纸资源的开发利用，江西图书馆学刊，1997 年第2 期，52-53 页。

THE BRITISH LIBRARY NEWSPAPER COLLECTIONS DEVELOPMENT AND FUTURE ACCESS

Geoffrey Hamilton

The British Library

The Buildings

- BL Newspapers Facts/ History   See: http://www.bl.uk/collections/newspapers.html

Northern façade of BL Newspapers building: 1980s
Permission British Library

History

1822 : Newspapers transferred to British Museum from Commissioners of the Stamp Office
1869 : Newspaper Printers and Reading Rooms Act: newspapers to be deposited by publishers at the British Museum.
1897 : Space for newspapers in the British Museum at Bloomsbury exhausted.
1902 : British Museum Act authorising purchase of the Colindale site.
1903 : British Museum Newspaper Repository completed as a warehouse for English provincial, Irish, Scottish, and Welsh newspapers.
1922 : Newspaper Repository is full.
1928 : Royal Commission on National Museums and Galleries Interim Report recommends that the Colindale Repository be enlarged to contain all newspapers published later than 1800 and that a reading room be built.
1930 : Building of the library commences.

1932, Aug 23 : British Museum Newspaper Library is opened.

1940, Oct 20 : A Luftwaffe bomb destroys the 1903 building. An estimated 6,000 volumes of newspapers are also destroyed and a further 15,000 volumes are damaged.

1971 :   New Microfilm building is completed.

1975 :   *Catalogue of the Newspaper Library Colindale*, compiled by P.E. Allen, is published in eight volumes.

1986 :   First of the NEWSPLAN reports is published (South West).

1991 :   Newspaper Library becomes responsible for the Newspaper Legal Deposit Office at 120 Colindale Avenue, formerly administered by the Copyright Receipt Office.

1995 :   Conversion of the catalogue is completed.

1996 :   Final NEWSPLAN report is published (London and South Eastern Library Region).
           Newspaper Library website is established on The British Library's Online Information Server.

1999 :   An online catalogue of the collections is made available in the Reading Rooms.

2000 :   The Newspaper Library catalogue of over 52,000 newspaper and periodical title holdings is launched on the web.

British Library Newspaper Collections

- Complete Runs of UK newspapers from 1800
- Some 660,00 volumes and parcels
- Estimated 330,000 reels microfilm
- Time consuming to access
- Possibility of missing material
- Lack of indexes to newspapers (some notable exceptions)

Consulting newspapers:

- London: 16,239 titles; Redbridge – 82 titles; Sutton 45 titles
- Manchester: 1,204 titles; Bristol 203 titles
- Readers search for information by title, by date
- Page by page, column by column
- Accuracy of retrieval depends upon concentration
- Stamina needed to concentrate
- Powers of observation enhanced to reduce risk of missing information
- Readers can spend months/ years upon a line of enquiry
- Tangential discoveries beneficial
- Many readers wish for the enquiry process to be speeded up
- Finding aids largely absent for most printed newspapers

Manual Indexing of Newspapers

- Work done on a surprising scale for UK Newspapers in several UK regions
- Limited indexing carried out on selected portions of newspapers
- Highly labour intensive
- Exclusion of material of research interest

Automatic Indexing of Newspapers: problems

- Complexity of multiple fonts
- Closeness of fonts on same page

- Imperfections of letterpress inking
- Imperfect registration of text recto/verso
- Bleed through of ink recto/ verso
- Great quantity of text
- Need to index continuous runs of issues
- Spine binding curvature on film

«The reprographic revolution»

Strands that have come together:

- Scanning of originals or microfilm
- OCR improvements
- Huge gains in access to low cost storage in computers
- High grade software to recognise OCR text
- The advent of the world wide web
- Software to improve access to large quantities of text

«Historic newspapers» digital scanning

- British Library projects:
- Pilot Project: http://www.uk.olivesoftware.com
- Collect Britain: http://www.bl.uk/collectbritain
- Commercially funded work:
- Gale – The Times (London)
- Proquest – New York Times
- Many other examples

Images

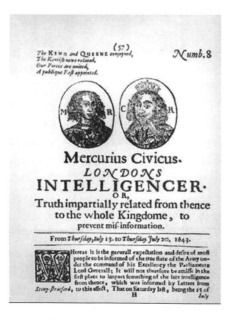

Mercurius Civicus. Londons Intelligencer
13-20 July 1643
Permission British Library

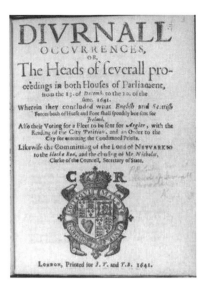

Diurnall Occurrences ... from the 13. of Decemb. to the 20. of the same. 1641 (London, 1641) British Library, E.201.(3.) *Permission British Library*

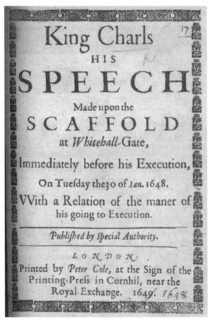

The final speech of King Charles I, given at his execution in January 1648/9. Shelfmark: E.540.(17). *Permission British Library*

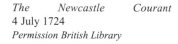

The   Newcastle   Courant
4 July 1724
Permission British Library

The   Calcutta   Gazette;   or,
Oriental Advertiser
17 February 1785
Permission British Library

New-York Price Current
Saturday August 31st 1799
Permission British Library

The Poor Man's Guardian
July 5th 1834
Permission British Library

The Norfolk and Norwich Satirist September 21st 1839 Permission British Library

The Family Circle Edition of the Christian World January 1892 Permission British Library

The Graphic
31 May 1884. *London and Westminster, 1584.*
Permission British Library

Police News
14 April 1888
*Permission British
Library*

Ísland
24 July 1897
Permission British Library

Seeing
Pears Annual 1897.
Permission British Library

The Mafeking Mail
December 7th 1899
Permission British Library

The Daily Mirror
16 April 1912
Permission British Library

All Picture Comic
16 April 1921
Permission British Library

The Evening Standard
17 February 1940: fake
copy
Permission British Library

Penny   Illustrated
Paper
August 14 1869
*Permission British
Library*

The End

Newspapers always excite curiosity. No one ever lays one down without a feeling of disappointment.
Charles Lamb. *Detached Thoughts on Books and Reading.*
****

Possible? Is anything impossible? Read the newspapers.
Duke of Wellington. *Words of Wellington*

LEGAL DEPOSIT OF NORWEGIAN INTERNET NEWSPAPERS

Jonny Edvardsen

Director, Collections and Bibliographic Services
National Library of Norway

[Note: the following is the text contained in a Power Point Presentation – Ed.]

National Library of Norway

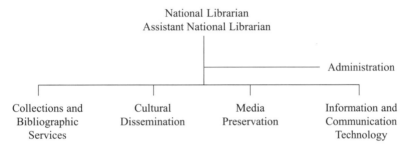

Act relating to the legal deposit of generally available documents

* came into force on 1 July 1990
* includes all kinds of documents regardless of medium
* States that the main criterion for legal deposit is whether the document is generally available

The Legal Deposit Act

* Paper
* Microforms
* Photographs
* Combined documents
* Sound fixations
* Film
* Videograms
* Digital publications
* Broadcasting programmes

Two main criteria for legal deposit

* The document is made generally available
* The document is made for a Norwegian publisher or specially adapted to the Norwegian public

Digital material

- The National Library of Norway administrates the Law of Legal Deposit, this means that the responsibility of storing and giving access to publically accessible digital documents rests on our shoulders.
- The law says that digital documents that have been made available for the public should be deposited.
- The documents can be on physical carriers, for example CD-ROM or diskettes, or they can be available to the public via telecommunication-, television- or computer networks.

Project 2000-2004 PARADIGMA

Preservation Arrangement **&** Retrieval of Assorted **DIG**ital **MA**terials
Project Leader: Carol van Nuys
carol.vannuys@nb.no

All types of digital documents:

- Fixed media
- The Norwegian web-space (.no)
- Databases
- All media types

Internet Newspapers

Important part of the work in Paradigma
Several challenges:
- How
- What
- How often
- Navigation in the collected material
- Digital preservation
- Legal rights
- Access

Started harvesting of 40 web-sites in august 2003, now 67 are collected daily.
Collects the newspapers once a day from the web, in addition we get the changes in the publication database from the publishers.
Harvesting is easy, making the rest work is difficult!

Harvesting .no

- 4,200,000 URLs last August
- Planned this spring: app. 5 mill URLs
- We are also discussing legal deposit of the biggest photo-database in Norway: +5,000,000 pictures

NB's Digital Repository

- The storage capacity in the Digital Repository is approximately 100 Tbyte today.
- This is the equivilent to ca 230 years of playing time for MP3-sound (96 kbps), 24 hours a day!
- The storage capacity can easily be expanded.

NEWSPAPER COPYRIGHT DEVELOPMENTS:
A EU AND UK PERSPECTIVE

Charles Oppenheim

Loughborough University, Loughborough, UK

Abstract

This paper examines how copyright has an impact on a newspaper librarian attempting to preserve copies of newspapers by copying, and attempting to provide ready access to newspapers for patrons. The perspective is from UK law, with recent development in EU law being highlighted. It is concluded that the law provides only limited help to newspaper librarians, and restricts their ability to make digital copies of newspapers. Recent EU Directives are unlikely to significantly change the situation, which is a microcosm of problems all librarians face when trying to preserve, sand allow access to, cultural materials to their patrons.

Introduction

In this session, I will be discussing UK copyright law issues involved when someone makes copies of newspapers for the purposes of preservation, provides access to such copies, and under what circumstances they can lend newspapers to other libraries to let them copy. It is worth stressing that in general, the law ignores the content – the law does not distinguish newspapers from other types of publications, such as books or journals – in other words, my remarks are applicable to all types of published materials and not just newspapers. It is also worth stressing that although copyright law is similar in most countries of the world, it most definitely is not identical, and therefore you should only assume what I am telling you is correct for the UK.

Copyright

As I am sure you are aware, the owner of the copyright has the right to prevent anyone else from doing certain acts to his work without his express permission. These acts include copying, selling, lending or hiring out or amending the work. These are the so-called *restricted acts*.

Copyright in most works lasts for 70 years from the end of the calendar year when the author died. Thus, if a newspaper article has an identified author, the lifetime of the work depends on when that author died.

If the work is anonymous, or if it has been created as part of employee duties, then in the UK the lifetime is 70 years from the end of the calendar year when the material was first published. Each individual article or news story in a newspaper is a separate copyright work. In addition, the contents of the newspaper as a whole enjoy copyright. Also in the UK, there can be copyright in the typography and layout of the printed words, though that only lasts for 25 years. There is also copyright in each image in the newspaper, such as photographs, sketches, graphs, etc. So, copyright law says no-one may copy a work – and copying includes photocopying, scanning, faxing, microfilming it, etc. If you do copy all, or a substantial part of the work without permission, you are *infringing* the copyright in that material and can be sued for the damage you caused the copyright owner, or for the profits you made out of your infringing action. In addition, in cases of severe wilful infringement, such as outright piracy, you can be sent to prison. As you can see, copyright law is not helpful to those wishing to provide access to newspapers. Notwithstanding the best efforts of Nicholson Baker (Baker, 2002) to persuade me otherwise, I accept that newspapers are fragile documents that are easily damaged, especially by repeated re-use, and therefore if libraries are to provide reasonable access, and at the same time ensure the long term preservation of such a crucial part of our cultural, social and political history, they should be offering *copies* to readers rather than the originals.

This difficult situation is not helped by the aggressive attitude towards libraries adopted by the Newspaper Licensing Agency, the Reproduction Rights Organisation that represents many UK national and local newspapers.

Exceptions to copyright

However, all is not gloom and doom. One reason is that there are a number of important exceptions to copyright in UK law. In particular, there are special rules about libraries and archives making copies for preservation purposes, and it is this I now want to look at.

Section 42 of the 1988 UK Copyright Act permits libraries or archives, under certain conditions, to make copies of copyright material to preserve or to replace the original. Any library can supply the copy, but only «prescribed libraries» can receive them.

A «prescribed library» is, in essence, one that is not for profit, such as public libraries, University libraries, school and college libraries, libraries of learned societies and professional associations, government libraries, national libraries such as the British Library, and hospital libraries. Only material permanently held by the donating library may be copied and even then, it should be reference material only.

So, newspapers that are on loan to the archive or library, or electronic materials it simply has a licence to access, cannot benefit from this provision of the law. And any newspapers that can be lent to patrons cannot be copied.

Libraries can copy their own newspapers providing they fulfil all these requirements. Finally, the newspapers in question must be out of print and unobtainable. The copy must enter the receiving library's permanent collection as a reference only item. Copies can only be made in this way to help preserve an item that has been lost or damaged, or is in severe danger of doing so. Not for profit archives that are associated with a commercial body can also make copies in this way.

Note that this exception only applies to literary, dramatic or musical works or to illustrations that happen to be embedded in a literary work. You cannot therefore use this exception to make preservation copies of artistic works, or to preserve sound recordings, TV broadcasts, video and film. Thus, you could not use this exception to preserve multimedia items that combine, say, text, music, still images and moving images.

Furthermore, digital copies can only be made under strictly controlled conditions; this is because the law allows the making of a single copy only, whereas digital copies are potentially multiple copies as anyone can access and download the item. If the digitised copy of the newspaper were held on just one non-networked PC, it would be OK, but most PCs are networked these days! Overall, then, Section 42 provides some help, but probably insufficient for scanning and digitising the old newspapers.

So how does one deal with the issue of digitising materials for preservation, making copies of electronic items for preservation, or making preservation copies under other circumstances where section 42 does not apply – for example, if you work in a non-prescribed library or the material in question can be borrowed, or is merely on loan to your library? You have to ask for permission from the copyright owner – in other words, you have to get a licence. There are certain steps you have to go through.

Firstly, you have to discover who the copyright owner is, i.e., who can authorise the copying. This is not always straightforward in the case of newspapers, as copyright ownership may reside with individual journalists and/or the newspaper proprietor (and remember, the owner might have changed hands over the years) and/or with news agencies. You then need to work out what actions you need to take to be able to preserve the newspaper and what level of access you wish to offer your patrons. It is particularly important to distinguish in your mind preservation and access.

A copyright owner may well give you permission to preserve, but refuse permission for access, or make access conditions so difficult that in practice it is hardly worth your while.

Think in advance why the person who could authorise your request to preserve an object might refuse to do so, and then prepare reasoned arguments and explanations of preservation methods you will adopt, and the access conditions you can impose, to persuade them that authorising preservation and access will not cause them any harm.

It is worth trying first with an informal letter, but it is likely that this will not work and you will need to negotiate a licence instead. Either way, you should consider the following points:

- Ensure that all actions necessary for the preservation process are permitted.

- Consideration should be given to the type of permission requested, e.g., access for the purposes of preservation only, and for no other purposes.

- You may have to display a notice to authorised users accessing the preserved object. The notice could warn them of the rights status of the object, or permitted actions, or both.

- Rights owners will be concerned to ensure the integrity of the object. You need to consider the technical and administrative means by which this can be guaranteed.

I cannot emphasise enough the problems that are involved in gaining permissions like these from copyright owners. The difficulties of tracking them down and getting them to agree to things are tremendous. You should bear in mind also, that if they fail to respond to an approach, that means «no», and any approach along the lines of «unless I hear from you to the contrary, I shall assume it is OK for me to copy for preservation and to allow patrons access» has no validity in law. Indeed, I have developed a Universal Law on this (Oppenheim, 2000).

This simply states: Whatever your most pessimistic estimate is for the time it will take to get a licence agreement sorted out, it will take twice as long.

The EU and copyright

The EU has an active and long-standing interest in copyright. It believes, rightly, that anomalies in copyright law between member states are inhibiting the development of the single market. It also believes that a strong copyright regime is necessary for its vision of an information society to come about. To this end, it has passed a number of Directives in the copyright arena. I want to briefly describe two of the EU's Directives that are of relevance.

The first is database right.

There is now a special type of literary work called «databases». This is a collection of independent works, data or other materials that are arranged in a systematic or methodical way and are individually accessible by electronic or other means, *each of which may or may not be subject to individual copyright.* A newspaper is certainly a database in this definition.

The newspaper itself gets protection over and above any copyright in each news item. So a newspaper gets double protection. Without going into the complex details, the result is that in a newspaper, each individual article has copyright, and the newspaper as a whole has copyright and a new right called database right. In practical terms, however, this makes little difference to the situation I have outlined to you in this talk so far.

The second example of the EU's activity that is of relevance to today's discussion is its Directive on Copyright and Related Rights that was passed in summer, 2001 and at the time of writing was due to become law in the UK in late Spring 2003. *(An update will be provided at the session itself)*

The Directive updates copyright law to take account of the Internet environment, and includes a list of possible exceptions to copyright, that is to say, things that may be done by users without having to ask permission or pay any fees. One of these exceptions allows for reproduction made by «publicly accessible libraries, educational establishments or museums, or by archives».

It is reasonable to assume that all libraries currently considered to be prescribed will continue to be so.

Quite what the implications of this for copying for preservation purposes will be is currently uncertain, but bearing in mind the approach taken by the British Government throughout the passage of this controversial piece of legislation, almost certainly it will mean that there will be little or no change in the current legal position under Section 42 of the Act.

Summing up

Let me sum um what I have been telling you today. Under UK law, it is possible under limited circumstances to make copies of newspapers for preservation purposes. Once lawfully copied, you are then free to provide those lawful copies to patrons, who can, if they wish, make their own copies of the newspapers under the well-known fair dealing exception to copyright, so long as it is for non-commercial research, or for their private study.

However, the law limits newspaper libraries in some regards; firstly, only prescribed libraries can create such preservation copies, and secondly, the possibilities for making digitised copies for preservation purposes is very limited. It is therefore quite probable that a UK newspaper library will have to approach the copyright owners for permission to copy for preservation, and/or to provide access to patrons. As I have indicated, this can be a stressful and time consuming process, and you may not get the permissions you want in the end.

Furthermore, the recent EU Directives do not, in my view, have much impact on the current somewhat unsatisfactory situation.

So there we have it; a less than ideal situation for UK newspaper librarians to have to work in, and one that is unlikely to change in the near future. But copyright has always caused problems for librarians attempting to serve their patrons and preserve the cultural heritage as best they can. The problems facing newspaper librarians are merely a microcosm of these problems.

References

Baker, N. (2002). *Double Fold.* London: Vintage.

Oppenheim, C. (2000). Legal issues for information professionals VI: copyright issues in digitisation and the hybrid library. *Information Services and Use*, 20(4), 203-210.

WHAT HAS COPYRIGHT GOT TO DO WITH NEWSPAPERS? – A SOUTH AFRICAN PERSPECTIVE

Denise Rosemary Nicholson

Copyright Services Librarian, University of the Witwatersrand,
Johannesburg, South Africa

Abstract

This paper gives a brief overview of the current copyright legislation of South Africa and its international and regional commitments with regard to copyright. It also focuses on the practical implications and complications that copyright creates for newspapers, libraries and archives depots, as well as for newspaper clipping services and preservation projects.

International Commitments

South Africa is a signatory to two international copyright agreements, namely, the Berne Convention and the Agreement on Trade-Related Aspects of Intellectual Property Rights, known as the TRIPS Agreement. It is also a signatory to the World Intellectual Property Organization (WIPO) Treaties, namely, the Copyright Treaty and the Performances and Phonograms Treaty, which came into effect during 2002. However, South Africa can only accede to them when its copyright legislation has been amended to address digital technology and related issues.

Regional Situation

South Africa is the most developed country in the Southern African Development Community (SADC), which consists of 14 developing countries.[1] With regard to industrial property (i.e. intellectual property excluding copyright), there is co-operation amongst SADC members, as well as with the various African countries belonging to the African Regional Industrial Property Organization (ARIPO). South Africa also cooperates closely with the United Kingdom Patents Office, the European Union Patents Office and several Middle East countries with regard to industrial property.

However, with regard to copyright, there are no co-operative copyright treaties amongst the SADC countries, nor is there any harmonization of copyright laws in the Southern African region. Thirteen of the fourteen member countries have some form of copyright protection and legislation, but in many cases the laws are very outdated.[2] South Africa's legislation is the most up-to-date, having been amended in 2002. As a result, the importance, application and interpretation of copyright principles in this region differ from one member country to the next.

---

1 Countries of the Southern African Development Community are: Angola, Botswana, Democratic Republic of Congo, Lesotho, Malawi, Mauritius, Mozambique, Namibia, Seychelles, South Africa, Swaziland, Tanzania, Zambia and Zimbabwe.
2 According to WIPO's website, Mozambique does not have any copyright legislation to date.
URL: http://www.wipo.int/about-ip/en/ipworldwide/pdf/mz.pdf) [May 13, 2003]

Domestic Situation

South Africa has its Copyright Act No. 98 of 1978 (as amended) and Copyright Regulations, which have limited exceptions for education. Foreign works, including newspapers, published by signatories to the Berne Convention also have full copyright protection in South Africa.

Since 1999, the educational sector has presented a number of copyright position papers and has made various recommendations to the South African Government, with regard to issues affecting education, e.g. electronic copyright, provisions for the disabled, the distance learner and the illiterate. However, to date, the copyright legislation has not been amended accordingly.

Also, initiatives by the educational sector to discuss copyright issues with the Publishing Association of South Africa (PASA), as well as with the International Publishing Association (IPA), have unfortunately not been successful.[3] The main reason is that there are major differences of opinion with regard to fair use and multiple copying for nonprofit educational purposes. The educational sector is currently drafting proposals addressing these issues and in due course, will present this document to Government and other stakeholders, for further discussion and debate. It is hoped that this will lead to amendment and updating of the copyright legislation in due course.

Fair Use

Regarding «fair use», South Africa modelled its «fair dealing» provisions on the United Kingdom's copyright laws. Fair dealing is permitted in Section 12 of our Copyright Act. «Fair dealing» permits the reproduction of literary or musical works (as well as works in some other categories), for the purposes of research or private study, or for personal or private use, or for criticism or review, or for reporting current events in a newspaper or similar periodical, or by means of broadcasting, or in a cinematograph film. [4]

Section 12 (7) of the Copyright Act provides that the copyright in an article published in a newspaper or periodical, or in a broadcast, on any current economic, political or religious topic, shall not be infringed by reproducing it in the press or broadcasting it, if such reproduction or broadcast has not been expressly reserved, and the source is clearly mentioned. [5]

Section 13 of the Act provides limited exceptions for reproduction by libraries and archives depots and also by teachers at educational institutions, but these do not extend to electronic media. These include limited copies for handouts for students in a classroom situation, but do not make provision for distance learners or for conversions to other formats for persons with disabilities.[6]

Regarding «fair use» in the electronic environment, and in the absence of appropriate legislation, cognizance is taken of the statements made by the World Intellectual Property Organization (WIPO) and IFLA that «digital is not different».[7]

---

3   Meeting held with IPA, together with PASA, in Cape Town, South Africa, in October 2001
4   Dean. O. *Handbook of South African Copyright Law.* Rev. Service 11. Juta, Cape Town, p. 4-138
5   Ibid. p. 4-138A
6   Ibid. p. 4-139.
7   www.wipo/int.treaties/ip/copyright/statements.html and www.ifla.org/V/press/copydig.htm

In the absence of appropriate legislation for electronic media, the educational sector and libraries find the following guidelines useful:

- *Guidelines on Fair Dealing in the Electronic Environment* by the Joint Information Systems Committee and the UK Publishers' Association; [8]

- *Publishers and Librarians promote common principles on copyright in the electronic environment* by IFLA and the International Publishers' Association; [9]

- *Fair use Guidelines for Educational Multimedia* by the American Distance Education Consortium. [10]

How Copyright Protects Newspapers

Newspapers are protected under the category of «Literary works» in our Copyright Act, but they also contain «Artistic works» such as cartoons, photographs, graphics, images and advertisements. When reproducing newspapers or information in newspapers, the term of copyright term has to be considered. In case of literary or musical or artistic works, other than photographs, the term is the life of the author and fifty years from the end of the year in which the author dies, with certain provisos. The term of copyright in the case of photographs is fifty years from the end of the year in which the work is made available to the public with the consent of the copyright owner, or is first published, whichever term is the longer; or failing such an event within fifty years of the making of the work, fifty years from the end of the year in which the work is made. [11]

This means that very old newspapers are already in the public domain and are not subject to copyright.

Copyright Ownership

Although the copyright law provides that works created within the course and scope of one's employment belong to the employer, newspapers do not always hold copyright in the works that they publish. They generally own copyright in articles written by their own staff, e.g. full-time reporters and journalists. This is seldom the case with regard to works by free-lancers or artists, unless the relevant copyright owners assign their rights to the newspapers.

Copyright in artistic works usually belongs to the artists. With regard to photographs, the copyright holder is the person who is responsible for the composition of the photograph, and not the person who physically presses the camera button. The person, who undertakes the arrangements necessary for the creation of a computer-generated literary or artistic work, is the copyright holder. [12]

8   The Joint Information Systems Committee and the UK Publishers' Association. *Guidelines on Fair Dealing in the Electronic Environment*: URL: http://www.ukoln.ac.uk/services/elib/papers/pa/fair/ [May 13, 2003]

9   IFLA and the International Publishers' Association. Joint Press Release: IFLA/IPA – *Publishers and Librarians promote common principles on copyright in the electronic environment*. URL: www.ifla.org/V/press/ifla-ipa.htm [May 7, 2003]

10 The American Distance Education Consortium. *Fair use Guidelines for Educational Multimedia* URL: http://www.adec.edu/admin/papers/fair10-17html [May 13, 2003]

11 Dean. O. *Handbook of South African Copyright Law*. Rev. Service 11. Juta, Cape Town. p. 4-133

12 Dean. O. *Copyright*. Presentation delivered at DALRO workshop at Kempton Park, South Africa, on February 21, 2003. p. 3

Copyright in readers' letters remains with the writer as author, but the editor can alter or shorten it as long as these amendments do no affect the credit or literary reputation of the writer.[13]

There is no copyright in «news of the day» nor in speeches of a political nature, although the author of the speech has the exclusive right of making a collection of his/her speeches.[14]

In the course of sub-editing, a sub-editor may change a work considerably or he/she may impart to the work a quality or character which it previously did not possess. This would result in copyright in the amended article being vested in the sub-editor, whilst copyright in the original article would remain with the journalist. Where the contributions are both substantial in the resultant work, it will be one of joint authorship with copyright vesting in the co-authors.[15]

A copyright holder may grant non-exclusive licences, to another party, by verbal or written agreement. However, an exclusive licence must be reduced to writing and must be signed by or on behalf of the licensor. Assignment of copyright must be reduced to writing and signed by or on behalf of the copyright holder/assignor. Copyright may also be bequeathed by will, and in circumstances where ownership in property devolves through operation of law, as on death or insolvency, ownership of copyright will likewise devolve.[16]

Copyright Clearance

South Africa does not have a Newspaper Licensing Agency to clear copyright for newspapers. Also, the Johannesburg-based Dramatic, Artistic and Literary Rights Organization (DALRO), which clears copyright for reprographic reproductions, has no mandate to clear copyright for newspapers.

Under legal regimes such as South Africa's (i.e. voluntary collective licensing), newspapers customarily do not entrust their rights to collective administration, in view of the complexities involved. As newspapers feature material from various external sources, copyright in each article, image, artistic work or photograph needs to be researched individually to establish the copyright clearance source.[17]

Newspaper publishers themselves need to obtain permission to publish material in their publications. In the absence of a Licensing Agency, they have to apply directly to rightsowners.

In the case of international media, they often have to enter into individual licence agreements before the material can be used. They cannot reproduce, re-format or digitize material unless they hold the copyright or have been mandated to do so.

---

13 Bell, Dewar & Hall. *Kelsey Stuart's The Newspaperman's Guide to the Law*. 5th Ed. Durban. Butterworths. p. 231

14 Dean. O. Handbook of South African Copyright Law. Rev. Service 11. Juta, Cape Town. p. 4-138A

15 Bell, Dewar & Hall. *Kelsey Stuart's The Newspaperman's Guide to the Law*. 5th ed. Durban, Butterworths. p. 225

16 Bell, Dewar & Hall. *Kelsey Stuart's The Newspaperman's Guide to the Law*. 5th ed. Durban, Butterworths. p. 226

17 Robinson. G. (November 7, 2002). *Newspapers and Copyright*. [Email to D. Nicholson], [Online]. Available email: Nicholson.D@library.wits.ac.za

Internationally, the controversial case of Tasini vs. New York Times is an example where the newspaper was sued for publishing freelancers' works electronically, when it only had the rights to publish them in print.[18]

Sometimes newspapers do not permit other newspapers to reproduce or re-format fulltext versions, but they may allow links to their websites. Newspapers also have to be very prudent when using material from other sources. A local newspaper editor gave me the following example. A newspaper once slightly altered an item in a picture from another newspaper to suit the context of its story. There was no malicious intent to infringe and was done quite innocently by the artist concerned. The other newspaper took exception and threatened legal action on the grounds of intentional copyright violation. The matter was resolved without litigation, but a formal apology was demanded and further editions containing the «infringement» had to be withdrawn.

Permission is sometimes denied for reproduction of a whole item (especially images) or portions of it (e.g. the text may be used but not the images), or the usage conditions may be impractical, which means that the desired information cannot be reproduced. This can cause serious gaps in a digital collection, for instance.

Only if a newspaper holds copyright, can it grant permission and charge copyright royalties. Some newspapers in South Africa do charge, but the majority of them waive fees for non-commercial or educational purposes. They naturally require full acknowledgement. However, international newspapers charge high copyright royalties, which are obviously payable in foreign currency.

If a newspaper does not hold copyright and has no mandate to grant permission for reproduction of works, it has to refer users to rights holders/owners directly. This is timeconsuming and problematic, especially if the rights-holder's whereabouts are unknown, or where there is more than one author/artist. Also, where rights holders/owners are deceased, their heirs have to be contacted. Establishing who the heirs are and their whereabouts presents many problems. It is also difficult to trace rights holders/owners if, for example, they are defunct entities or have merged with other entities, or have assigned their rights to third parties.

Copyright and News-Clipping Services

In South Africa, there are many media monitoring services or news-clipping services provided by libraries and commercial firms. I visited two firms in Johannesburg, namely, Newsclip Media Monitoring and SA Press Group, to find out how copyright affected them.

Newsclip subscribes to over 800 periodical and newspaper titles and provides mainly *original* clippings to their clients. Copyright is not a problem, except in cases where it is necessary to photocopy an article. A representative of this firm confirmed that the provision of original clippings to their clients was in accordance with fair dealing, as provided for in Section 12 of the Copyright Act.

SA Press Group also subscribes to a large number of journal and newspapers, but provides *photocopied* clippings to its clients. It finds copyright fees very expensive and the clearance process very slow and problematic. In recent years, the Group has entered into many formal licence agreements with rights holders/owners, to enable it to provide an efficient service to its clients. It also provides an online article service, which is licensed. A representa-

---

18 Tasini v New York Times – http://www.jmls.edu/cyber/cases/tasini1.html

tive of this firm said that he would like to see the establishment of a Newspaper Licensing Agency in South Africa, as this would be a solution to the ongoing copyright problems. The process could then be streamlined and the collection of royalties would be centralized.

I also spoke to a Johannesburg-based corporate librarian of a large international firm. She provides a clipping service for staff only, via the Intranet. She confirmed that copyright clearance is problematic and very slow and that royalties are excessive. Users require information virtually immediately and cannot wait for weeks to obtain permission. She suggested that newspapers should rather include a copyright fee in their subscription fee to allow for copying and scanning of articles, particularly for in-house or Intranet purposes. Alternatively, she felt that a Newspaper Licensing Agency might resolve the problems, but only if the fees were reasonable and requests could be submitted retrospectively and not prior to reproduction.

Copyright and Digitization Projects

Our copyright law does not permit multiple copying (other than in the limited exceptions in Section 13 of the Act). It does not permit adaptations or conversions, without prior permission. In most digitization projects, the goal is to provide better access to more users. This involves multiple copying, which is not permitted in the legislation. Also, the technical process of digitization automatically creates more than one copy, so for digitizing a whole or large portion of a newspaper collection, copyright clearance is necessary. Rights holders/owners are reluctant to give permission for digitization projects, especially since they can be accessed by millions of people all over the world.

There are also practical problems involved in obtaining permission for such projects. For example, the Digital Imaging Project of South Africa (DISA) experienced problems with copyright when digitizing a previously banned collection of anti-Apartheid periodicals for the period 1960 to 1990.[19] The clearance process was exceptionally slow. Some rights holders/owners did not respond to requests for permission. Others could not be traced, so some works could not be cleared for copyright. These works had to be excluded from the project, thus leaving gaps in the collection. Copyright fees were waived for this project, because of the nature of the material, but for other projects, copyright clearance could become an expensive budgetary item. One of the problems facing librarians, when seeking digitization rights, is the very considerable variation in pricing, which they experience from different sources. Many smaller publishers appear willing to grant permission without charge, while large publishers' methods and rates of payment vary considerably. [20]

Digital preservation is a vital part of the creation and management of any digital collection. Invariably, any preservation strategy will require the occasional re-mastering of the digital images (possibly onto new storage media) or re-formatting (to accommodate new technological changes). This will also require permission from the copyright holders/owners. It is therefore good practice to negotiate rights to move and change file formats «in perpetuity» where possible, so that the project does not have to seek permission each time such a change is made as part of the preservation strategy. [21]

---

19 DISA website: http://disa.nu.ac.za

20 Copyright Clearance and Digitisation in UK/Higher Education: Supporting Study for the JISC/PA Clearance Mechanisms Working Party. *Unpredictability of pricing.* Ch. 4.3. p. 7 URL: http://www.ukoln. ac.uk/services/elib/papers/pa/clearance/study.doc [March 13, 2003]

21 Managing Digitisation Projects. *Copyright Strategy.* p. 1 URL: http://www.tasi.ac.uk/advice/managing/ copyrights.html [May 13,2003]

When negotiating contracts for copyright clearance and usage of material, provisions must be made for fair use, inter-library loans, archiving, hyperlinking, and multiple copying, if possible. Indemnities against litigation or prosecution should also be secured. It is important that any digitization project (and its host institution) considers issues such as ethics, data protection, the intellectual property of the works in the collection, as well as the intellectual property of the project itself. This includes providing simple, concise copyright notices on the project's web page, stating how and for what purposes the material can be used.[22]

Barriers to Accessing Information

Unfortunately, copyright creates problems for news-clipping services, but more so, it creates barriers for libraries and archival services, especially with regard to preservation projects, including microfilming and digitization. Most libraries or archives depots have newspaper collections and many are in a poor condition caused by various factors, e.g. brittle or inferior paper, damage by worms and other pests, poor atmospheric conditions, constant usage or inadequate storage space, etc. Many are too fragile to be handled any more and unless they are preserved properly, they will not be accessible at all.

Newspapers are an important part of a country's heritage and history and are used by consumers from all walks of life, for all different purposes. They should not be allowed to deteriorate to the extent that the information contained in them is lost forever. Although most libraries in South Africa, as well as in other developing countries, do not have the resources to convert newspapers or other collections to other formats, e.g. microfilm or digital formats, some have been fortunate to receive donations from international donors to address special collections. Because of the many problems associated with copyright, libraries needing to microfilm or digitize newspaper collections can only include very old material, which is already in the public domain. If the collection is split into different formats, based on which sections have been cleared for copyright, there will be problems with storage, preservation and maintenance of the split collections. Moreover, access to the information contained in the collections will be hampered.

For preservation purposes and accessibility purposes, newspapers need to be microfilmed and digitized. However, libraries and archives depots are faced with copyright clearance and associated problems with regard to material that is not yet in the public domain. Very often, there is a lack of funds for copyright clearance too. This means that part of or whole collections of newspapers will eventually be lost to everyone. Newspaper publishers themselves do not keep back-runs of their publications for any length of time and have effectively transferred the responsibility and financial burden of maintenance and preservation of newspapers to libraries and archival services. In fact, many newspapers refer users to libraries when they receive requests for their earlier publications. Libraries are expected to maintain, preserve and make these publications available to users, but receive little or no resources or assistance from newspaper publishers. This problem needs to be addressed. Newspaper publishers need to play a more responsible role if they want their publications to serve the citizens of South Africa, as well as other interested users around the world, for more than one generation.

---

22 Managing Digitisation Projects. *Copyright Guidelines and Ethics.* p. 2. URL: http:// http://www.tasi.ac.uk/advice/managing/copyrights.html [May 13, 2003]

Conclusion

Copyright has various practical implications and complications for newspaper publishers themselves, as well as for consumers and collectors of newspapers. Although copyright has its positive aspects for creators and authors, it is often a barrier to accessing information for users. It retards the dissemination of information, e.g. in libraries, as well as in archival and news-clipping services. It definitely creates a barrier to microfilming and digitization projects and in the process, it affects access to information in newspaper collections.

It is clear that a more streamlined copyright clearance system is necessary in South Africa, but newspaper publishers should still be allowed to waive copyright fees for non-commercial and educational purposes.

Newspaper publishers also need to work closely with libraries and archival services to ensure that newspaper collections are maintained, preserved and stored in the best possible way to serve all users, for this generation and for future generations.

I believe that appropriate provisions for the microfilming and digitization of information for archival and library preservation purposes should be included in our legislation, either in the Legal Deposit Act or in the Copyright Act. Apart from libraries and archival services, the Government itself has a responsibility to preserve the country's heritage and historical treasures, including newspapers, for future generations. I have therefore suggested to our National Library that formal proposals should be submitted to the Government to amend the relevant legislation accordingly.

Newspapers give us yesterday's stories, today's news and tomorrow's wealth of information. Copyright laws need to facilitate, not restrict, access to these treasures.

OPPORTUNITIES FOR NEWSPAPER PRESERVATION AND ACCESS IN SOUTH AFRICA

Opening Address

George Claassen

Deputy Editor, Die Burger, Cape Town, South Africa

When I grew up in Mpumalanga province – those days it was called the Eastern Transvaal High-and Lowveld – my parents daily bought three newspapers, one an Afrikaans morning paper, one an Afrikaans afternoon paper, and one English afternoon paper. Unfortunately only the English paper has survived.

When my grandfather died in the mid-seventies I inherited an edition from the Cape Argus of January 1896 that described the Jameson Raid into the Transvaal Republic in detail. That impressed me, that I could read a newspaper published that long ago to see how they reported an important historical event that would eventually lead to the Ango-Boer War three years later.

The word «daily» or «journal» (from the Latin diurnalis) has been an important part of newspapers ever since the acta diurna, bulletins of daily events or transactions which were first posted in 59 ad in the Roman Forum on the orders of Julius Caesar. According to the Roman historian Suetonius, Caesar also ordered an official version of the daily proceedings of the senate (much like the modern-day Hansard) to be posted in public. The acta senatus included speeches made and decisions taken in the senate.[1]

The contents of the acta diurna was very similar to today's newspapers, containing information about Caesar as head of state, his family, the birthdays and funerals of important Romans, and trials and executions. Also information on aspects of special interest to the Romans, such as the fall of a meteorite, and even sports news – the outcome of gladiatorial contests – were included.

As the actus diarnus comprised official information only, it should be seen as as the forerunner of government or official propaganda publications, rather than newspapers as such. However, it was not long before an enterprising Roman named Chrestus began collecting information (from news about bumper crops to the burning of witches at the stake) and selling this on the contemporary local markets. In this sense he became one of the first journalists (from Latin diurnarius, diary writer). The Roman writer and orator Cicero who died in 43 ad, was quite upset about the sensational news that Chrestus published – not unlike the reactions of many present-day heads of state, the Flemish communications historian T. Luykx wrote in his book Evolutie van de communicatie media.

The earliest newspapers from which more closely resembles the modern-day version can probably be traced to China where a publication similar to a court journal, entitled Tsing Pao, appeared about 500 ad.[2]

---

1   Pedro Diederichs and Arrie de Beer, Newspapers: the Fourth Estate – a cornerstone of democracy, in A. S. de Beer *Mass media towards the Millennium: the South African handbook of communication* Pretoria: J. L. van Schaik Publishers, 1996, p.86

2   ibid., p.87

But it was only in the 15th century with the invention of moveable type by German gold-smith Johannes Gutenberg (1398-1468) that the printing industry developed. This led to the publication of what are now known as newspapers.

By 1620 primitive newspapers were being published in Germany and Holland with the Dutch presenting news of the Thirty Year's War in English in London in 1621. These publications were known as «diurnals» or corantos (from the French courant, English «running» and Afrikaans lopend. Note the Afrikaans word koerant and Dutch krant). It is commonly accepted that the first weekly was the German Avisa Relation oder Zeitung (1609). Historians seem to agree that the first daily newspaper was the German Leipziger Zeiting of 1660. And Oxford saw the first truly English newspaper when the Oxford Gazette was published in 1665 and the first daily became the Daily Courant in 1702.

In South Africa there were no real newspapers for the first 150 years after the founding of the Cape by the Dutch in 1652. Even before the start of the first newspapers, the diaries of the Cape «freedom fighter» Adam Tas caused an uproar, due to his chronicles of the unjust policies of governor Willem-Adriaan van der Stel. But the first small bilingual newspaper, The Cape Town Gazette and African Advertiser/Kaapsche Stads Courant en Afrikaansche Berigter, was published on 16 August 1800. This was the only newspaper that was allowed and it was printed on a government-owned press. The editors, Alexander Walker and John Robertson, undertook to «make it their particular and anxious study to collect the most authentic materials, and lay before the public the information thus obtained, in the fair Simplicity of Truth,» writes the Afrikaans historian Christoff Muller in his press history of Nasionale Pers, Sonop in die suide[3].

Today South Africa has more than 200 weekly newspapers, mostly bilingual Afrikaans/English papers of towns or suburbs, as well as 17 daily papers, and 6 Sunday papers. And these are all testimony that prophets of doom who predicted during the height of the dot.com years that newspapers would die, were wrong, in the words of Mark Twain in a telegram in 1897, «The reports of my death are greatly exaggerated».

Today newspapers fulfil the needs of the curious, what the former publisher of The Washington Post, Phil Graham, described as follows:

I am insatiably curios about the state of the world. I am constantly intrigued by information of topicality. I revel in the recitation of the daily and weekly grist of journalism.[4]

And in many instances, the newspaper has since the 17th century become one of the most important documents providing an insight into events of the past. That's why, for future generations, that although this morning's Die Burger and Cape Times may be old news by this afternoon when the Cape Argus gives us an update of news, all three will be the best testimony of important news, as well as advertisements reflecting our age, announcements of social events and other not so important trivia of this day.

To quote Phil Graham again, newspapers have the «inescapably impossible task of providing every week a first rough draft of a history that will never be completed about a world we can never really understand …[5]»

We indeed provide the first rough draft of history and it is important for future generations to be able to access those first drafts to understand the past and their own era and lifetime.

3　C. J. F. Muller *Snoop in die suide – geboorte en groei van die Nasionale Pers, 1915-1948*. Cape town: Nasionale Boekhandel, 1990, p.3

4　Katharine Graham 1997. *Personal history*. New York: Alfred A. Knopf, 1997, p.324

5　ibid., p.324

CURRENT INTERNATIONAL NEWSPAPER WORK

Hartmut Walravens

Berlin State Library, Germany

Newspapers have a bad reputation with many librarians and archivists – they are bulky, difficult to assemble as full sets, hard to catalogue because of different editions and frequent title changes, awkward to collate and to preserve. Readers love them but complain about the difficulties of tracking newspaper holdings and accessing them. Newspapers often have the lowest priority in libraries and archives, not only in times of shrinking budgets. To stimulate international interest in newspaper work and promote their preservation and improve access to them, the International Federation of Library Associations (IFLA) sponsored a Round Table of Newspapers under its auspices, which comprised a small group of newspaper experts who met during IFLA general conferences, and in addition arranged extended business meeting at changing venues. The current reorganisation of IFLA demanded that newspaper work be elevated to the official status of a Section, or to downgraded to a short-lived Discussion Group. As newspaper work will not cease in the foreseeable future, the status of a Section was adopted. This will mean a change from informal membership to the requirements of IFLA, which include defined terms for officers, as well as appointment and election of members for certain periods of time. Considering the small number of co-operating newspaper specialist worldwide this may cause practical problems in future.

The Newspaper Section is involved in a number of activities and projects:

At the forthcoming IFLA General Conference, it will hold an open session on the subject of Newspapers and Copyright – a really hot item at national as well as international level. Digitization projects and electronic document delivery practices, to name just two relevant issues, must be supported by copyright legislation, otherwise there will be grave limitations. It is not always just the legal situation – sometimes it is a matter of practicality: who would be able to track all the people (journalists, photographers, correspondents) who contributed to a newspaper and get their approval for digitization?

After the main conference the Section will organize a Post Conference entitled «Newspapers in central and Eastern Europe» (August 9-11). Four main subject areas will be introduced by keynote speakers and then dealt with in a number of individual contributions. A visit to the local newspaper department as well as an excursion to Leipzig (National Library, Institute for Preservation) are on the agenda.

The next business meeting, which by tradition will combine visits to local newspaper collections and meetings with newspaper experts, will probably take place in Shanghai in 2004.

A very important event will be a hands-on workshop on newspaper digitization to be run in Mikkeli (Finland) by invitation of the Centre of Microfilming and Preservation of Helsinki University Library. The excellent results that the Centre's staff presented at the end of the TIDEN project (see www.tiden.kb.se) which was a joint Scandinavian undertaking, and the current popularity of digitization projects worldwide seem to call for such a seminar. Our Scandinavian colleagues have top-ranking experience in such difficult projects, both from the technical and the organizational sides, and it would save people a lot of effort preparing projects of their own if they could gain the necessary experience beforehand, instead of trying to reinvent the wheel at high cost. Therefore a hands-on presentation was preferred to giving lectures. Participants will be directly and practically involved in the scanning, digitizing, OCR-ing and managing newspaper texts.

A project which is very closely connected to the above-mentioned seminar is the preparation of guidelines for the best practice of microfilming for digitization. It is quite obvious that good quality results from scanning newspaper microfilms can only be expected if the films themselves are of a high standard. The guidelines are therefore intended to lay the basis for successful projects in the future.

Achievements in the recent past include:

The compilation of guidelines for preservation microfilming of newspapers and others serials. They were published as an IFLA publication and alerted specialists to basic conditions which must be observed when doing microfilming. Unfortunately, it cannot be taken for granted that filming companies follow the latest developments and requirements, at least not worldwide, and reports of low quality work reaches the Section only too often.

The organisation (together with IFLA PAC) of a conference on Preservation and Access to Serials and Newspapers in Paris in 1999. The proceedings have just been published by K. G. Saur: *Proceedings of the IFLA symposium managing the preservation of periodicals and newspapers.* Bibliothèque Nationale de France, Paris, 21-24 August 2000. Edited by Jennifer Budd, IFLAPAC. Munich: Saur 2002 (IFLA Publications.103).

The development of a questionnaire to be used internationally for the creation of a topography of newspaper holdings. It had to be concise and precise, yet it needed to be intelligible by «ordinary» librarians and not only by newspaper specialists. The result is a two-page questionnaire which has been tried out in Germany, with feedback being mounted on the internet in an attractive searchable file. (URL http://daten.zeitschriftendatenbank.de/projekte/zeitungstopographie/allgemein.html).

On-going activities of the Section include:

The preparation for publication of the collected papers presented at recent IFLA conferences. As the venue changes every year, and as the Section – in the interest of better outreach – has often focussed on that particular area, the publication of these papers is expected to be of much interest.

A newsletter is disseminated in printed form but also available on the IFLA website (www.ifla.org), where further information on the Section is available.

The Section has profited enormously from the enthusiasm and expertise of its members, especially those in North America, Great Britain, France, and Scandinavia where newspaper work has a relatively high priority and where holdings are well catalogued and microfilmed (e.g. NewsPlan, US Newspaper Project, Bibliographie de la presse française). Nevertheless, even there much work still needs to be done. More so in many other countries where the holdings of newspapers are inaccessible or even unknown, not to speak of proper measure for preservation microfilming.

The best way to improve the newspaper situation is co-operation and exchange of information. Therefore the Section invites interested colleagues to join and co-operate.

Having its business meeting in Cape Town, in co-operation with the National Library of South Africa, has not only given the members of the Section new ideas and impressions, but meeting colleagues from all over South Africa, and even Namibia, has also given us a much better understanding of the region's situation and needs, and fostered good relations.

A few words on the newspaper situation in Germany

Some of the earliest newspapers were published in Germany, and so it has a rich tradition. Owing to political decentralization, however, newspapers were not collected centrally, and there was no national library until 1912, which, founded by book publishers, excluded newspapers from their collection profile. World War II wreaked havoc on German newspaper collections, and only a part survived; others which escaped destruction were held by Polish libraries, and still others were removed to the Soviet Union.. The year 2003 was a highlight as the Russian State Library in Moscow returned several tons of German newspapers to Germany, realizing that they had neither readers, nor means to preserve them.

Germany has its union catalogue of serials, ZDB (*Zeitschriftendatenbank*) which, among its 1.1 million titles also boasts about 60,000 newspapers and similar publications. ZDB includes electronic newspapers, digitizations and microforms (masters and user's copies). There is a national preservation programme supported by the German Research Association (Deutsche Forschungsgemeinschaft) but owing to insufficient holdings information, its practical application is by no means systematic. German libraries and archives are therefore trying to implement a national newspaper project along the lines of the United States Newspaper Project as the only way to take stock of what is extant.

Nevertheless, many newspapers are available in microform, through the good offices of Mikrofilmarchiv der Deutschen Presse (Microfilm Archives of the German Press), a not-for-profit organisation that accumulated over the years approximately 25,000 reels of microfilm. So far no major digitization project has taken place. Recently the Austrian National Library embarked on such a project after studying the Scandinavian Tiden model.

A few years ago, K. G. Saur in Munich published its *International Newspaper Holdings in German Libraries* (3rd ed. 2001, 2 vols., with geographical index), comprising about 54,000 records.

Another useful tool is *Zeitungen und zeitungsähnliche Periodika, ihre Beschreibung und Erfassung in der Zeitschriftendatenbank* (Newspapers and similar publications, their description and cataloguing in the German Union catalogue of serials), also published by K. G. Saur (1998). This is not so much a cataloguing code but an illustrated newspaper handbook for cataloguers and newspaper experts.

NEWSPAPERS AT THE NATIONAL LIBRARY AND ARCHIVES OF CANADA

Sandra Burrows

Newspaper Specialist, Library and Archives Canada

[Note: the following is the text contained in a PowerPoint presentation – Ed.]

1. Newspaper Collections

Print:

- all first, last and special (supplements, historical) issues of Canadian newspapers.
- a select number of Canadian dailies since 1967 (10 titles).
- a representative number of Canadian dailies maintained in print until the microform arrives.
- all ethnic and native newspapers.
- a large number of student newspapers.
- a select number of foreign newspapers.

The NLC has an archival collection of 18,000 bound volumes of print newspapers

Microform:

- Newspapers in print form are not subject to legal deposit.
- All newspapers published on microform after 1988 are subject to legal deposit.
- If a run of 4 to 100 is produced, the publisher must send one copy.
- If a run of over 100 is produced, two copies are required.

The NLC collects all Canadian newspapers on microform. We purchase titles filmed for preservation purposes (under 4 runs produced) as funds permit.

Accommodation:

The Library and Archives has submitted a report to Treasury Board for an interim collections facility to house print newspapers, presently stored in one onsite and two offsite locations. The facility would also house Archival Federal Records Centre documents.

2. Newspaper Access

AMICUS : The Canadian National Catalogue on the Web: http://www.nlc-bnc.ca/amicus/index.html

Search via:

* Title
* Subject
* AMICUS number.

Newspapers at NLC Web Site http://www.nlc-bnc.ca/8/16/index-e.html

* Canadian ethnic newspapers currently received – alphabetical list.
* Canadian ethnic newspapers currently received – language-group list.
* Canadian newspapers currently received – alphabetical list.
* Canadian newspapers currently received – geographical list.
* Canadian newspapers on microform held by the National Library of Canada.
* Checklist of indexes to Canadian newspapers held by the National Library of Canada.
* Engine of Immortality: Canadian newspapers from 1752 until today – A new feature!
* Native newspapers currently received.
* Non-Canadian newspapers currently received.
* Special editions of Canadian newspapers.
* Student newspapers currently received.

3. Library and Archives of Canada Newspapers National Strategy

The report Canadian newspapers online: a national consultation (October 2002) is available at: http://www.nlc-bnc.ca/8/3/r3-650-e.html. It aims to explore co-operative strategies to strengthen, on a national basis, online access to contemporary and historical newspaper content for Canadians. The ultimate goal is to begin to articulate a national strategy to strengthen access and preservation of Canadian online newspapers. Approximately 80 participants came from all sectors, including newspaper publishers, commercial information providers, researcher institutions, and libraries.

Recommendations re: Leadership:

* In the short term, the Library and Archives of Canada should initiate a working group of representative stakeholders to continue the dialogue begun with the consultation. This working group would flesh out the issues, define required actions, and develop a national digital newspaper preservation and access strategy.
* Consider establishing a Canadian Newspaper Centre. With the new Library and Archives of Canada in a leading role, such a Centre could address on a more permanent and high-

profile basis the strategies developed by the working group, including legislation, standards, and preservation. It would lobby for funds, be a research centre of excellence, and develop digitization toolkits and other resources.

* Promote the value of digital newspapers as a source of information for Canadian education, research and innovation at all levels through advocacy by a coalition of leaders.

* Monitor newspaper access and preservation initiatives in other countries, including the goals and activities of the American working group on newspapers formed under the OCLC Digital and Preservation Co-operation.

Recommendations re: Canadian Digital Newspaper Content:

* Comprehensive historical coverage should be the overarching goal, both for the preservation of currently-produced online newspaper content and for retrospective digitization of historical Canadian newspapers.

* Respect the current complementary approach, whereby the private sector digitizes those Canadian dailies for which they see a market, and public-sector-based projects digitize newspapers of more local or limited reach.

* Strengthen pan-Canadian coverage by developing a strong provincial approach, building upon and extending the scope of the original Decentralized Plan for Canadian Newspapers.

* The Library and Archives of Canada or Canadian Initiative on Digital Libraries (CIDL) should inventory all online newspapers and retrospective digitization projects, including those of libraries, historical societies, genealogical and other associations so that the full extent of gaps in coverage can be better known.

* Prepare an integrated, pan-Canadian strategy to address retrospective newspaper digitization. The focus should be on needs assessment, funding priorities, a business model, coordinated collaborative applications for funding, and a plan for funding the digitization of newspapers of limited or niche-market interest. Such a document would assist in the development of private/public sector partnerships.

Recommendations re: a National Strategy:

* Compulsory legal deposit of electronic newspapers is recommended.

* A business case for the digitization of Canadian newspapers should be prepared, and special government funding sought.

Recommendations re: National Technical Standards:

* Inventory standards employed in current projects.

* Develop a set of recommended practices. For example, digitization projects in Canada should support, as a minimum, full-text keyword searching and the ability to view the original page image.

* The Library and Archives of Canada should continue to provide leadership in dialogue/ discussions on technical standards, which should be vendor neutral to allow maximum interoperability.

NEWSPAPER ACCESS AND PRESERVATION IN FRANCE, MARCH 2003

Else Delaunay and Isabelle Rollet

Bibliothèque nationale de France, Paris

Before trying to present to you what is done concerning the access and preservation policy of France and, especially, the French National Library, the Bibliothèque nationale de France (BnF), it may be interesting to give you some historical background. The BnF has its roots in the King's Library of the 15th century. Legal deposit was established in 1537 by King Francis I and the holdings have been kept in the vicinity of the Richelieu building since 1666. The library's organization into five sections hardly changed until the middle of the last century. It was only in 1936 that a special section was created dedicated to periodicals and newspapers, and was given its own stacks and reading room in 1960. The first historical newspaper is *La Gazette* by Théophraste Renaudot (30 May 1631) and its call-number is «Lc2 1» (Lc2 is the classification number for «The Press»). We have around 350,000 titles of periodicals, from the 17th century to the present day, kept on 60km. of shelving. The periodical collection alone is growing by 1km. a year. We receive between 50,000 and 60,000 current titles by Legal Deposit, adding 5,000 new titles each year.

In 1992, after some controversy, the Authorities decided to move all the printed materials to the new building in Tolbiac. It was not only the transportation of more than 10 million items we had to perform but also the re-organization of the holdings coming from the former books and periodicals sections into four new sections: «History and Social Sciences», «Law, Economics and Political Science», «Science and Technology» and «Literature and Arts», with each section now keeping periodicals as well as books. Newspapers are now kept in the «Law, Economics and Social Science» section, together with Official Publications, among the 25,000 running titles which we have to deal with. This section houses 40 to 50% of our Legal Deposit acquisitions.

Access

Access to newspaper collections in France has been improved especially through bibliographic control.

Databases

BN-OPALE PLUS is the general database of the Bibliothèque nationale de France. It also provides bibliographic information on all French newspapers. Most microfilms available in the BnF to date are included in BN-OPALE PLUS. This may be accessed through our website http://www.bnf.fr.

The database of the Union Catalogue of Periodicals («Catalogue Collectif National» or CCN) also provides bibliographic records of newspapers. Normally the catalogue goes back to 1960 but one may find records long before that date. In fact it is intended that the Union catalogue should include all periodical holdings from the beginning of the 17th century. «Myriade», its CD-ROM edition, when it was updated in 2001, contained some 360,000 entries and 1,500,000 locations. Now the catalogue has been merged into the National

Union Catalogue of France (Catalogue Collectif de France) http://www.ccfr.bnf.fr which includes information on all holdings of monographs and serial publications in about 3,000 French libraries and institutions. It is updated regularly. At present it includes 15 million entries.

Printed catalogues

The *Dictionary of newspapers published from 1600 to 1789* (*Dictionnaire des journaux 1600-1789*), by Jean Sgard is a union catalogue of some twenty European libraries and archives recording 1,267 titles

French local newspapers

The Bibliography of French Local Newspapers (*Bibliographie de la Presse française politique et d'information générale*) is both a national bibliography and a national union catalogue. Department by Department (France is divided into ninety Departments), political and general information newspapers published between 1800 and 1944 are recorded here together with the holdings kept by different libraries and archives. Each volume includes an historical introduction, an alphabetical list of bibliographic records with information on holdings in various institutions, and a chronological index. Fifty-four volumes have been published so far. When the bibliography has been completed it will include more than 40 000 newspaper titles and give information on holdings kept by hundreds of institutions in France – such as local city libraries, National, district or city archives, learned societies, the BnF, etc.– in original format or on microfilm.

The catalogue of Alsatian Newsprint (*La Presse alsacienne, 1870-1918*) deals with the period between 1870 and 1918 when Alsace was governed by Germany. This was a very important time for newspaper publishing. The catalogue contains complete bibliographic records of original or microfilmed files available at the Section for Alsatian items of the National and University Library in Strasburg which keeps a unique collection of more than 200 newspapers from that period as it was a legal deposit library. The catalogue was published in 1982 with grants from the Regional Council of Alsace.

In 1990, the Direction du Livre et de la Lecture (DLL) (Direction of Books and Reading), linked to the Ministry of Culture, published the second edition of French Local Newspapers (*La Presse régionale française, catalogue collectif des périodiques microfilmés*), a union catalogue of newspaper files available on microfilm. It is a catalogue resulting from the microfilm programmes conducted and completed by the DLL in co-operation with different local public libraries in France, assisted by the Bibliothèque nationale de France when complete holdings could not be located within the regions concerned. The Bibliothèque nationale de France would then lend missing issues for microfilming and also buy a duplicate positive of the titles filmed.

French former colonial territories

During the last fifteen years numerous new catalogues have been published in France on various categories of newspapers and their location in libraries and archives. There has also been a regular updating of already published catalogues (new editions of printed catalogues) or databases.

Serials published in Senegal between 1856 and 1982 (*Les Publications en série éditées au Sénégal, 1856-1982*) and kept by the Bibliothèque Nationale de France. It is a kind of preliminary list of periodicals from Senegal. Each record includes title, subtitle, title changes, BnF's shelfmark and holding with missing issues or gaps. It was compiled by Marie-Elisabeth Bouscarle in 1986 and published in BnF's series Etudes, Guides et Inventaires, no.7.

In 1982 Gil-François Euvrard published a dissertation for the French State School of Librarians in Lyon, concerning newspapers in the French West Africa colonies from the eariest times until their independence, and kept by the Bibliothèque nationale de France (*La Presse en Afrique occidentale française, des origines aux indépendances et conservée à la Bibliothèque nationale*). This bibliography records 674 titles of which some 60 % were published in Senegal. Indexing is by UDC. The bibliography concludes with a list of titles missing in the BnF. All records follow international standards and all holdings were verified in the stacks beforehand.

The *Catalogue of Malagasy Periodicals* («Catalogue des Périodiques malgaches») covers the period from 1874 until 1970. Some 1,000 periodicals in Malagasy or published for Malagasy people in France or elsewhere are recorded in the catalogue with precise information about BnF's holdings. It includes newspapers.

Another catalogue concerning the African area is the *Catalogue of Periodicals published at the Reunion Island from 1794 until 1900* («Catalogue des Périodiques réunionnais de 1794 à 1900») including historical facts on Reunion newspapers during the 19th century. It was published in 1990 by Olivier Caudron, head of the University Library of Reunion. During the 19th century the Reunion people were particularly keen readers of newspapers. Although the BnF keeps a great number of files, many have been lost. One hopes that some titles may yet be rediscovered somewhere in the possession old Reunion families. Titles which are not available any more on the island have been microfilmed (BnF, National Archives Overseas Section, individual collections). The catalogue contains records of 114 newspaper titles.

A catalogue on newspapers and periodicals from the Guadeloupe Island was published in 2000 by the District Archives of the Guadeloupe entitled *Newspapers and periodicals, a catalogue of the newspaper collection* («Journaux et revues, catalogue des collections de presse, Archives départementales de la Guadeloupe», 2000), with a comprehensive introduction by Ghislaine Bouchet, head of the Archives. This catalogue includes several indexes : alphabetical title index, chronological title index, index of editors, index of publication places, thematic index, numerical index of microfilmed newspapers and, finally, a list of illustrations. The catalogue records some 200 titles kept by the Archives in Basse-Terre. It covers publications from Guadeloupe and the West Indies, even those published in other islands with links to Guadeloupe and the West Indies, from the end of the 18th century right up to the present day. The Archives has received legal deposit material since 1946 as the French law did not include the overseas departments until that date. The administrative deposit made by the printers started in 1881 according to the Act on the freedom of the press.

The *Catalogue of Vietnamese Periodicals* («Catalogue des Périodiques vietnamiens de la Bibliothèque Nationale»), compiled by Jean-Claude Poitelon and Nguyen Tat Dac, was published by the BnF in 1993 on microfiche. BnF's holdings of Vietnamese periodicals makes up one of the most important collections worldwide. It probably ranks first in regard to the items published during the first half of the 20th century, especially between 1922 and the end of World War II. The catalogue records periodicals published in Vietnam, or written in Vietnamese, or meant for Vietnamese people, or dealing with Vietnam. It gives information about 2350 publications. The microfiche edition reproduces recent and accurate inventory cards. However, the catalogue should be considered to be a kind of working file. A printed catalogue may be published later.

Commercial catalogues of periodicals on microfilm, especially newspapers

The *ACRPP* Catalogue, 16th edition, Paris, 1998. ACRPP stands for «Association for the Conservation and Photographic Reproduction of the Press», a non-profit agency founded by the BnF and some other institutions and newsprint companies. The catalogue gives information on around 6000 files of French periodicals (including French overseas periodicals), newspapers and magazines being reproduced on 35 mm unperforated silver halide films up to international standards for archival microfilming. The records include information on BnF's holdings when used for microfilming. Gaps in the holdings have been completed prior to filming whenever possible. Collection origin is indicated in the catalogue as well as on the films. From 1958 to 1991 ACRPP was BnF's almost exclusive microfilming agency for newsprint. At present newsprint microfilming is carried out by a few more agencies. Microfilms can be ordered directly from ACRPP acrpp@compuserve.com.

A small Catalogue published by *ARMELL*, a former local microfilming and restoration unit for the Loire departments (that is Western France) registers newspapers, serials and other items available on microfilm. The first edition was published in 1987, updated with yearly supplements (the last of which was published in July 1994). On the whole, the catalogue contains some 50 local papers available on 35 mm unperforated silver halide films. ARMELL was located in BnF's technical centre in Sablé (300 km west of Paris) taking advantage of technical assistance from BnF's staff in Sablé when needed, so as to ensure a high quality level for the films.

As to EROMM (European Register of Microform Masters), the microfilmed newspaper holdings of the BnF have not yet been recorded in that database. France (that is to say, the BnF) conducted the pilot project which is now complete. It involved four countries: the United Kingdom, Portugal, Germany and France. Control of EROMM has passed to Germany (the University Library in Göttingen) which is now responsible for further development of the project. Technical microfilm data should be added to the BN-OPALE PLUS database soon. That means for each title title: name of the owner of the master negative, filming agent's name, number of images and reels, type of film used, vertical or horizontal placement of the frames, reduction ratio, etc.

Preservation policy

In the perspective of the new library building, special grants were allocated for microfilming programmes. And indeed, from 1991 to 1995, 250 back files were microfilmed resulting in some 2,5 million images covering various types of newspapers: national and regional dailies, financial papers, fashion magazines, sport papers and illustrated children's papers. But since 1995, serious financial cuts have forced us to cut back our ambitious plans. On average we now get 300,000 euros (2 million rands) a year for the microfilming of our back files, 150,000 euros (1 million rands) for the microfilming of current local dailies (17 titles with numerous local editions), 40,000 euros (300,000 rands) for purchases (mostly from the ACRPP catalogues), and 300,000 euros (1 million rands) for current acquisition of microfilm (subscription to 53 current titles: 12 national papers, 17 local papers and 24 foreign papers). This means 800,000 images for back files and 200,000 images for local papers. In the library workshop, in Sablé-sur-Sarthe, we produce 500,000 to 600,000 images a year (microfilms of newspapers only).

The figures could seem impressive, but it means approximately only 30 to 40 meters of volumes transfered to microfilm a year. Up to now, since 1958 when microfilming began, 2,5km. of volumes have been copied onto microfilms, representing 80,000 reels (100,000 including acquisitions). So you understand easily that there is still a lot to do to preserve efficiently more than 10km. of our newspaper holdings.

As in any library, most of the material printed between 1870 and 1960 is in poor condition and requires swift intervention. From 1982 to 1999, all heavy restoration of newspapers was carried out in the workshop of the BnF in Provins, which has now closed down. Each year, around 60,000 sheets were deacidified and laminated with a polyamid layer. However in 18 years, we treated only 900,000 sheets when ten times as much needed treatment.

The paper restoration is now carried out in the new workshop at Bussy-St-Georges, but on a smaller scale. Fewer than 10,000 sheets were treated last year by Japanese tissue covering. Some curators are reluctant to carry out polyamid covering as a long-term preservation method.

To my mind, if we can extend the life of the items by 40 or 50 years, it is worth doing. We already know that numerous volumes in our stacks are highly embrittled and some have been lost, but we don't know to what extent.

Digitisation

Our digital library already offers 640 periodical titles (hhtp://www.gallica.fr). The current programme consists of the digitisation of 33 titles of literary and satirical newspapers up to 1914. In prospect is a set of 32 newspapers (national 19th century titles) and nine illustrated weekly supplements (3,800,000 frames).

French newspapers on the web

The two major websites are Europresse (http://www.europresse.com) and Le Portail de la presse (http://www.portail-presse.com).

THE UNITED STATES NEWSPAPER PROGRAM

http://lcweb.loc.gov/preserv/usnppr.html

Ed King

The British Library

(The following is the Editor's realisation of a Power Point presentation.)

The United States Newspaper Program is a massive, coordinated national effort to locate, catalog, preserve, and make available to researchers newspapers published in the United States from the eighteenth century to the present. The program is supported with funds from the National Endowment for the Humanities and with technical and management support provided by the Library of Congress.

USNP cataloging

USNP cataloging is done following Program guidelines and is entered into the CONSER (Cooperative Online Serials Project) database, maintained by OCLC. (See http://lcweb.loc. gov/acq/conser/)

- Detailed holdings data collected by project staff is recorded and maintained in the OCLC union list subsystem.
- Preservation microfilming is done following guidelines and standards developed by Library of Congress.
- Management and coordination of project activities carried out jointly by NEH Division of Preservation and Access and LC USNP Coordinator, following protocols stated in a Library of Congress/NEH interagency agreement signed in 1984.
- Project teams in each state, territory, and the District of Columbia survey every possible repository to locate every U.S. newspaper published since colonial times.
- Complete a full issue-by-issue inventory of all holdings found, including general condition reports.
- Teams survey collections in research libraries, archives, historical societies, publishers offices, and private collections ... And conduct a full inventory of the collections, noting missing issues, title changes and variant editions, and bibliographic relationships.
- Catalogers also note the physical condition of the papers, in order to establish priorities for filming ... Yet too often find that other organic actions have preceded them. This is our one example of a petrified newspaper, discovered in a public library in the «wilds» of Wisconsin.
- Catalogers prepare CONSER bibliographic records for each «title».
- Title changes are dealt with as efficiently as possible, using a single record approach for multiple formats.
- Catalogers also prepare detailed holdings records that assist researchers in locating specific issues for interlibrary loan.

Microfilming

Each state project selects appropriate titles for preservation microfilming, often with the advice of local historians, librarians, archivists, and publishers. Preservation microfilming may be done by an agency within the state, or may be contracted to a preservation micro-filming vendor or service bureau. In all cases, preservation microfilming by USNP projects is governed by established guidelines. Those guidelines can be viewed on the web at: http://lcweb.loc.gov/preserv/usnpguidelines.html.

Quality preservation microfilming

«The aim of the U.S. Newspaper Program is to produce high-quality microfilm records of newspapers that will satisfy the needs and requirements of researchers, archivists, librari-ans, and the general public for all reasonably anticipated purposes, including the use of both text and image material for general and scholarly research, as well as the use of newspaper images for display or exhibition purposes. Every effort shall be made to record in the new format all information contained in and issued with the original newspaper, and to maintain the integrity and authenticity of the representation of the original document on microfilm.» (USNP Microfilming Specifications and Inspection Guidelines.)

- USNP project staff have been accused of mutilating «pristine» bound newspapers in order to preserve the text on microfilm. The reality is quite different. Here's an example of the popular yardstick binding.

- Dealing with brittle materials is a daily task, and heroic efforts are made to retrieve and preserve the content of these newspapers – even when preserving the original is simply not possible.

- Poorly produced microfilm is nothing more than tiny little pictures in a row.

- Objective is to reformat to a more permanent medium, while maintaining as much as possible the integrity and completeness of the information as originally recorded.

- Selection of materials for filming, design of workflow, and choice of vendor varies from state-to-state, depending upon internal factors such as previous experience, resource requirements, and pre-existing regulatory requirements, all done under Program-wide guidelines.

Library of Congress and New York Public Library began microfilming in the late 1930s. At that time, the life expectancy of early film was less than a generation. Current life expectan-cy, when film is produced, processed, and stored in accordance with national and interna-tional standards is 500 years.

- Without training and support, standards can't become practice.

- Without skills, experience, and collaboration, best practices won't emerge.

In the U.S., improvements in preservation microfilming practices in the past decade-and-a-half can be directly credited to support provided by

- NEH Division of Preservation and Access.

- Brittle Books Project Managers meetings.

- RLG publications and training.

- NEDCC publications and workshops.
- SOLINET, AMIGOS training.
- Image Permanence Institute research and development.

In addition, many of the same preservation professionals who developed guidelines for NEHfunded projects have been active in standards work under NISO, AIIM, and ISO. Representatives of Brittle Books Program projects and the USNP have collaborated, both formally and informally, in a wide variety of international preservation microfilming projects, e.g.,

- UK NEWSPLAN.
- European Commission on Preservation and Access.
- EROMM

In spite of the difficulty in reproducing the full page image on most microfilm readers, newspapers are easier than many other text materials to use for research in microfilm format. Newspapers are analog; one moves naturally through the reel as one would through the calendar. Too often, poorly maintained microfilm readers are the real source of dissatisfaction with the format.

Lessons learned

Much of the microfilm produced during the 1950's and 1960's, and even later, is substandard – thus extreme care should be taken before discarding brittle originals.

- Page-by-page collation with film and original.
- USNP projects have been able, in many cases, to create new high-quality film to replace inferior film produced in the past.
- If readers are maintained properly, high-quality microfilm of newspapers is actually easier to use than bulky bound volumes of brittle text.
- Satisfaction is possible, in spite of the critics.

Reformatting onto microfilm is «republishing»: significant effort must be extended in selection, preparation, and editing.

- Garbage in, garbage out.
- Be selective.
- Maintain integrity of the page, issue, illustrations, etc.
- Completeness, including supplements, added materials, editions, «change pages».
- Bibliographic information, including title histories, relationships, etc., must be provided.
- Targets and guides to assist reader in «experiencing» the original.

As of 2002, NEH support for USNP projects totals $48.2 million (U.S.) Additional contribution from state and private funds of approximately $19.3 million (U.S.) We project completion of USNP by 2007, but each project has made the commitment to maintain the database and to continue preservation microfilming of current publishing output. Complete and current projects will produce bibliographic records for 163,300 titles (in more than 60 languages,) and will microfilm 63.3 million pages of newsprint.

What's next?

Ultimately, researchers want access to the CONTENT of newspapers. Manual indexing is tedious and laborious, yet requires intellectual skill. In the U.S., the most successful non-commercial projects have been produced by volunteers (genealogists or retired history faculty) or with student «labor». PC-based indexing «databases» exhibit thesaurus problems; local indexing can't be generalized. Clipping files mutilate newspapers, and filing/subject arrangements are not widely applicable or understood.

Making the digital leap

Convergence in OCR, information retrieval, and user interface tools and software in the past decade make possible what was heretofore only a set of research goals. A variety of «pilot» projects in the past five years provide ample evidence of alternate pathways. Commercialization of «most desired» titles – the titles the public is willing to pay the most for – is proceeding quickly, with competition weeding out weaker or slower players. We assume – with growing evidence – that formats will be proprietary, and thus both an access and preservation problem. For the rest, consensus among producers/users is needed to define best practices and to assure access over the long term.

What we know we want or don't want:

- Garbage in – garbage out.
- No more tiny little pictures.
- Already we see examples on the web that are the digital equivalent of bad microfilm.
- We need to preserve access both to the content and the CONTEXT.
- We need to be able to represent the parts and elements of the newspaper page, and how that changes over time.
- Retrieval should not dis-aggregate the page (clipping excludes context).
- Success will require expertise (like image analysis or multi-language OCR) in areas that we have traditionally assigned to obscure corners of our IT departments, as well as expertise in information retrieval, history, and journalism.

Requirements

- A Framework of Guidance for Building Good Digital Collections (http://www.imls. gov/pubs/forumframework.htm).
- Persistence: «Objects principle 2: A good object is persistent. That is, it will be the intention of some known individual or institution that the good object will persist; that it will remain accessible over time despite changing technologies».

- Interoperability: «Objects principle 3: A good object is digitized in a format that supports current and likely future use or that supports the development of access copies that support those uses. Consequently, a good object is exchangeable across platforms, broadly accessible, and will either be digitized according to a recognized standard or best practice or deviate from standards and practices only for well documented reasons.»

- Authenticity: «Objects principle 6: A good object can be authenticated in at least two senses. First, a user should be able to determine the object's origin, structure, and developmental history (version, etc.) Second, a user should be able to determine that the object is what it purports to be.»

Next steps

- Technical development.

- Content development.

- Management, organization, governance.

- Repository agreements/ assurances.

- Access management.

- Sustainability.

More next steps

- Gain consensus – broaden dialogue.

- Innovate: don't wait to try something; there is still much to be learned through experimentation and demonstration.

- Take advantage of already-converted material to experiment, test, enhance – build research data.

- Create value and innovation through collaboration.

- Prove quality of product through continuing evaluation and innovation.

THE UNITED KINGDOM NEWSPLAN

Beti Jones

Acquisitions Librarian, National Library of Wales

From a personal point of view may I say how happy I am to be in this beautiful city. When I tell you that this is my third visit to Cape Town, you will appreciate my high regard for it, and were it not for the distance that divides us, I would be a far more frequent visitor.

I will be presenting today an overview of NEWSPLAN UK. My part in the project was to be research officer for Wales between 1989 and 1990, working from the National Library of Wales at Aberystwyth. The National Library is situated on a hillside overlooking the town of Aberystwyth, which developed around the castle begun in 1277. From the south side of the building one can see the first evidence of a settlement in the area, the remains of an Iron-Age Fort called Pendinas, dating approximately from 500BC.

Newspapers are an invaluable and heavily used source for many kinds of research, both academic and non-academic, into subjects such as local and family history, social and political history, advertising and sport. By their very nature they are not intended to last indefinitely, and the effects of chemical changes and of wear and tear on their files present libraries with a preservation problem on a large scale.

NEWSPLAN is a comprehensive programme for the identification as well as microfilming and preservation of the local newspapers of the British Isles, including the Republic of Ireland. The programme is based upon co-operation between the British Library, the National Library of Scotland, the National Library of Wales, the National Library of Ireland, and other major research libraries, public and academic libraries, record offices, museums and any other individuals and institutions holding newspaper collections, as well as the newspaper industry itself. All these work together for the preservation of a major element of the printed record of life in the British Isles over the last two hundred years. It seeks, also, to harness the goodwill of the newspaper industry. NEWSPLAN is widely recognised as an example of successful co-operation.

The regions of England are:

East Midland

West Midlands

South West

Yorkshire and Humberside

North Western

Northern

London and South Eastern

The UK NEWSPLAN Panel

Each of these countries, Northern Ireland and the Regions of England had its own committee, with one member from each sitting on the Panel. This devolved structure allowed for local arrangements to be gathered within a centrally controlled framework, allowing the

Project to work effectively with all the library services, and other organisations such as archives and museums, universities and publishers.

The UK NEWSPLAN origins

A pilot NEWSPLAN project was undertaken in the late 1970s by the South-Western Regional Library System (SWRLS), with the support of the British Library. The result was published in 1986 as *NEWSPLAN: report of the pilot project in the South-West,* by Rosemary Wells (Library and Information Report 38. British Library, 1986. ISBN 0-7123-3057-7). This report undertook

- to make a survey of the present holdings of newspaper collections paying special attention to their quality and to the completeness of the existing lists and catalogues and to check their accuracy by examining the holdings of the various repositories.

- to identify the scale of the preservation needs relating to local newspapers, arising from the combination of heavy use, fragility of the newsprint medium, and the often inadequate storage conditions in which newspaper collections are kept. In addition, the report included background information on the history of newspaper development and publishing.

This led to the setting-up of research projects in the regions of England as well as, Scotland, Wales, Northern Ireland and the Republic which was on an all-Ireland basis (a rare situation, one may add and usually restricted to the field of Rugby Union) jointly funded by the relevant regional library system and the British Library. Ten Reports were published listing every local and regional newspaper published in the UK and Ireland.

It was recognised that microfilming to archival standards offered the best medium for preserving and ensuring the long-term survival of the newspapers' contents. It also realised that tackling the problem was likely to be beyond the capacity of any single organisation, that limited resources could be used most effectively through co-ordinated and co-operative programmes.

Microfilming has continued steadily in Aberystwyth, Dublin and Edinburgh, where they continue to produce microfilms of newspapers from the national collection, together with titles from libraries elsewhere. The British Library Newspaper Library (BLNL) website has details of the NEWSPLAN project and reports: www.bl.uk/collections/newspaper/

Since 1992 the BLNL has offered a concessionary rate for NEWSPLAN microfilming. It is important that microfilming is done to the appropriate standard to ensure archival quality and longevity. To assist in this, *Guidelines for the microfilming of Newspapers* by Jennifer MacDougall was published by NEWSPLAN in 1994.

Systematic collection of newspapers did not really begin until 1822. From 1869 onwards newspapers were included in the legal deposit legislation and were deposited directly at the British Museum as it was then known. Currently about 2,600 UK and Irish newspaper and weekly/fortnightly periodical titles are received. This includes the main London edition of the national daily and Sunday newspapers, and free newspapers, with the exception of those consisting entirely of advertising.

Major overseas newspapers in European languages are collected, where possible on microfilm, selectively to complement the UK and Irish collections. About 250 titles are currently received, including the most significant newspapers from most English-speaking countries and from western and eastern Europe.

Over 52,000 separate newspaper, journal, and periodical titles are currently held in the BLNL. The Newspaper Library's collections in Colindale extends for 20 miles; with over 664,000 bound volumes and parcels. Most Commonwealth and Colonial newspapers, which were formerly received through copyright deposit, as well as those from other overseas nations are currently purchased on microfilm rather than in the original.

The first national NEWSPLAN conference was held at Stoke Rochford Hall in Lincolnshire in 1991. It dealt mainly with problems involved in implementing recommendations in Reports. Both the 1994 and 1998 Conferences were held at Durham, the theme of the former was «Current perspectives on newspaper preservation and access» and latter «NEWS-PLAN, Millennia and Grids: the digital challenges». The papers given at this conference highlighted some of the prospects for libraries in an increasingly digital environment. They drew attention to the practical difficulties, to the costs, and to copyright issues that have to be confronted in considering projects to digitise newspapers. The most recent conference was held in London in April 2002 to show «Diversity and Opportunity». The Conference aim was to show the range and diversity of UK and other countries' newspapers that are being preserved. This conference underlined the need to think more about newspaper projects which are taking place in many countries, and how to benefit from the experiences of those involved in their set up and implementation.

To date ten issues of a *Newsletter* have been produced during the period when this section was a mere Round Table. However, the future of the *Newsletter* in its present format is in doubt and the next issue could possibly be online.

In 1998 the Heritage Lottery Fund (HFL) awarded funding for a feasibility study into an archival microfilming programme. An application for £16 million for the first phase was made in 1999. The Trustees of the UK Heritage Lottery Fund provided £5 million in 2001 to save local newspapers in peril. This was by far the largest preservation grant ever made in the United Kingdom. The application was made on behalf of NEWSPLAN to support the programme of microfilming historic files covering, in the main, the period between 1800-1950 and to investigate the digitisation of newspaper text through the preservation medium of archival-quality microfilm to provide enhanced on-line access to them. John Lauder was appointed Director to the NEWSPLAN 2000 Project.

Once the priority lists were completed, work at the national level continued steadily. Units are based in Aberystwyth, Dublin and Edinburgh. Preparation for microfilming then began. In the case of Wales all the targets were to be bilingual Welsh / English (25% of the population are bilingual). The National Library of Wales undertook the preparation work on the volumes to be filmed, and the Library drew on its own collections and, those of local libraries and archives. The same is true of Dublin and Edinburgh, but it must be recognised that the BLNL is the major contributor as it provides about 75% of all titles required for filming.

Digitisation

Microfilm is regarded as the principal preservation medium for newspaper texts, rather than digital files. However, the matter of digital archives of local newspapers is being monitored; the recommendation of the Panel is for individual local authorities to engage with newspaper proprietors in the first instance, as copyright permission may be required to hold digital archives. Advice should also be sought from a national library, from the Newspaper Licensing Agency, or from the Newspaper Society.

It is hoped that the next step is the digitisation of pre-1950s newspapers which will open up these newspapers to new and future generations. The most impressive development for newspaper librarians is the quantity of current newspapers available via the internet. Recently, there has been increasing interest in opening up access to older newspapers, which has resulted in projects to scan and index them, and make the results available on the web e.g. the BLNL's project to scan and index 19th and 20th century newspapers.

Storage

In its Phase 1 operation lasting until 2004, the NEWSPLAN 2000 Project plans to film some 1,700 local newspaper titles. The problem of what to do with the original runs, once a microfilm has been made of the newspapers, becomes increasingly acute.

The four national libraries, the British Library, the National Library of Scotland, the National Library of Wales, and the National Library of Ireland are all committed to the permanent retention of newspapers published in their countries. It is also expected that local authorities will make adequate provision for the collection, storage and preservation of hardcopy local newspapers published in their area.

It has been my priviledge to be a part of the NEWSPLAN programme for the last 15 years, and I would like to record my appreciation of having been a member of the Round Table for almost as many years, during which I have learnt so much, and established so many friendships which I hope will flourish for years to come.

A NORDIC DIGITAL NEWSPAPER LIBRARY

Majken Bremer-Laamanen

Helsinki University Library, Mikkeli, Finland

Newspapers on microfilm will in a short time be a part of the overall digitisation programme in our libraries. With the turn of this millennium we are experiencing a totally new way of using newspapers, of using our historical collections. During the next few years it is possible for us all, with large newspaper collections on microfilm, to digitise our collections, to build «Digital Newspaper Libraries» for our users.

The Project

The aim of the Nordic TIDEN-project was to test criteria for microfilm as a platform for digitisation and full text searching. As a result a Nordic Digital Newspaper Library has been established in October, 2001, with Nordic newspapers from 1640-1860 on the Internet, http://tiden.kb.se. We have launched a digital newspaper library with several hundred thousand pages, for the public and for researchers interested in the Nordic Countries. The libraries participating in TIDEN were the Royal Library of Stockholm, the National Library of Norway and the State and University Library of Århus. The co-ordinator for the project was Helsinki University Library, the Centre of Microfilming and Conservation. This project, was supported by the Nordic Council of Scientific Information (NORDINFO) and the libraries during 1998-2001.

To support the Nordic project the Library in Finland started an additional project AURORA in 1999, cofinanced by the Finnish Ministry of Education.

The project TIDEN stretch both geographically and in a time perspective. In 2000 financing was granted by NORDINFO also to Iceland, Greenland and the Faroe Islands to start digitising their newspapers, under the project name VÄSTNORD.

Some newspaper publishers did show an interest in the project, which in Norway has resulted in including a local newspaper Nordlands Avis from the years 1893-1978 into the project and making it available in the Internet. In Finland the largest newspaper publisher Sanoma Oy will make indexes of their newspaper collections to the 1990's available at Helsinki University Library.

The Objectives of the Nordic Project

The main objective of the project has been to use microfilm as an intermediate for future digitisation.

Microfilm enables large-scale production of digital images. In Norway and in Finland we have built production lines for digitisation of newspapers from film. The objective has been to start with a part of the newspapers and when this project is finished, integrate the digitisation of the newspapers to the libraries' ordinary functions.

In Denmark and Norway the objective has been to get as much of the collections on the web as possible – with minimal search possibilities. That is search on title, date and place.

In Finland and Sweden we have included full text search, which enables search on each word in the textual content. In addition in Finland an Index of articles with hierarchical search terms from 1771-1890 will be available.

The Newspaper Contents

The contents in the Digital Newspaper Library of TIDEN have been chosen according to the importance of the newspapers and copyright possibilities in the member countries.

Kungliga Biblioteket chose to digitise *Post- och Inrikes* from 1640-1721 in Sweden. Some predecessors to this actual first newspaper have been digitised from 1620-1630's. This means that information starting from the 30-year war in Europe is included and available today for full text searching until 1721.

In Finland we chose to build a digital platform for the day-to-day life in the 18th and 19th centuries. In this project every newspaper, containing 44 titles, is digitised for full text searching from 1771-1860, starting with our first newspaper *Tidningar utgifne af et Sällskap I Åbo* in 1771 containing 140,000 pages. This project has been continued by a second project, which will include all newspapers until 1890, with 800,000 pages more.

Denmark continues in the TIDEN project, almost where Sweden stopped, with *Adresseavisen* from 1751-1890. Shorter periods of other titles have also been included, like *Berlinske Tidende* 1863-1865, *Dannevirke* 1862-1864 and *Faedrelandet* 1863-1865.

Norway is covering almost two centuries, the 19th and 20th century with *Den norske rigstiden* 1815-1882, *Adresseavisa* 1802-1900 and *Norlands Avis* 1893-1978.

The number of pages we have on the net at this point is actually of minor importance. More value lies in the development and innovations we have made to build the production line, for digitisation and full text searching, for our large library collections.

As I know the Finnish project best, and as it is the most complete I will introduce it to you.

The Finnish part of the project

Helsinki University Library – the Finnish National Library – was established in 1640 and has had legal deposit rights since 1707. Our Library is carrying out most of its preservation services in the Centre for Microfilming and Conservation. It was established in 1990 in Mikkeli, 250 kilometers from Helsinki. Digitisation and microfilming, supported by the Centre's conservation and preservation expertise, will constitute the Library's reformatting activities. As the responsibility of library's digitisation services are here, the work for both the TIDEN and AURORA projects are situated in the Centre. website: http://digi.lib. helsinki.fi.

Helsinki University Library had in 1997 chosen digitisation of all newspapers – due to their high demand – as one of the main targets of its reformatting programme. The digitisation of newspapers was also ranked as first priority by the research libraries in Finland. And as practically all newspapers in Finland have been microfilmed, it was possible to use microfilm as intermediary for digitisation needs. Due to copyright restrictions the digitisation had to be focused on pre 1890-material.

The work flow

The production has to be as fully automated as possible. However, human intervention is needed at some stages of digitisation, indexing and OCR treatment.

The individual steps of the process are as follows:

* Microfilming – refilming the newspapers if the quality of the present microfilms is not good enough

* Digitisation – scanning of the microfilms; today films are scanned automatically.

* OCR – conversion of the images to text files; requires many adjustments and training of the software especially for text in Gothic letters.

* Identification – identification of title, issue, date, pages and attachments of the newspaper takes place in principle automatically but requires some human treatment.

* Database import – Importing the prepared material to the database system.

Microfilming

When using microfilm as intermediary, the quality of the microfilms is the key to the success. Of course, the quality is crucial also for the preservation in general because we have to accept that in the long run newspapers will survive only on microfilm. It is a stable medium with a life length in centuries. It is readable by the human eye and offers a very high resolution, good enough for conversions onto new carriers in the future.

Digitisation

The preservation microfilms in our collections have advantages and disadvantages relating to digitisation. High-contrast microfilms have a limited dynamic range, which in many cases is a good thing. This is a good feature especially if you compare the scanning result of the text which is quite sufficient, favouring 16x or lower reduction originals and the microfilms of grey text on brittle and brownish paper. Smaller shades, spots or wrinkles in the paper are eliminated in the film. The text is clearly extinguishable from the base. It makes the OCR-process easier, using bitonal images and 400 dpi.

In an economic perspective scanning from film is much faster than using the originals when oversized items like newspapers are concerned.

On the other hand photographic material is best when digitising in greyscale from the original. But there is also a clear difference between the different kinds of microfilm copies used for digitisation, because the negative direct duplicate gives the poorest results for the photographs in the newspapers.

OCR

In addition to making the newspapers available on the Internet digitisation has also to create a new powerful search tool because an improved access was the main reason of the whole exercise in Finland.

The basis for full text searching is that the words in the text files are searchable which again requires that the images have to be converted into text files with the help of an Optical Character Recognition process.

Because of the poor quality in the original newspapers and the Gothic letters much used in Northern Europe, the OCR conversion has required much effort. Problems are encountered as many types of fonts and languages are used on the same pages in one paper. Today six persons at our Library are involved in OCR conversion of Gothic script at a yearly rate of 150,000 pages.

After investigating the available OCR softwares we chose Fine Reader 5.0. in 1999. It is able to handle the columns of the newspapers fairly well and is not too sensitive to react too much to the unevenness of the quality of the original pages. In addition to these features the software also can handle the text in batches, once it has been «trained». Still the columns in old oversized newspapers give us extra work.

The results of testing the text for OCR on eight different newspapers have shown that there are several factors influencing the quality of the conversion, the most important of them being the text font, language and reduction ratio. Roman style, Swedish language and a low reduction rate gave the best results in our newspapers. At the moment we have OCR'd 44 titles that have been available since March, 2002 at the Digital newspaper library in the three main languages used in our newspapers during the 18th and 19th century: Finnish, Swedish and German.

Identification

The last point in this process, the entering of each image and its textual version should aim at automation when dealing with large quantities of material. Usually, every image has to be described by the title, date, number and page.

We have constructed software for the identification of large quantities of images. The title and ISSN of a publication can automatically be used for all chosen newspaper numbers. Each newspaper number, when chosen, automatically gets the correct page numbers.

When the identification step has been completed the software creates an XML file that is copied to the server along with images and text files.

Database import

The server picks up new files from server and processes them automatically. At this point surrogate images in various formats are created. Database importing is done by custom Java software.

The Engine Room

Much effort has been put into developing a proper functional architecture for the digital newspaper library, as a part of an overall digital architecture. This will include all kinds of materials and the production of the digital versions as the digital original, the digital master and the digital image on the web and the textual versions for full text searching. URN identifiers are generated automatically.

We have also information on articles and the authors of them together with search words. The database structure is combined with permanent archiving and retrieval. Solutions have to be applicable for other types of material such as maps, periodicals and books.

Text search software

From the very beginning it was obvious that a hundred per cent OCR conversion is impossible. It was equally obvious that it was unthinkable to start proofreading the great mass of the converted text manually. That is why the following two decisions were made:

The first one was that the basic tool for the users of the digitised newspapers would be the digital facsimile of the original pages. The ASCII version would be used for searching purposes only.

The other decision was to find a retrieval software which could manage a limited percentage of errors. This is also needed for the retrieval of the old-fashioned language used in the newspapers. For this the Convera Retrievalware by Excalibur was chosen. It processes the words as bit-strings and uses pattern recognition to find matches. One to three letters can differ from the original word and is still searchable. Finnish and Swedish language support has been added to the normal search functions.

In action

The Nordic Digital Newspaper Libraries opened to the general public on 25 October 2001 in a press conference in Mikkeli along with the joint project website. The Nordic and the Finnish Historical Newspaper Library was prominently featured on the largest Finnish newspaper *Helsingin Sanomat* and later on in Finnish television. During the first year of use about one million pages were searched on, which is a lot in a population of 5 million inhabitants. We have received plenty of user feedback on the system. Most of it has been positive along with some error reports and improvement suggestions. The website of Finnish researchers of history AGRICOLA has noticed the TIDEN-project and been most enthusiastic about it. It will be an important cornerstone of the virtual library of the future. Based on the experience and the infrastructure developed with the help of these projects the National Library of Finland is creating a national digitisation service, which will be strong enough to assume the responsibility for large national projects.

Conclusions

There is a great demand for Digital Historical Newspaper Libraries. There have been newspapers published for almost half a millennium now. The TIDEN project covers almost four centuries, one and a half of these with full text search. For the Nordic project the interfaces of the participating libraries will be searchable via the TIDEN web page http://tiden.kb.se. We are still working together to enhance full text fuzzy search possibilities between the Nordic newspaper databases including the Icelandic VÄSTNORD-project. This pre-investigation has been funded by Andrew Mellon Foundation and will be ready in spring 2003.

With microfilm, researchers have used a limited number of titles for historical research. By full-text searching, the sources are widely extended. Research will focus in other new directions. The history on everyday life is now searchable as never before. Borders are abandoned.

MANAGING COLLECTIONS OF NEWSPAPER CLIPPINGS

Lesley Hart

*Special Collections Information Services,
University of Cape Town Libraries, South Africa*

How to deal with collections of newspaper clippings and newspaper clippings that are part of manuscript collections is a vexing question; at least, it is one that has vexed me for some time. I shall probably raise more questions today than provide answers to the problems of managing such collections. There does not seem to be a great deal in the literature about these collections. What I did find shows that I am not alone in finding them a problem. Duckett in his Modern manuscripts states:

Newspaper clippings, loose or mounted in scrapbooks, form another general category of printed material that tries the curator's patience.

Collections of newspaper clippings take many forms. They may be a loose assemblage of clippings kept by an individual or organisation on a few or several subjects of interest. They may be ordered or in a disorganised jumble. They may be systematically pasted into scrapbooks or onto individual sheets of paper. If pasted into scrapbooks, they can be in an orderly form, or pasted one over the other in overlapping layers. They may be carefully annotated as to date and source, but quite often this information is missing.

They are vexing because of format, because of fragility, because of problems of housing and also vexing because the question must be asked: if the intellectual content of the clippings can be found by searching the relevant newspapers, why keep the clippings?

My reply to this question would be that my experience has shown that subject-ordered collections of newspaper clippings provide an extremely useful and convenient source of information for the researcher.

In older collections or collections that span time or countries, accessing the information in its original form is often not a practical solution.

In my own repository, the boxes of clippings on the unrest that followed the Soweto riots of 1976, a student project initiated through the prescience of the late Robin Hallett, are referred to year after year by students. Our collection of newspaper clippings on University of Cape Town staff and activities provides a very useful part of the archive of the University and is consulted regularly. The scrapbooks of clippings that reflect the career of a composer, such as Erik Chisholm, whose career spanned at least three continents, very conveniently provide access to a source that would be almost impossible to obtain as comprehensively if the researcher had to refer to the original newspapers. The newspaper clippings that form part of the archive of the Surplus People Project provide a record (as published in the newspapers) of forced removals in South Africa. These are just some examples.

If we keep our collections of clippings, do we need to keep them in their original format? These collections often take up a great deal of space. They are a medium that will not last indefinitely, as other speakers have or will confirm. Continued handling, especially of loose clippings, has two negative effects: the clippings become increasingly tatty and, inevitably, they start getting out of order. Is it not a good strategy to reformat them? If so, what sort of reformatting should we choose?

Photocopying them will partially solve the problem of long term preservation, and is possibly cheapest in the short-term, but will not solve the problem of bulk, and therefore becomes an expensive solution in the long-term. Microfilming or digitisation would seem to be a better alternative and the choice between these technologies would depend on several factors.

Our own decision, with regard to the newspaper cuttings in the Surplus People Project archive, is to microfilm them, but with another collection we may well have decided otherwise. The choice of microfilming was made for several reasons. In this case, it would seem to be a cheaper option, as it can be outsourced and a very simple form of indexing will enable quite effective searching. The collection consists of about 15,000 to 20,000 clippings. Most are from South African newspapers, so it would not be as difficult to find the articles in the original newspapers as might otherwise be the case. There is therefore not the same advantage in making them accessible electronically, as might be the case with a collection less easily consulted in the original. After microfilming, we shall discard the clippings themselves, gaining a significant savings in space in the process.

With the scrapbooks of clippings on the career of composer Erik Chisholm, on the other hand, I would choose to digitise them. As mentioned, they span several decades and at least three continents and were they to be digitised, it would make a very useful resource if combined with photographs and letters from the collection. In this case, we would not discard the original scrapbooks.

The decision to reformat would have to be based on the informational value of the collection, its contribution to the total holdings of the institution, its rarity value, and how it fits into the institution's collection development policy. There are other practical criteria that would also need to be considered. How much preparatory work would be necessary before reformatting – to either microfilming or digital format? Would a considerable amount of sorting need to take place before reformatting begins? What sort of indexing or metadata is necessary to allow effective searching of the microfilm or database? How much physical preparation is needed, such as in the case of scrapbooks where clippings have been pasted into overlapping layers?

It seems to me that there is no one answer to the questions I have raised, but that reformatting – to microfilm or digital format – is an option that should be considered if the collection is one that has been assessed as worthy of long-term retention. The decision as to which of the two formats to use can be based on a whole range of factors and is one for the individual institution to make.

DIGITIZATION OF NEWSPAPERS:
THE SOUTH AFRICAN EXPERIENCE

Dale Peters
(with Pat Liebetrau and Colleen Goldsworthy)

Digital Imaging Project, Durban, South Africa

[Note: the following is the text contained in a Power Point Presentation (15,3 Mb)]

DISA objectives:

- Make accessible online South African material of high socio-political value.
- Collate serial literature scattered across collections.
- Develop local expertise in use of digital technologies.
- Set standards for digitization initiatives in South Africa.

DISA Phase 2:

- Identification of appropriate collections.
- Distributed digital production.
- Gateway to federated digital collections.
- Develop policies, strategies and guidelines in support of South African initiatives.
- Comply with international standards.

Campbell Collections:

- Digital microfilm scanner.
- Obsolete technology.
- Preservation of microfilms.
- Newspapers and MSS of microfilm.
- Data transfer.
- Application to DISA 2.

Indexing for the project:

- Digitised a selection of newspapers – indexed in the same manner as journals.
- Encoded using the international Text Encoding Initiative (TEI) standard with an xmi DTD and the Encoded Archival Description (EAD).

- Metadata capture: publisher, place and date of publication at journal/ newspaper level.
- Indexing of title, author and keywords at article level
- Articles over several pages.

Processing:

- Indexed skeleton xml file created by indexer.
- Page images scanned from paper originals or microfilm.
- OCR processing.
- Automatic insertion of OCR-ed text into the skeleton xml file.
- One issue = one xml file.

Searching:

- Browsing facilities.
  - -- browse the text images.
- Searching facilities.
  - -- full text searching.
  - -- article title, author and keyword searching.
  - -- thesaurus online.
  - -- acronyms online.
- Readability and advanced searchability.

Indexing results:

- Human indexing has enabled advanced searchability on all the encoded elements.
- By using terms from a thesaurus, language usage is standardised.
- Higher relevance of returned hits.
- Added intellectual input.

However,

- Human indexing is time and labour intensive.
- Training is required.
- Quality control is needed.
- Thesaurus management software is essential.

DigitisingMicrofilm ... :

Samples were tested using the following:

1 bit at 300 dpi

1 bit at 400 dpi

1 bit at 600 dpi

8 bit greyscale at 300 dpi with thresholding at 128

8 bit greyscale at 400 dpi with thresholding at 128

8 bit greyscale at 600 dpi with thresholding at 128

Metadata Input

- Easy access to information
- Value added over and above date: access to at least ARTICLE headings
- The quality of OCR Intellectual input that will always be human reliant: subject indexing
- Research is reliant on a more contexual search basis than full text searching, thus the success of any digital project remains fully reliant on the quality of the OCR output

What is the solution?

Use both –

- Microfilm for preservation at this time until technology has moved forward.
- Digitization for access to and searchability of materials by researchers.

Digitizing from microfilm –

- Essential that microfilming adheres to internationally accepted standards.
- Technical training is ongoing.

OCR and Bitmap recognition:

It would be obvious that the rate of word return from the previous two samples would be far greater in the first image than it would be for the second image, even if bitmap recognition software was used in the case of the second example.

Conclusion: some microfilms are better than others, thus re-microfilming is required in those instances.

Primary objective of digitization:

* Search ability.
* Access to hitherto inaccessible publications.

Languages:

* Many newspapers in Africa are in the vernacular and these present very specific OCR problems which require a great deal of time and labour to teach the software to recognise.

Costs:

* Storage space – one tabloid page at 8bit greyscale at 50% = +-8Mb
* One issue of approx. 20 pages = 160Mb
* 1 CD will therefore only hold 5 issues of archival quality tiffs

Outcome of investigation:

* Reliance on OCR success rate.
* Level of metadata complexity.
* Minimal manual indexing.
* Cost of staff time.
* Service on demand.
* Preservation of microfilm.

Conclusions:

The massive amounts of information reproduced in newspapers suggests improved organisation thereof by means of computer automation. Given the sheer volume of data, the digital conversion of newspapers also makes good sense in separating the information from the poor substrate, by reformatting degraded heaps of acid hydrolysis into a digital bit stream. Nicholas Negroponte in his book, Being Digital (New York: Knopf, 1995, P. 179), writes that computing machines of the future will no doubt be as capable as you or I of understanding narrative text, but at present, machine understanding of content is limited to optical character recognition and content recognition of grouped alphabetical characters. To fully expoloit the immense value of metadata asscoated with newspapers, we need those bits that describe the other bits – the tables of contents, indexes and keywords laboriously inserted by humans, to be more efficiently aided by computers.

Our experience in investigating the digitisation of newspapers both for the Campbell Collections and for the DISA project has shown that while it is technically feasible, even profitable for some, until the basic digtial networking requirements of the digital era are met – scalability, interoperability and open systems – the social fabric of the South African society does not support the general adoption of the technology. The DISA project went the laborious human indexing route. The Campbell Collections will provide a limited service on demand, passing on the cost to the user. We simply cannot afford the disk space or labour costs required to create the metadata necessary in a systematic conversion programme. Instead, we conclude that the successful application of digital technologies to the enormous preservation problem, demands a substantial injection of grant funding of a well structured and dedicated project, similar to the successful TIDEN project presented at this workshop, in which work processes can be refined for maximum efficiency.

This strategy calls for a collaborative national response to establish a dedicated digitisation project, preferably linked to the existing microfilm technologies established at the National Library of South Africa. The recommendations resulting from the investigation presented today need to be developed in a forum of national consultation to ensure that the newspaper heritage of South Africa is preserved. A primary objective of national collaboration is the rationalising of functions and elimination of unnecessary duplication, as in the establishment of a South African version of the EROMM (European Record of Microfilm Masters). Our investigation has indicated an urgent need to review the image quality of existing microfilm holdings, and to implement international standards in microfilm quality control. A national forum would be well placed to develop a programme of systematic digital conversion, prioritised according to common criteria.

The success of a collaborative approach is related to the support of ia.:ntified stakeholders. We would strongly support a grant funding proposal by the National Library of South Africa to co-ordinate such national consultation, which must include the regional copyright libraries, who are legally responsible for much of our newspaper holdings. We also recommend that publishers have an important role to play in funding the future preservation of their «offspring» in newspaper production, indeed, they have already seen the benefit of digital production and electronic reference services within their own operations. Finally, a primary objective of the DISA project is to develop local expertise in use of digital technologies in participating institutions. The DISA project has conducted this investigation with the view to develop standards and guidelines and would be able to contribute to a national consultative forum to make South African heritage more accessible online.

PRESERVING NEWSPAPERS IN NAMIBIA

Johan Loubser

National Librarian, National Library of Namibia

To compare publication of newspapers in Namibia with other countries here present I have to inform you that we only have three daily and four weekly country wide newspapers. The National Library of Namibia (NLN) receives two copies of all Namibian newspapers on legal deposit. It has the biggest and most complete newspaper collection in Namibia. Although we have in theory been receiving two copies, in reality there is only one bound copy in the stack rooms for preservation. The second copy is maintained for microfilming. We bind all newspapers yearly and these copies are not for use but for preservation in supposedly dust free, climate and humidity controlled stack rooms. With a few exceptions all newspapers titles and runs have been microfilmed up to 1995 at the National Library of South Africa with the financial assistance of the Social Science Research Council of the United States of America. At the moment we are aiming at eliminating the backlog by ensuring that all newspaper titles have at least been microfilmed up to 1995. Once this has been achieved we will microfilm on a yearly basis. We have a 35mm master negative film and a 35mm diazo (non archival) copy for consultation.

The functionality of our microfilm reader/printers has been a problem for years resulting in preservation copies of newspapers being made available to users for consultation and photocopying. Hopefully this problem will be solved once all reader/printers are on lease only, and it will then be the responsibility of the commercial company to maintain these machines. Neither the NLN nor the National Archives have binding facilities. We use commercial binders resulting in cumbersome tender procedures and fluctuating binding standards and even irreparable damage through glue and cropped margins. The legal deposit privileges were expanded in 2001. Five copies of each title must now be deposited and there are three places of deposit. Unfortunately these additional three places of deposit are reluctant to preserve newspapers due to the binding cost and space requirements. The future of these three newspapers will have to be seriously debated.

Unfortunately digitization is not being considered at the moment.

The Sam Cohen Library in Swakopmund is the only other library in Namibia that collects newspapers for preservation. They bind the newspapers three times a year. Between the Sam Cohen Library and the NLN a complete set of all printed newspapers has been preserved. They co-operated in our 1990-1995 microfilm project.

The Namibian Scientific Society in Windhoek, the counterpart of the Sam Cohen Library in Swakopmund does not preserve newspapers but concentrates on collecting cuttings on various subjects. The Library of the University of Namibia states in its collection development policy that they do not preserve newspapers. The newly established northern campus library is not yet reflected in their policy document.

In the light of the new legal deposit privileges for the UNAM Northern Campus this policy will be revised.

The producers of the three main daily newspapers are preserving the originals as well as providing a cutting service. Indexing is very limited. These papers have been available in electronic format on the internet since 2000 but archival images or digitized copies have not been preserved. The information is available through online searches on their websites. The possibility exists that printed, digitized and microfilmed versions of our three daily newspapers will be made available to the National Library. I must give credit where credit is due and this information only became known when I prepared for this seminar.

In conclusion I would like to mention the collection and preservation of Namibian newspapers outside Namibia. The National Library of South Africa has played an important role in collecting, preserving and microfilming Namibian Newspapers. The Basler Afrika Bibliographien's Namibia Resource Centre & Southern Africa Library in Basel, Switzerland is also collects and preserves Namibian Newspapers.

THE CAPE TOWN ENGLISH PRESS INDEX PROJECT (CEPIX)

Peter Coates

formerly National Library of South Africa

Preparing my address for today, I realised that it would not be appropriate to try and teach you how to index newspapers. Included in your Conference Pack is the introduction to the 1876 edition of the Cape Town English press index which goes a long way towards providing all those boring details. Today I shall simply review how the project began and what I hope to achieve. When I joined the staff of the South African Library in 1964 I was shocked by the condition of its very large and comprehensive newspaper collection, and when-ever I could get away from my Legal Deposit duties I systematically catalogued and repaired the volumes, and in 1971 was able to move the whole collection to a suitable store with horizontal shelving. During my 36 year career at the Library the collection grew from about 30,000 volumes to an estimated 70,000 both from normal accessions as well as transfers of entire newspaper collections from the National Archives and from other libraries. The newspapers were always my «children»!

A large proportion of the fragile bound volumes were beyond further physical use and researchers were obliged to use microfilm – when it was available – and it did not take a wily researcher long before he started investigating which titles had not been microfilmed and began requesting those. As a matter of principle I also used microfilm for my own researches, so I was aware of the difficulty of the medium, and users had my sympathy. I would observe successions of researchers each going though the same papers looking for their own fragments of information. I believed I had a «calling» to undertake an indexing project so researchers could go directly to the report they needed and find it with certainty. Searching microfilm, reel after reel, is guaranteed to dispirit the most ardent researcher, and often material which is there is not found.

Microfilm is a librarian's solution to the problem of disintegrating newspapers, but no-one at that time felt any responsibility to make the contents available by means of indexes. From the middle of the 20th century newspaper libraries compiled amazing clipping files which have recently been superseded by online electronic searching of the digital text from which newspapers are now made. But the period before about 1930 is not covered, and newspapers in the period between 1880 and 1930 are in the most fragile condition and most likely to be available only on film.

I set out to producing a detailed index to all African news in the English-language Cape Town newspapers. I am not a sociable person and live alone, so no-one could be offended by my solitary work, I am both a history and librarianship graduate, and a trained indexer, and (as I said) the newspapers were my «children». When I began the project I lived in an apartment across the road from the newspaper store and would work in that dark, locked building until the early hours of the morning. When I moved to the suburbs, I was given permission by the Library to borrow the volumes as well as a few essential reference works like directories, to use at home. This made to project viable, for without this concession the work could not continue.

At the outset I thought the work would be quick, and expected to cover five years of newspapers in one reasonable-sized volume. How mistaken I was! Instead of five years per volume, the first index, for 1871, filled 698 pages, and each year the size of a volume has grown, until the 1876 edition had reached 1066 pages, and I am certain that I have already exceeded that mark in August 1877.

I use manual methods: the reliable, crash-proof 5x3 paper slip and ballpoint pen, and have avoided using the world's most time-wasting technology. I do not wish to get into an argument about the potential of computerizing my methods. I actually produce an index manually, single-handedly, without any financial support; computer-philes do not get further than speculating about the possibilities. But then I am producing pre-coordinate indexes which evolved through hundreds of years of manual methods, while computer methods are better suited to accessing information in post-coordinate searches. I know that with my methods everything I index will be findable; it is well-known that in the humanities the hit rate with computerized free text searching is quite disappointing.

The subject headings I favour are user-friendly headings such as those found in an encyclopaedia, rather than the pedantic Library of Congress headings. Names of people have to be verified, and I can put in an hour's work trying to determine «Mr Smith's» full name, and possibly also birth and death dates, place of residence and occupation – indeed I now spend so much time on this kind of research that the job is in danger of coming to a halt. Variant spellings of names have to be cross-referenced. To ensure consistency from one volume to the next, I maintain an authority file with all cross references and background notes for my guidance.

I chose to start with the year 1871, because my knowledge of South African history made it clear that this was the turning point when the country ceased to be a pastoral backwater and became an industrial nation. Diamonds were first exploited in 1870, and the area was seized from the Orange Free State by Britain in 1871, then gold was discovered, followed by coal and iron, which led to Britain taking over the Transvaal as well in 1877. Telegraph lines and railways were built. Labour and racial laws appeared on the statute book, and the South Africa which we are now trying to bury was born.

Public affairs were remarkably well reported in those days: full texts of speeches in Parliament, full proceedings in the Supreme Court, Circuit Courts and Magistrates' Courts; full reports of Town Council proceedings; verbatim reports of speeches at public meetings, and even church sermons and addresses at temperance meetings! All in 8 point type without headlines or illustrations on two of the four pages which made up the newspaper.

Indexing work has slowed down year by year: I began with two newspapers, and I now index four; with twice the number of newspapers in Cape Town, their reporters vied with each other to gather news, and more things were happening to be reported. It takes a surprising amount of time to combine in one entry all the references to the same story appearing in the four papers, which often reported the story days (even weeks) apart. Added to this, my increasing insistence on researching the people who appear in the news has considerably slowed down the work.

The indexes for 1871 to 1876 may be bought from the National Library on microfiche, and I am hoping against hope that they will be willing to publish the 1877 index in the same manner.

Indexing principles used for the Cape Town English press index

Introduction. Indexing the English language newspapers of nineteenth century Cape Town is done manually using 5x3 inch slips of paper and a ballpoint pen. The computer is only used to type out the finished product. Whether preco-ordinate indexing of this kind has a future may be questioned, but indexers know very well, and users are beginning to admit also, that in fields other than the sciences, recall rates by means of postco-ordinate electronic searching of full-text are remarkably poor. Whether preco-ordinate indexing becomes obsolete will not be decided on grounds of its effectiveness but rather on account of the prodigious amount of indexing time it requires. That indexing may be done quickly, even automatically, by computer is a mirage. True indexing is a painstaking, precise, monotonous task demanding a high degree of insight, skill and broad general knowledge.

Method. Four Cape Town English-language newspapers are indexed: The Cape Argus, Cape Times, The Cape Town Daily News and The Standard and Mail. The Cape Mercantile Advertiser is not indexed apart from a few items needed to expand reports appearing in one of the other papers. Certain categories of text are indexed selectively or ignored. These included overseas news items not relating to Africa, its off-shore islands or Antarctica; routine advertising and commercial reports; names of individuals on shipping lists; proceedings in the inferior courts; names of candidates who passed lower level examinations without distinction, and persons who, though named, acted in their official capacities (such as policemen giving evidence in court). Summaries of previously-published news intended for distribution overseas are ignored. Poetry, which was inserted more often than not to fill up unused space, is ignored unless it has an African connection.

No limit is placed on the number of entries arising from one article. By way of example, the Liquor Licensing Boards' proceedings, reported in an article 100mm. long, produces about 300 entries, including the general subject (liquor trade), special pleadings before the Board (by Good Templar and other temperance organizations), and details of the licences granted (street name, hotel or canteen name and name of licensee).

Parliamentary proceedings are indexed fully by subject, name of Bill and name of Member, but papers laid on the Table are ignored if their contents were not reported, while notices of motion are ignored if the motion was subsequently debated and reported. Occasionally, Members' speeches are so insubstantially reported that these, too, are ignored. Questions are ignored unless a substantial reply was reported.

Local authorities' proceedings are usually indexed by topic only. Superior courts' proceedings are indexed fully by subject and names of prosecutors, defendants and non-official witnesses.

Ideally, citations to the same event reported by the several newspapers are brought together in one entry, but if there was strong divergence of point-of-view between the different reports, separate entries are made. This was particularly true of the «burning questions» of the day.

Definitions. A newspaper index is made up of three main elements, headings, cross-references and entries.

The terms chosen as headings dictate the alphabetical sequence. subheadings and sub-sub-headings form alphabetic subsets, whereas chapter headings provide a means of breaking up long strings of entries according to some other sequence, usually chronological. Headings may consist of names (persons, places or things) or subjects (activities, processes or concepts). Subheadings are typically used with main headings for places, for «natives» and for economic activities. Except in the case of Cape Town, place names are not used as subheadings in cepix.

Cross-references are a form of heading which direct users to a different heading where all or additional entries may be sought. Normal indexing practice uses cross-references to other headings of equal or greater specificity (eg. «Botany», see also «Carnivorous plants»), while referencing to broader headings (eg. «Trees», see also «Botany») is not considered good practice; however, this has been done to a limited extent in cepix.

Entries provide the substance of the index. They consist of two components: the modification which is an abstract of the portion of the text relevant to the heading or sub-heading, together with the citation which indicates precisely where in the source document that item may be found. If space permits, the nature of the source (eg. editorial, letter, full-text of a document, obituary or advertisement) is also indicated. Choice of terms used for the entries is determined by the language and tone of the source text of the time, and reflects a world where hunting rhinoceros was a pleasurable manly pastime, the country districts were populated by «boers» and «kafirs», and women had no rights and needed little education except so far as it would contribute to their husbands' domestic comfort. The system of headings was created by the compiler, choosing popular rather than academic terminology. Library of Congress usage is always considered, but not necessarily adopted. In doubtful cases, the usage of the indexes to The Standard Encyclopædia of Southern Africa and Chambers's Encyclopædia was preferred.

Personal names were very inconsistently spelt in newspaper reports and completeness ranged from surname only to surname plus initials to full name. Sometimes no name appeared in a report but the indexer was able to supply this from personal knowledge and context. While it was not feasible to check all names in all accessible reference sources, the following were frequently consulted: The General Directory, the Cape Blue Book and the later Civil Service List, the Dictionary of South African Biography (5 volumes and the «prospectus»), The New Dictionary of South African Biography (volume 1) and Southern African Dictionary of National Biography, the alphabetical lists of Death Notices in the Cape Archives Depot, 1834-1916 and 1917-1928, and general biographical reference works like Who was Who and A Dictionary of Universal Biography. Even these disagree as to spellings. As a last resort, dubious spellings were checked in the modern telephone directory. I need to make every effort to avoid listing different people with the same name together or the same person under several different forms. Compound surnames are entered under the first element of the compound, whether or not they are hyphenated.

Place names are given in the old orthography as they appear in the source newspapers, such as «Blaauwberg», «Piquetberg» and «Zwartkops». Some exceptions are made.

Point of view. The Compiler of an index is obliged to respect the points of view of his source. Although each newspaper targeted a specific audience, this was on the whole, the white, English-speaking Cape Town male. As explained above, this influences the wording of entries. At government level the viewpoint is Cape unless otherwise stated (hence «Finances: public sector (Cape Colony)» but «Transvaal – finances».) At local level Cape Town is assumed (hence «Post Office (Cape Town)», but «Worcester – postal service».) For relations between the Cape Colony and other Colonies or States, entries will be found only under the name of the other Colony or State (eg. «Natal – Cape relations»), but mutual relations between any other two Colonies or States will be found in both places. The form used for the Cape's relations with the Mother Country is «Cape of Good Hope – British relations».

Filing rules. Word-by-word filing has been adopted (De Witt precedes Deafness), persons precede places of the same name (the rule being to follow a sequence from smallest to largest). Arranging identical names of different people is generally according to precedence of first appearing. De, Van and Von are used as filing elements for personal and place names, and Malay and aboriginal names are generally entered straight, eg. «Abdol Magiet». The Dutch dipthong «ij» is filed as «y» but when these letters appear in English and other words, eg. «Bijou», they file as printed. Titles such as Col., Dr, Miss, Mr, or Mrs are ignored for filing purposes. Hyphens used linguistically, as in «co-operative», are disregarded and the word is filed as one, whereas compounds linked by a hyphen, as in «horse-racing» are filed as two words. Numerals are filed as spoken, eg. «Eighteen-twenty Settlers» or «Thirteenth Regiment».

Abbreviations. Words are spelled-out in full whenever space permits, but abbreviations which have been used are explained in the Introduction.

Symbols. The following symbols have been used in citations:

Left of the colon

On this side will be found the date. Months are abbreviated Ja, F, Mr, Ap, My, Je, Jl, Ag, S, O, N, and D.

Right of the colon

On this side is the title, A: *Cape Argus*, M: *Cape Mercantile Advertiser*, N: *Cape Town Daily News*, S: *Standard & Mail*, and T: *Cape Times*, pages 1-4, columns a-g. A citation «21N:A3f*(letter)*,N3g?,S*(sup₂)*1b,T3a*(ed)*» means 21st November, *Cape Argus* page 3 column 6 (letter to editor), *Daily News* page 3 column 7 (two citations), *Standard* supplement no.2 page 1 column 2, and *Cape Times* page 3 column1 (leading article). Misdated newspapers occurred several times during 1876. The error did not usually occur on all four pages, and the following citation style was used only for items appearing on the incorrectly dated page: «10[11]Mr:N3a» means that a misprinted date 10th March ought to have been 11th March.

General remarks. Each edition includes a general introduction to the main events of the year, and concludes with the year's calendar.

CREATING A PORTAL OF DIGITAL JOURNALS IN SOUTH AFRICA

Pierre Malan

SABINET, South Africa

[Note: the following is the text contained in a PowerPoint presentation – Ed.]

South African «e-publications»

Background:

- Project started 2001.
    - -- Identified 350 scientific and scholarly journals.
    - -- Approached 270 publishers (70% interest).
    - -- Today we have around 120 contracts.
- July 2002 – launched with 40 journals.
- January 2003 – 101 journals online.
- 14 publication Web sites.
- African Journals Online (AJOL) agreement.

Production:

- Online publication – Adobe (.pdf).
- Publishers provide data in .pdf, WordPerfect, MS Word, or hardcopy.
- Indexing.
- Difficulties.
    - -- Volumes.
    - -- File sizes.
    - -- Future standards.
    - -- Sustainability of process.

Future:

- Continue with process of data acquisition.
- Group titles into collection.
    - -- Legal.
    - -- Theology.
    - -- Medical and Health Sciences.

    -- Business.

    -- Education.

    -- Humanities.

- Enter international market.
- Adapt pricing models.
- Enhanced product administration.
- Publisher relationship.

URL: http://journals.sabinet.co.za/

THE NEWSPAPER AS A SOURCE OF INFORMATION

Niel Hendriksz

Stellenbosch University Library Services,
South Africa

Newspapers are used daily by a wide variety of researchers and students:

1. Economists at Stellenbosch use newspapers to play a Stock Exchange game in which the daily share prices are noted. Prices of products and the history of the markets can be researched. At least 50% of our queries on SA Media are for economic articles in the press.

2. Political Scientists have daily recourse to the press to trace events in the world and especially hotspots i.e. Zimbabwe and Iraq and not forgetting globalization. At least 35% of the SA Media queries are political.

3. Journalism students obviously use them daily as a base for practical work for layout and how articles are presented.

4. Genealogical Researchers use the older stock where records of shipping are of great value. Lists of new arrivals in the country as well as births and deaths, especially in times of war where casualty lists are avidly researched.

5. Biographers also use the back copies as well as files of clippings kept in our Special Collections departments. An especially fine collection on the Anglo Boer War of 1899-1902, compiled and donated by the Secretary of State of the Z.A.R., dr W. J. Leyds, is kept in the Africana collection.

6. Archaeologists, and more especially maritime archaeologists use the older papers for reports of wrecks, cargo lists and sales of flotsam.

7. Newspapers carry essential information for the conservation of our cultural heritage. Buildings and artifacts that are in danger of being destroyed can also be saved by publicity and research on their past can aid to keep lost memories alive.

8. Artists use the media for research on cartoons and cartoon strips. Graphic artists do research on advertisements, as do fashion designers.

9. Sport historians use older papers for the history of especially rugby, football and cricket clubs at the Cape as well as visits by overseas teams. Sometimes papers are the only remaining sources of information on long defunct clubs and the development of multiracialism in South African sport.

10. Scientific research, astronomical happenings and weather forecasts are also popular items of research gleaned from papers.

11. Schools visit us to research specific days in history – usually the birthdays of their students as a time capsule of what else happened on those days.

Long live the newspaper! It is of essential value to the researcher and its preservation cannot be overemphasized.

NEWSPAPERS AND COPYRIGHT

Denise Rosemary Nicholson

*Copyright Services Librarian, University of the Witwatersrand,
Johannesburg, South Africa*

South Africa is bound by international copyright commitments and domestic legislation. Unfortunately electronic copyright has not yet been addressed. As time is limited, my brief today is to focus on some practical copyright issues which affect newspapers, e.g. fair use, copyright ownership, clearances, and reformatting of information.

Newspapers are protected under «literary works» in our Copyright Act, but they also contain «artistic works» such as cartoons, photographs, images and advertisements.

Subject to exceptions, copyright endures for the lifetime of the author and 50 years after his/her death, or the first posthumous publication of his/her work. This means that very old newspapers may already be in the public domain and are not subject to copyright.

Regarding «fair use», South Africa uses the UK model of «fair dealing». This is permitted in Section 12 of the Copyright Act, which permits reproduction of literary or musical works (and some other works), for the purposes of research or private study, or for personal or private use; or for criticism or review; or reporting current events in a newspaper or similar periodical; or by means of broadcasting, or in a cinematograph film.

Section 13 provides limited exceptions for reproduction for educational purposes, but these do not extend to electronic media.

Regarding «fair use» in the electronic environment, and in the absence of appropriate legislation, South Africa takes cognizance of WIPO's and IFLA's statements that «digital is not different». The websites are www.wipo/int.treaties/ip/copyright/statements.html and www. ifla.org/V/press/copydig.htm. You may also like to consult the following website addresses for some useful guidelines, namely

- Guidelines on fair dealing in the electronic environment by the Joint Information Systems Committee and the

- UK Publishers' Association (www.ukoln.ac.uk/services/elib.papers/pa/fair/intro.html); Publishers and Librarians promote common principles on copyright in the electronic environment by IFLA and the International Publishers' Association www.ifla.org/V/press/ifla-ipa.htm, and

- Fair use guidelines for educational multimedia by the American Distance Education Consortium www.adec.edu/admin/papers/fair10-17html.

Newspapers generally own copyright in articles written by their full-time reporters/journalists, but this is seldom the case with freelancers or artists, unless they are assigned the rights. Copyright in artistic works usually belongs to the artists.

The person who is responsible for the composition of a photograph, and not the person who physically presses the camera button, holds copyright in the photograph.

The person, who undertakes the arrangements necessary for the creation of a computer-generated literary or artistic work, is the copyright holder.[1]

---

1. Dean. O. Presentation at DALRO's Blanket Licence Workshop held in Kempton Park on 21.2.2003

There is no Newspaper Licensing Agency in South Africa and the Reprographic Rights Organization, DALRO, does not clear copyright for newspapers either.

Under legal regimes such as ours (i.e. voluntary collective licensing), newspapers customarily do not entrust their rights to collective administration, in view of the complexities involved. As newspapers feature material from various external sources, copyright in each article, image or photograph needs to be researched individually to establish the copyright clearance source.

Newspapers themselves need to obtain permission to publish material and in the absence of a licensing agency, they have to apply directly to rights-owners. In the case of international media, they often have to enter into individual licence agreements before the material can be used. They cannot reproduce, reformat or digitize material unless they hold the copyright or have been mandated to do so. The controversial US case of Tasini vs. New York Times is an example where the newspaper was sued for publishing freelancers' works electronically, when it only had the rights to publish them in print.

Sometimes newspapers do not permit other newspapers to reproduce or re-format full-text versions, but some allow links to be created to and from their websites.

Recently, a local newspaper editor told me that newspapers have to be very prudent when using material from other sources. He gave the following example. A newspaper once slightly altered an item in a picture from another newspaper to suit the context of its story. There was no malicious intent to infringe and was done quite innocently by the artist concerned. The other newspaper took exception and threatened legal action on the grounds of intentional copyright violation. They resolved the matter, however, by formally apologizing and by withdrawing the altered picture from all further editions.

Only if a newspaper holds copyright, can it grant permission and charge copyright royalties. Some newspapers in South Africa do charge, but the majority waives fees for non-commercial or educational purposes. They naturally require full acknowledgement. However, international newspapers charge high copyright fees.

If a newspaper does not hold copyright and has no mandate to grant permission for reproduction of works, it has to refer users to rights-owners directly. This is time-consuming and problematic, especially if the rights-owners' whereabouts are unknown, or where there are more than one author/artist. Also, where rights-owners are deceased, their heirs have to be contacted. It is also difficult to trace rights-owners if, for example, they are defunct entities or have merged with other entities.

Permission is sometimes denied for reproduction of a whole item (especially images) or portions of it (e.g. the text may be used but not the images), or the usage conditions may be impractical, which means that the desired information cannot be reproduced. This could cause serious gaps in digital collections, for instance.

Our law does not permit multiple copying (other than in Section 13 of the Act). It does not permit adaptations or conversions to other formats, without prior permission. Although microfilming has been done for years, it is not provided for in the law. Libraries could argue that the preservation exceptions for libraries and archives in the Regulations possibly include microfilming, but this is a matter of interpretation and could be a valid one. I would suggest, however, that one gets legal advice on this if one wishes to embark on a microfilming or reformatting project of any kind. As the process of digitization creates more than one copy, copyright clearance is necessary. Rights-owners are often reluctant to give permission for digitization projects and there are also practical problems involved in getting permission. An argument for preservation, as with microfilming, may be made but again legal advice on this would be preferable.

The Digital Imaging Project of South Africa (DISA)[2] experienced copyright problems when digitizing a 30-year collection of Anti-Apartheid periodicals. The clearance process was exceptionally slow; some rights-owners did not respond; others could not be traced. Some works could not be cleared for copyright and they had to be excluded from the project. Copyright fees were waived because of the nature of the collection, but for other projects, copyright clearance could be very expensive. Overseas newspapers, for example, charge high copyright fees.

Digital preservation is a vital part of the creation and management of any digital collection. Invariably, any preservation strategy will require the occasional re-mastering of the digital images (possibly onto new storage media) or re-formatting (to accommodate new technological changes). This will also require permission from the copyright holders. It is therefore good practice to negotiate rights to move and change file formats «in perpetuity» where possible, so that the project does not have to seek permission each time such a change is made as part of the preservation strategy.[3]

When negotiating contracts for copyright clearance and usage of material, provisions must be made for fair use, inter-library loans, archiving, hyper-linking, re-formatting and multiple copying, if possible. Indemnities against prosecution should also be secured.

It is important that any digitization project (and its host institution) considers issues such as ethics, data protection, the intellectual property of the works in the collection, as well as that of the project itself. This includes providing simple, concise copyright notices on the project's web-page, stating how and for what purposes the material can be used.[4]

In South Africa, there are many media monitoring services or news-clipping services provided by libraries or commercial firms. I recently visited two such firms in Johannesburg, namely, Newsclip Media Monitoring and SA Press Group, to find out how copyright affects them.

Newsclip subscribes to over 800 periodical and newspaper titles and mainly provides original clippings to their clients. Copyright is not really a problem, as they do not use photocopies very often. They confirmed that what they do is in compliance with Section 12 of the Copyright Act.

SA Press Group also subscribes to a large number of journal and newspapers, but provides photocopied clippings to its clients. It finds copyright fees very expensive and the clearance process very slow. In recent years, the Group has entered into many formal licence agreements with rights-owners, to enable it to provide an efficient service to its clients. Its online article service is also licensed. A representative of the Group said that the establishment of a Newspaper Licensing Agency would be a solution to the problem, as the process could then be streamlined and collection of royalties would be centralized.

In conclusion – copyright has various practical implications and complications for newspapers themselves, as well as for consumers and collectors of newspapers. It is clear that a more streamlined copyright clearance system is necessary, but newspapers should still be allowed to waive fees for non-commercial and educational purposes. I believe that provisions for re-formatting and digitization for archival and library preservation purposes should be included in our legislation, either in the Legal Deposit Act or in the Copyright Act. Perhaps formal recommendations should be submitted to the Government to amend the

2. http://disa.nu.ac.za
3. www.tasi.ac.uk/advice/managing/copyrights.html P1 -5.3.03
4. www.tasi.ac.uk/advice/managing/copyrights.html P2 -5.3.03

legislation accordingly? For a useful South African reference tool, you may like to consult The Newspaperman's Guide to the Law (5th ed), by Kelsey Stuart, published by Butterworths, South Africa.

MICROFILMING OF NEWSPAPERS IN SOUTH AFRICA

David Farrant

MicroFile (Pty) Ltd, South Africa

In the late 1960s I was instrumental in establishing the first Mainframe Computing Bureau in South Africa. While in the United Kingdom before this I was exposed to microfilm and its many benefits to commercial institutions and realized that my computer bureau would definitely need the backup of microfilm to avoid the loss of information due to the continuous head crashes which we experienced in those days. Every printout, cheque, etc. was microfilmed using a Kodak Recordak Rotoline, and the film was processed by ourselves. This was and still is the only legally accepted form of the original. Microfilm only taking 2% of the space of the paper originals resulted in great savings to our clients who then offered us other microfilming projects.

In 1946, Strathmore Holdings, with the co-operation of all the major newspaper groups commenced microfilming English and Afrikaans newspapers published in the major cities of Southern Africa. This resulted in the compilation of the most comprehensive bibliography of South African history ever made available. African Consolidated Films (controlled by the Schlesinger family of cinema fame), later Kinekor Organization, took over and continued with a full microfilm bureau service to commerce and industry (35mm, 16mm, jacketing, aperture cards, microfiche diazo copies, as well as the hardware for viewing and printing). Microfile, as this company was called, was then acquired by myself in the early 1970s and merged with my Computer Bureau microfilm division, to operate independently as a one-stop microfilm and micropublishing company.

I should stress at this point that after attending thirty CeBit Hanover Fairs and watching the growth and evolution taking place within the microfilm industry, and its progression into the computer industry prompted me at great expense (R300 000) in 1992 to import from Germany the first A2 newspaper scanner into South Africa. This made it possible for us to scan cuttings and past newspaper articles and thus provide a full clipping service to our many microfilm customers. To our amazement, not one of these customers was willing to change from the microfilm format due to its archival stability over a hundred years as against their fears about the ever-changing computer storage medium and its related expense.

Today, as you are aware, it is possible to scan newspaper microfilm images and convert them into easily compressed TIFF Group 4 images which can be stored on a number of different media. For example, a CD could hold between 2000 and 3000 images. The images can then be printed or e-mailed at will.

Example the NEWSPLAN 2000 project by the British Library (which is one of our most prominent customers) will create an archive containing some 65 million pages for the public at large to view at will. The project is a 7.8 million pound initiative.

I end by saying that archival microfilm is with us today and will stay with us for many, many years into the future. It has served its purpose with distinction and will continue to do so.

«CAMP» AND AFRICAN NEWSPAPER MICROFILM PRESERVATION AND DIGITISATION

Peter Limb

Michigan State University, USA

Introduction

Librarians and archivists have long been interested in the successful preservation of newspapers in order to meet both the needs of present and future researchers and the interests of heritage.

Newspapers, as journals of record, remain a major primary source in humanities and social sciences research. In many African countries, attempts to preserve the national newspaper heritage face major obstacles, notably limited resources and the vagaries of climate. In South Africa, the work of the National Library and other libraries and archives has preserved a very sizeable proportion of the newspaper heritage, though gaps in holdings remain for some historical black newspapers, such as the ANC's founding organ *Abantu-Batho*.

Microform and/or Digitization

For the present, microfilm still appears to many to be the most reliable form of preservation. Doubts persist about the reliability and longevity of web sites. However, stable web-storage projects such as JSTOR suggest the possibility of solutions. New technology does offer some hope to address the chronic problems of newspaper preservation in Africa. Digital cameras can transcend problems of disintegration of original copy during scanning. Equipment exists to combine the microfilming and digitizing processes. Most importantly, digitized newspapers offer superior access by means of full-text searching. Anyone who has spent long hours pouring over print or microform newspapers in search of vital data will agree that full-text e-newspapers will be a great boon to researchers.

Digitization, however, does not come without considerable costs – start up, processing, and digital preservation (server) – or without technical problems related to the poor quality of either originals or microfilm copies. Therefore in the Digital Age, African countries will still face the same problem of limited resources. Partial solutions to these problems lie in partnerships that are more effective and in the combination of microform and digital approaches.

Partnership or Perish?

In the face of recurring problems of acquiring Africana, a number of successful co-operative Africana acquisition and preservation schemes emerged in the early 1960s among U.S. and British librarians, developed primarily for their own national needs. These included the Cooperative Africana Microfilm Project (CAMP), the Standing Committee of Library materials from Africa (SCOLMA), and the Cooperative Acquisitions Program of the Library of Congress.

Sometimes these approaches had unintended deleterious effects on local publishers or libraries. African journals relying on scarce foreign income through overseas subscriptions to survive could find at their door agents of Western libraries buying journal issues in local currencies. CAMP was careful to work in a spirit of cooperation with African partners. Yet, an unintended result of the Project was a decrease in direct sales of microfilm copies of South African newspapers to individual U.S. libraries, which naturally enough exploited the scheme's co-operative lending power. These are complex problems, which can be partially resolved by better coordination. However, it is important that Western librarians and scholars appreciate the substantial differences between the African library and publishing worlds and their Western counterparts and do not try to reproduce solutions to collection development problems more appropriate in a Western setting. The ethical dimension is crucial here because, left to private market forces, the value of African publications would depreciate markedly.

Nevertheless, co-operation offers the best prospects for securing the needs of both scholars and libraries in both arenas.

The Cooperative Africana Microform Project (CAMP)

CAMP promotes the microform preservation of African documentation between research libraries in many countries and the repository at the Center for Research Libraries (CRL) based in Chicago. Founded in 1963, CAMP acquires expensive or hard-toobtain microform sets and authorizes original filming of unique research materials in North America, Africa, and Europe. Materials preserved by CAMP include newspapers, government publications, personal and corporate archives, and works in African languages.

The CAMP web site http://www.crl.edu/info/camp.htm summarizes the aim of the Project:

The microform collections of CAMP form a large pool of historical, political, linguistic, economic and geographical data and primary source materials that are not available elsewhere. Member libraries can rely on the vast microform collections of newspapers and journals and, thereby, avoid the high costs of acquiring, cataloging, and storing these materials locally.

CAMP participants pay an annual fee, with overseas libraries paying a much lower fee than their North

American counterparts. Participants make selections of new newspapers to film. The CAMP Executive Committee is composed of elected members and ex-officio members of the Africana Librarians Council (affiliated to the African Studies Association, (ASA)) and two faculty or academic representatives from member universities, with public meetings held twice a year.

The very extensive holdings of CAMP comprise one of the largest collections of African newspapers and archival papers on microfilm in the world. The 1985 *CAMP catalog* already comprised 642 pages and has long since moved to an online version at CRL http://catalog.crl.edu/

Recent CAMP projects include the Liberian newspapers scheme (which has enabled the filming of extensive runs of newspapers despite the ongoing serious conflict in that country) and the Timbuktu Manuscript Digitization Project http://wwwcrl.uchicago.edu/info/camp/timbuktu.htm. Other successful recent CAMP initiatives include the Senegalese Archives Project (in co-operation with the National Archives of Senegal and involving local training in microfilming and other preservation techniques), the ongoing filming of Tanzanian, Nigerian, Malian, Somali and Malawi newspapers, and the Cooperative African Newspapers Project sponsored by the AAU/ARL Global Resources Program.

The Cooperative African Newspapers Project

As part of the Cooperative African Newspapers Project, CAMP has created the African Newspapers Union List (AFRINUL), an electronic database of holdings information for newspapers (in all formats and eventually in all relevant languages) published in Africa. This database, maintained at CRL http://www.crl.edu/info/camp/afrinul.htm aims to meet the needs of researchers by providing greatly enhanced access to African newspapers. It builds upon an earlier project, *African newspapers currently received by American libraries* (also now online). AFRINUL consolidates holdings information for collections of African newspapers in North America and aims to also include holdings elsewhere. AFRINUL lists print, microfilm, and online holdings at CAMP, CRL and, progressively, other libraries. CAMP is interested in the preservation of fragile newspaper resources not only by microfilming titles but also by exploring digitization of newspaper content, thus facilitating research.

South African Newspapers and CAMP

Among the extensive South Africa-related holdings of CAMP are the Carter-Karis and Karis-Gerhardt Collections, Abdurahman Papers, Xuma Papers, Black Sash Papers, Leo Kuper Papers, Treason Trial transcripts, and runs of many newspapers. Most of these are microfilm copies of originals held in South Africa. Many of the guides or inventories of these collections are now being digitized (for example the Kuper and S.A.I.R.R. collections). CAMP describes its microfilm holdings on the Southern African region thus:

CAMP has built an important collection of microforms of archives, journals, newspapers and government publications at both the national and local levels. This includes documents on the independence movements such as the African National Congress (ANC) in South Africa and the South West Africa People's Organisation (SWAPO) in Namibia. CAMP's filming of the «Carter-Karis Collection, 1920-1965» and the subsequent publication of its index by Susan G. Wynne as *South African political materials: a catalogue of the Carter-Karis Collection (… 1977)* has made these source materials on the Black political movements in South Africa one of the most heavily used archive sets that CAMP has acquired. The collection includes microfilm of about eighty South African current and retrospective newspapers. Other acquisitions are microfilm of the archives of the South African Institute of Race Relations, the Trade Union Congress of South Africa, publications in the Tswana language, records on the death of Steve Biko and on South African political trials. http://wwwcrl.uchicago.edu/info/camp/campov.htm

CAMP thus maintains a valuable preservation repository for South African research materials. It can be posited that the existence of overseas copies might discline researchers from visiting South Africa. Certainly, part of the uniqueness of South African archives is lost with copying. And Western libraries should not be involved in removal of original documents from Africa (rather, they should follow the example of CAMP, which has made copies of microfilmed materials available to African libraries). However, the timing of copying can be adjusted to accord with research agendas such that material is only copied after scholars have made good use of local sources. Moreover, overseas (or African) researchers can use CAMP copies to better plan their research visits and give them more time to uncover new materials. The inexorable march of scholarship pushes on to new frontiers of knowledge, making use of both microfilms and local sources.

CAMP is particularly rich in South African newspaper holdings. Currently, a CRL/AFRIN-UL web search reveals 181 South African newspapers ranging from *Abantu-Batho* to the

Zululand Times. It also holds 29 microfilmed newspapers from Namibia, 26 from Mozambique, 10 from Botswana, 84 from Nigeria and 38 from Zimbabwe.

Recent suggestions for new newspaper acquisitions, to be done in conjunction with South African partners, include three early Zulu-language mission newspapers associated with the American Board Mission: *uBaqa Lwantwana* (1877-1883), *Ikwezi* (Pietermaritzburg, 1861-1868), and *Inkanyezi Yokusa* (1850). This could be a fruitful small co-operative preservation microfilm project with South African repositories.

Today, talk of co-operative newspaper projects invariably involves the magic word «digitization».

In South Africa, the Digital Imaging Project of South Africa (DISA) has embarked on an exciting digitization project that involves newspapers and other periodicals of the anti-apartheid movement.

In its first stage, DISA successfully digitized over 30 periodicals, some in a newspaper format. It is possible that newspapers will be included in its more extensive second stage, starting in 2003. If so, then interesting possibilities for national and international cooperation may arise in the combination of microform and digital approaches that could, for the first time, make available electronically to researchers the historic treasures of the South African press. DISA is a South African initiative that has deftly deployed national skills but it also has drawn on overseas funding and expertise. By developing effective national and international partnerships, DISA has maximized its potential. Future developments in the field of newspaper preservation in South Africa can learn from this successful model.

Conclusion

For successful newspaper preservation, many African countries, including South Africa, continue to face the problem of limited resources. One solution to this problem lies in more effective partnerships and in the combination of microform and digital approaches. Partnerships must be based on mutual benefit and trust. CAMP's newspaper preservation operations seek to complement those in South Africa and elsewhere in Africa. CAMP seeks mutually beneficial projects based on equality in the interests of African and worldwide researchers. CAMP looks forward to sharing its expertise and resources and to learning from South African colleagues at this exciting time of changing paradigms and technologies.

THE CONSERVATION HOUSING, STORAGE AND (RE)BINDING OF NEWSPAPER CLIPPINGS ORIGINALLY BOUND IN A SCRAPBOOK OR ALBUM FORMAT, FOLLOWING CONSERVATION TREATMENT AND REPAIR:
The Fascicule System of Single Sheet Document Storage[1]

Mary Minicka

Conservator, Parliament, Cape Town, South Africa

1. Introduction

Today I am going to speak to you as a conservator about one of the specific concerns conservators have with regard to the preservation of newspaper clippings. Here, at Parliament, many of our newspaper holdings consist of newspaper clippings, as well as the more commonly held newspaper format(s). This institution's holdings consist of a number of scrapbooks and albums housing newspaper clippings. These clippings may have been compiled as a record of a particular subject matter (for example, the formulation of a particular piece of legislation) or event. In a number of instances, the newspaper clippings mingle with other forms of documentation (for example, letters, mass printed pamphlets, etc.) within the scrapbook or album's pages.

As a conservator, I am not only concerned about the preservation problems most commonly associated with the presence «inherent vice» due to the high acid content of news print. I am also concerned with other preservation-related issues that affect the preservation of newspaper clippings. Some of these issues concern the long term usage, secure housing and storage of newspaper clippings.

All of these inter-related issues regarding the preservation of newspaper clippings require the maintenance of the highest conservation treatment standards and regard for ethical considerations, while ensuring that the conserved newspaper clippings are easily accessible to researchers and other interested parties.

One of the issues related to the preservation of newspaper clipping collections, concerns the manner in which they are housed. Most commonly, newspaper clippings are glued into a large scrapbook or album book. These albums are unfortunately, frequently constructed of cheap materials. Furthermore, many of the album books are of a very poor and/or rudimentary construction.

Consequently, over time and with usage, both the binding structure and materials of many of the albums and scrapbooks have deteriorated to the point where individual volumes resemble little more than fairly neat piles of papers sandwiched between detached book boards.

---

1. The information presented here is an extract from a paper on the use of non-adhesive binding structures for conservation rebinding, presented at the Society of South African Archivists (KwaZulu-Natal Branch) Conference on the Preservation of Library and Archival Materials in Africa (10-13 December 2002). Structural considerations for the conservation (re)formatting or (re)binding of pamphlets and other mass produced multi-sectioned monographs, publication of which is currently pending.

The standard conservation treatment techniques of dry cleaning, tear repair, deacidification and other aqueous treatments currently available do work to counter the physical degradation affecting newsprint go a long way to extending the life span of the clippings. However, fresh challenges confront the conservator when s/he attempts to (re)bind or house the now conserved newspaper clippings and other document material contained in the erstwhile bound album or scrapbooks.

2. Reconsidering the album or scrapbook binding structure as housing for newspaper clipping collections

Due to the failure of the original album or scrapbook binding structure as a long-term secure and safe housing system for large parts of newspaper clipping collection(s) at this institution, it is not an unreasonable idea to reconsider the use of the same or similar binding structure to re-house or rebind the now conserved and repaired newspaper clipping collections.

When considering the use of a binding format or structure other than that of the original binding structure, considerable caution needs to be exercised. Cases need to be sympathetically evaluated on an individual basis, with due regard for the historical and archival context of the item(s). Conservation treatment ethics and a healthy consideration for the need to respect the integrity of the album or scrapbook as an object of material culture has to be exercised during the entire process of formulating a conservation treatment for the album or scrapbook(s) in question. Adequate documentation of the reasoning behind the decision to reformat an album or scrapbook needs to form part of the conservation documentation record, as well as a record of the original binding structure.

In considering the use of another binding structure for the conservation (re)binding of conserved newspaper clipping collections, certain criteria regarding the original binding structure need to be fulfilled before embarking upon a conservation (re)binding of a different format or structure. They include:

2.1 Failure of the original binding structure

The binding structure cannot be returned to its original format or composition. This can be caused by the inadequate protection provided by the binding structure for the contents (that is, newspaper clippings) of the volume. Or, the original binding structure failed so spectacularly in its function of keeping items together in a specific order and as a single unit. Alternatively, the original binding structure may have the potential to cause actual physical harm to the contents of the volume.

2.2 The contents have to be (re)bound as a unit

The contents of the volume have to be (re)bound or reformatted as a unit, not necessarily in the original binding structure. There are a number of reasons for the need to rebind, ranging from the need to reconstitute the original sequence in which the newspaper clippings were originally glued into the volume (or, simply found prior to conservation). Other considerations regard the facilitation of easy access to the information contained in the newspaper clippings. In most instances a straightforward boxing of the now loose clippings will not suffice as a long-term «keeping-things together-and-in-order» storage and security solution.

2.3 The (re)bound newspaper clippings will be housed in a protective enclosure

The new binding structure will be housed in a protective enclosure of some sort, for example a «clam shell» box. This allows for the possibility of using soft, or limp non- adhesive binding structures to house newspaper clippings. Using protective enclosures to house the now (re)bound clippings also allows for the possibility of breaking up the size of the original volume into smaller, more viable units. The tremendous thickness of many albums and scrapbooks are often a contributing factor to the disintegration of the bound volume. Here, there is a chance to avoid making the same structural mistake by thinning a large single volume into two or three thinner more stable structures. While bearing in mind that the reconstituted and smaller units are kept together through storage in a common enclosure.[2]

3. The *fascicule* document storage system: for the conservation housing of single sheet document items

The *fascicule* document storage system is a storage method was specifically devised for the storage of a large collection of single sheet and manuscript material at the Bodleian Library (Oxford, United Kingdom) by Christopher Clarkson.[3]

«Single sheet material» is the term used to describe manuscripts (that is, unbound pages of written or printed text), pamphlets, prints, letters, maps, early newspapers, and various other items of printed ephemera. The format of the majority of these items consists of a single printed sheet, which may be repeatedly folded or cut into smaller dimensions. The storage and care of collections of single sheet items (including newspaper clippings) has fallen to archival and library type institutions. These custodial institutions are, thus, confronted with the need to store and accommodate a wide variety of sizes and formats within an archivally acceptable storage system, while making these documents easily and readily accessible to their clientele.

Briefly, the *fascicule* system is a large format single section binding structure[4] composed of blank pages. Naturally, only archival/conservation quality materials are used for the construction of each fascicule, and its protective enclosure. The single sheet documents are attached to the fascicule's pages by means of a hinge of pasted Japanese tissue paper.

The beauty of this storage system is both its simplicity and flexibility as a storage system. The basic structure of the pamphlet «book», allows for the housing of a number of single

---

2. While due regard is given to ethical considerations when considering the division of a single large volume into smaller units, it is the information content and sequential order of the content, by and large, which is of primary importance. The binding structure (unless found otherwise) is very much a secondary consideration; in many cases it is the very binding structure itself that has a detrimental effect on the newspaper clippings it is supposed to shelter.
3. For a full description of how the system was devised, as well as a description of the technical and practical processes involved in the creating of such a storage system, see: Lindsay, H. & Clarkson, C. «Housing single sheet material: the development of the *fascicule* system at the Bodleian Library», In: *The paper conservator journal of the institute of paper conservation,* 1994, 18:40-48.
4. Single section binding structures consist of a grouping of folded pagers. This grouping (or section) of pages is held together by a single stitch that forms a sort of «figure of eight» which loops back on itself, using between three to five sewing holes (or sewing stations). This stitch is fixed in place with a double knot, usually in the centre of the booklet's spine fold (or gutter). The stitch typically runs the entire length of the book's spine fold. For more information consult Smith, K. *Non-adhesive binding: books without paste or glue* (New York: Sigma, 1993 – available from the author at 22 Cayuga St, Rochester, NY 14620-2153, USA).

sheet document items of disparate size, shape and format in the same volume. Some of the advantages of this document storage system are as follows:

3.1 An ability to accommodate a variety of items in a single storage unit

This storage system allows for the accommodation of a large number of single sheet document sizes, thicknesses and formats within a single fascicule binding structure. Even bi- or tri-folio pamphlets, can be accommodated within the fascicule structure. These pamphlets can be sewn onto a flange created by folding one of the fascicule pages a number of times to create a flange onto which the pamphlet can be sewn using a simple pamphlet binding stitch.

3.2 A secure storage system

The *fascicule* system is a secure storage system for a wide variety of sizes and formats. Documents are affixed to the fascicule's pages by means of a pasted hinge of Japanese paper. Thus, documents are securely fixed in a given sequence and cannot easily be removed, lost or mislaid. This is a far more secure and controlled system than just having loose documents contained within a box.

3.3 Reversibility

Despite the above-mentioned advantages regarding the security of the *fascicule* storage system, the hinging attachment is easily reversed by the careful application of moisture to release the paste adhesive. Thus there is no need for the use of expensive and harmful solvent chemicals to reverse the hinging attachment. The ease of removing documents reduces the danger posed by the use of chemical solvents and subsequent handling of the newspaper clippings (or any other documents) during the reversal process.

3.3 Minimized handling of contents

Similar to the principle of a scrapbook, the handling of the individual documents/ newspaper clippings is minimized by the fact that readers handle the fascicule's pages as they work (and turn pages), rather than repeatedly handling the actual documents. Yet, the hinging attachment used to affix individual documents to the fascicule's pages allows both/all sides of each document to be accessible to the user. The document can literally be turned over just like any other page within the fascicule binding.

3.4 Minimization of further damage to clippings

Documents of varying formats and sizes stored loose within a box can incur physical and mechanical damage as they slide and move around within the box. In a fascicule, each individual item is secured individually within the fascicule, removing the potential for such damage to occur.

The fascicule binding structure is a flexible binding, that is, its cover is not made of stiff board. The cover is made from a thin, but firm card. This gives the binding a «limp» quality. This «limp» quality provides a greater accommodation of the bulk (or thickness) resulting from the inserting of newspaper clippings into the fascicule. The flexibility of the fascicule has the potential to prevent much of the damage associated with the storage of numerous single sheet documents within the confines of a traditional rigid book binding structure.

3.5 A cost effective storage system

Clarkson considers the *fascicule* storage system to be a cost-effective means of storing a variety of documents of differing sizes and formats. This is due to the fact that any given single sheet document collection may need only, say, three or two different sizes of fascicules to accommodate the differing sizes and formats of the entire collection(s). These «average» sizes could be determined after a collection survey. The survey results can assist in the planning and budgeting stage of a large scale institutional re-housing or conservation (re)binding project.

The nature of the *fascicule* storage system allows for the affixing of more than one document per page, particularly if the clippings are small of a size. Obviously it would not be appropriate to load each page with the maximum amount (or more) of documents able to fit into the page space, as damage may well occur by the injudicious loading of pages with affixed documents.

4. Conclusion

In addition to the many advantages of the *fascicule* document storage system discussed above, the *fascicule* storage system has many additional advantages of interest to book and document conservators. Particularly with regard to the many advantages cited in conservation literature dealing with the application non-adhesive binding structures (into which this particular book structure falls). Non-adhesive bindings are increasingly recognized by conservators for their numerous conservation-related advantages for the conservation (re)binding of certain book formats.[5] Non-adhesive bindings are generally considered to be easy to construct; have friendly handling properties, and rely on little or no adhesive to hold the structure together. Removing the potentially harmful effects of adhesives, as a source of physical and material degradation, and as a source of structural failure should the adhesive fail.

I hope I have managed to convey some of the practical conservation applications of the *fascicule* document storage system as devised by Chris Clarkson for the preservation of newspaper clippings, via this presentation and display of model examples during the course of this presentation. A large number of the conservation-related questions concerning the long-term preservation storage requirements for newspaper clipping collections are answered by the *fascicule* system. Thus, it would seem that the *fascicule* storage system certainly has a place in the conservator's arsenal of conservation techniques when dealing with the preservation of newspaper clipping collections and other single sheet document items.

---

5. See the following two articles for discussions regarding the use of non-adhesive bindings for conservation (re)binding purposes: Arregui, C. «The crossed structure binding», In: *The new bookbinder: journal of Designer Bookbinders*, 1994, 14:101-107; Spitzmueller, P. «Long and link stitch bindings», (BGN XXI, 8). In: *Guild of Bookworker's journal*, 2000. XXXV:86-112.

CURRENT SOUTH AFRICAN NEWSPAPERS
WITH DATE OF COMMENCEMENT

Advertiser en Karoonuus- news. (Graaff-Reinet)

Aderdeen, Colesberg, Jansenville George) 2000

Alberton Rekord = Alberton Record (Johannesburg) 1974

Algoa Sun (Port Elizabeth) 1983

Aliwal Weekblad (Aliwal-North) 19--?

Athione News (Cape Town) 1986

Atlantic Sun, inc. City Express; Gardens Gazette (Cape Town) 1981

Barkly East Reporter, *The* (Barkly East) 1912

Beaufortwester (Beaufort West)

Bedfordview and Edenvale News (Edenvale)

Beeld (Johannesburg) 1974

Benoni City Times and Oosrandse Nuus (Johannesburg) 19--?

Berea Mail (Pinetown) 1984

Bloenmuus = Bloem News (Bloemfontein) 1982

Boksburg Advertiser (Johannesburg) 1982

Bonus (Rustenburg) 1992

Bosvelder nuusblad vir Potgietersrus en Naboomspruit Bosveld, en Springbokvlakte (Potgietersrus) 1993

Brakpan Herald (Johannesburg) 19--?

Breederivier Gazette, *Die* (Robertson) 199-?

Brits Pos (Brits) Bugle, *The* (Louis Trichardt) 1990

Burger, Die (Kaapstad) 1915

Burger, Die (Byvoegsels) (Kaapstad) 1916

Burger, Die (Oos-Kaap) (Port Elizabeth) 1993

Burgersdorper (Graaff-Reinet) 1986

Business Day (Johannesburg) 1983

Cape Argus, *The* (Cape Town) 1857

Cape Jewish Chronicle (Cape Town) 1984

Cape Times (Cape Town) 1876

Capricorn Voice (Ladaima) 2000

China Express (Johannesburg) 199-?

Citizen inc. Financial Gazette (Johannesburg) 1976

City Press (Johannesburg) 1983

City Vision (Johannesburg) 1998

City Vision (Cape Town) 1996

City Vision (Johannesburg) 1994-1998

Coastal Weekly (Tongaat) 1996

Constantiaberg Bulletin (Cape Town) 1979

Courier (Beaufort West) 1869

Daily Despatch (East London) 1872

Daily News (Durban) 19--

Daily News (Gaberone, Botswana)

Daller, *Die* (Middelburg) 1998-1999

District Mail = Distrikpos (Somerset West) 1927

East Cape Weekend (Port Elizabeth) 1998

Eastern, *The* (Menlo Park) 1998

Eastern Province Herald (Port Elizabeth) 1845

Echo, *De* (Bethal) 1914

Echo, *Die* = The Echo (De Aar) 1974

Eikestadnuus (Stellenbosch) 19--?

Estcourt and Midlands News (Newcastle) 1992

Excelsior Nuus = Excelsior News (Piet Retief) 19--?

Express (Bloemfontein) 1991

False Bay Echo (Cape Town) 1986

Focus (Vanderbijlpark) 2000

Franschhoek Tatler (Franschhoek) 1994

Galaxy (Pietermaritzburg) 1981

Gemsbok met Koerier (Upington) 19--?

George Herald (George) 1986

Germiston City News (Johannesburg) 1981

Go! & Express East London (East London) 1995

Great North News

Greytown Gazette, *The* (Greytown) 1903

Grocott's Mail (Grahamstown) 1872

Harrismith Chronicle (Harrismith)

Heilbron Herald (Heilbron) 19--?

Helderberg Sun (Cape Town) 1996

Herald, *The* (Port Elizabeth)

Herald Carltonville (Carltonville) 19--?

Herald Potchefstroom-Ventersdorp (Potchefstroom) 1980

Heraut Heidelburg-Nigel (Heidelburg) 1985

Hermanus Times (Hermanus) 1995

Highveld Voice supplement to Witbank News

Highway Mail, *The* (Pinetown) 1949

Hilltop, *The* (Hillcrest)

Hoevelder/ Highveld Herald (Ermelo) 1981

Ilanga Lihiuba udlubu akhasini (Durban) 1965

Independent on Saturday, *The* (Durban) 1998

Indicator, *The* (Lenasia) 1985

Kempton Express (Johannesburg) 1980

Klerksdorp Midweek (Klerksdorp) 2003

Knysna-Plett Herald (George) 1984

Kokstad Advertiser (Kokstad) 1982

Kontrei, *Die* (Prieska) 1990

Kosmos Nuusblad = Cosmos Newsletter (Balfour) 1996

Kowie Announcer (Port Alfred) 19--?

Krugersdorp News (Johannesburg) 1977

Kuruman Bulletin (Kuruman) 1986

Kwana News = Kwana Izindaba (Northway, Durban) 1999

Kwevoel, *Die* (Thabazimbi) 1983

KZN Newspaper = Ikuphathela ezaKwazulu-Natal. (Mobeni) 2000

Ladysmith Gazette (Ladysniith) 1904

Laudium Sun (Laudium) 1984

Leader, *The* (Durban) 1941

Lenasia Times (Lenasia) 1978

Lentswe Voice of Western Transvaal (Klerksdorp) 1980

Letaba Herald (Tzaneen) 19--?

Lowvelder, *The* = Die Laevelder (Nelspruit) 19--?

Lydenburg Nuus = Lydenburg News (Lydenburg) 1887

Mail Voice of the North West (Mmbatho)

Mail & Guardian (Johannesburg) 19--

Messenger (Victoria-West) 1876

Metroburger (Kaapstad) 1997

Meyerton Gazette, *Die* (Vanderbijipark) 1994

Meyerton Pos = Meyerton Mail (Vanderbijipark) 1996

Mid South Coast Mail (Pennington) 1985

Middelburg Observer (Middelburg) 1990

Middellander

Midland News = Midland Nuus (Cradock) 1891

Midlands Herald, *The* (Howick) 1998

Midlands Observer, *The* (Estcourt) 1990-1992

Midrand Reporter (Bramley View) 19--?

Mirror Venda! (Thohoyandou) 1988

Montagu Mail (Montagu) 1997

Mossel Bay Advertiser (George) 1971

Mpumalanga news (Nelspruit) 1995

Natal Mercury, *The* (Durban) 1852

Natal Midlands Herald, *The* (Howick) 1996-1998

Natal Withess, *The* (Pietermaritzburg) 1846

New Mirror (Port Elizabeth) 1997

Newcastle and District Advertiser (Newcastle) 19--?

Noord-Vrystaatse Herald = Northern Free State Herald (Parys) 1973-1993

Noordelike Pretoria Rekord = Northern Pretoria Record (Pretoria) 1986

Noordelike Review = Northern Review (Pietersburg) 19--

Noordwester, *Die* (Lichtenburg) 19--?

Noordwester an Oewernuus (Calvinia) 1916

North Coast Courier (Ballito) 1984

North Eastern Tribune (Johannesburg) 1975

Northcliff & Melville Times (Johannesburg) 1982

Northern Cape Gazette (Port Nolloth) 1995

Northern Natal Courier (Dundee) 19--?

Northern Transvaal Province (Pietersburg) 1995

Northglen News (Pinetown) 19--?

Ons Kontrei (Vredendal) 1968

Ons Lindleyer (Lindley) 1979

Oostelike Pretoria Rekord = Eastern Pretoria Record (Pretoria) 1986

Oudtshoorn Courant (George) 1879

Our Times (Jeffrey's Bay) 1987

Outlook Springs and Nigel (Springs) 1984

Overvaal (Wolmaransstad) 1997

Palabora en Hoedspruit Herald (Tzaneen) 1988

Petrusburger, *Die* (Petrusburg) 1988

Plainsman (Cape Town) 1980

Port Elizabeth Express (Port Elizabeth) 1983

Pos (Warmbad) 1982

Pretoria Moot Rekord (Pretoria) 1991

Pretoria News, *The* (Pretoria) 1898

Prince Albert Vriend (Prince Albert) 1994

Queensburgh News (Pinetown) 1981

Randburg Sun (Johannesburg) 1970

Randfontein Westonaria Herald (Johannseburg) 19--?

Rapport (Johannesburg) 1970

Record = Rekord (Klerksdorp) 1996-2002

Rekord Centurion (Pretoria) 1994

Rekord Mamelodi= Record Mamelodi (Pretoria) 1994

Rekord Noord = Record North (Pretoria) 2000

Rekord Sentraal= Record Central (Pretoria) 1992

Rekord Wes Nuus = Record West News (Pretoria) 1998

Representative, *The* (Queenstown) 1978

Ridge Times and Echo (Secunda) 1998

Roodepoort Record (Johannesburg) 1977

Rustenburg Herout = Rustenburg Herald (Rustenburg) 19--

Sandton Chronicle (Johannesburg) 1970

Sasolburger (Sasolburg) 1995

Seculo de Joanesburgo, *O* (Johannesburg) 1963

Sentinel News (Cape Town) 1980

Somerset budget & Pearson advocate (Somerset East) 1886

South Coast Herald 19--?

South Coast Mail (Amanzimtoti) 1988-1994

South Coast Sun (Amanzimtoti) 1981

Southern Courier (Johannesburg) 1970

Southern Cross (Cape Town) 1935

Southern Mail (Cape Town) 1986

Southern Suburbs Tatler (Cape Town) 1979

Sowetan (Johannesburg) 1980

Sowetan Sunday World (Johannesburg) 2000

Springs African Reporter (Springs) 1968

Springs and Brakpan Advertiser (Springs) 1981

Standard (Worcester) 1894

Standerton Advertiser (Standerton)

Stanger Weekly (Stanger) 1990

Star, *The* (Johannesburg) 1871

Stellalander (Vryburg) 1897

Stellenbosch Gazette (Stellenbosch) 1999

Ster (Vanderbijlpark) 1994

Sterkstroom Courier (Sterkstroom) 1984

Suid-Kaap Forum = South Cape Forum (Riversdale)

Suidernuus (Bredasdorp) 1983-1999

Sunday Independent, *The*; (Johannesburg) 1995

Sunday Times (Johannesburg) 1906

Sunday Sun (Johannesburg) 2001

Sunday Tribune (Durban) 1935

Sunday World (Wibsey) 1999-2000

Swartlander (Malmesbury) 1941

Tabletalk (Cape Town) 1996

Tembisan (Tembisa) 1990

Times of Ladysmith (Ladysmith) 199-?

Tygertalk Kraaifontein; Brackenfell & Kuil's River (Cape Town) 1996

Tygertalk Durbanville & Beliville (Cape Town) 1996

UD Nuus = UD News (Port Elizabeth) 19--?

Umafrika (Marianhill) 1929?

Umhlanga Globe, *The* (Durban) 1993

Vaal Vision (Vanderbijipark) 1989

Vaal Weekly (Vanderbijipark) 1998

Vaal-weekblad (Vanderbijlpark) 19--?

Village Talk (Pietermaritzburg) 1992

Village Voice (Ixopo) 1998

Vista (Welkom) 19--?

Voce, *La* (Johannesburg) 1975

Volksblad (Bloemfontein) 1915

Volksrust & Distrik Rekorder = Volksrust & District Recorder (Volkrust) 1994

Vryheid Herald (Vryheid) 1984

Vrystaat (Bethlehem) 1975

Vukani the voice of Khayelitsha (Cape Town) 2000

Weskus Nuus = Weskus News (Vredenburg) 1984

Weslander (Vredenburg) 1972

What's New (Stutterheim) 1972

Witbank News = Witbank Nuus (Middelburg) 19--?

Zambi (Sinoville) 1998

Zoutpansberger (Louis Trichardt) 1985

K·G·Saur Verlag

THOMSON

IFLA Series on Bibliographic Control

Edited by Sjoerd Koopman

IFLA Series on Bibliographic Control publications provide detailed information on bibliographic standards and norms, the cultivation and development of which has become indispensable to the exchange of national bibliographic information on an international level. The IFLA Series on Bibliographic Control publications also give a comprehensive and accurate overview of a wide range of national bibliographic services on offer.

Volume 25
Subject Retrieval in a Networked World

Proceedings of the IFLA Satellite Meeting held in Dublin, OH, 14–16 August 2001 and sponsored by the IFLA Classification and Indexing Section, the IFLA Information Technology Section and OCLC.
Ed. by I.C. McIlwaine 2003. IX, 193 pages. Hardbound
€ 78.00 / sFr 134.00
IFLA members € 58.00 / sFr 100.00
ISBN 3-598-11634-9

Volume 26
IFLA Cataloguing Principles: Steps towards an International Cataloguing Code

Report form the 1st Meeting of Experts on an international Cataloguing Code, Frankfurt, 2003
Ed. by Barbara B. Tillett, Renate Gömpel and Susanne Oehlschläger
2004. IV, 186 pages. Hardbound
€ 78.00 / sFr 134.00
IFLA members € 58.00 / sFr 100.00
ISBN 3-598-24275-1

Volume 27
IFLA Guidelines for Online Public Access Catalogue (OPAC) Displays

Final Report May 2005
2005. 61 pages. Hardbound
€ 34.00 / sFr 59.00
IFLA members € 26.80 / sFr 46.00
ISBN 3-598-24276-X

Volume 28
IFLA Cataloguing Principles: Steps towards an International Cataloguing Code, 2

Report form the 2nd Meeting of Experts on an international Cataloguing Code, Buenos Aires, Argentina, 2004
Ed. by Barbara B. Tillett and Ana Lupe Cristán
2005. 229 pages. Hardbound
€ 78.00 / sFr 134.00
IFLA members € 58.00 / sFr 100.00
ISBN 3-598-24277-8

www.saur.de

K·G·Saur Verlag
A Part of The Thomson Corporation

Postfach 70 16 20 · 81316 München · Germany
Tel. +49 (0)89 7 69 02-300 · Fax +49 (0)89 7 69 02-150/ 250
e-mail: saur.info@thomson.com   http://www.saur.de

K·G·Saur Verlag

IFLA Publications
Edited by Sjoerd Koopman

The *International Federation of Library Associations and Institutions* (IFLA) is the leading international body representing the interests of library and information services and their users. It is the global voice of the information profession.

109
Libraries as Places: Buildings for the 21st Century

Proceedings of the thirteenth seminar of the IFLA Section Library Buildings and Equipment together with the the IFLA Section Public Libraries Paris, France, 28 July – 1 August 2003
Marie-Françoise Bisbrouck, Jérémie Desjardins, Céline Ménil, Florence Poncé and
Francois Rouyer-Gayette
2004. Hardbound
€ 74.00 (for IFLA members € 55.50)
ISBN 3-598-21839-7

110
Newspapers in Central and Eastern Europe / Zeitungen in Mittel- und Osteuropa

Papers presented to the Newspaper Section at IFLA Post Conference, Berlin 2003
Edited by Hartmut Walravens
2004. 251 pages. Hardbound
€ 78.00 (for IFLA members: € 58.00)
ISBN 3-598-21841-9

111
Preparing for the Worst, Planning for the Best:
Protecting our Cultural Heritage from Disaster

Proceedings of a conference sponsored by the IFLA Preservation and Conservation Section, the IFLA Core Activity for Preservation and Conservation and the Council on Library and Information Resources, Inc. with the Akademie der Wissenschaften and the Staatsbibliothek zu Berlin, Germany, July 30 - August 1, 2003
Edited by Johanna G. Wellheiser and Nancy E. Gwinn
2004. 192 pages. Hardbound
€ 78.00 (for IFLA members: € 58.00)
ISBN 3-598-21842-7

www.saur.de

112-114
World Guide to Library, Archive and Information Science Associations
2nd edition. 2005. 510 pages. Hardbound
€ 168.00 (for IFLA members: € 131.00)
ISBN 3-598-21840-0

115
e-Learning for Management and Marketing in Libraries
e-Formation pour le marketing et le management des bibliothèques
Papers presented at the IFLA Satellite Meeting, Section Management & Marketing / Management
& Marketing Section, Geneva, Switzerland, July 28 - 30, 2003
Edited by / Edité par Daisy McAdam
2005. 165 pages. Hardbound
€ 74.00 (for IFLA members: € 55.50)
ISBN 3-598-21843-5

116
Continuing Professional Development - Preparing for New Roles in Libraries: A Voyage of Discovery
Sixth World Conference on Continuing Professional Development and Workplace Learning for
the Library and Information Professions
Edited by Paul Genoni and Graham Walton
2005. 307 pages. Hardbound
€ 78.00 (for IFLA members: € 58.00)
ISBN 3-598-21844-3

117
The Virtual Customer: A New Paradigm for Improving Customer Relations in Libraries and Information Services / O cliente virtual: um novo paradigma para melhorar o relacionamento entre clientes e serviços de informação e bibliotecas / Le usager virtuel: un nouveau paradigme pour améliorer le service à la clientèle dans les bibliothèques et services d'information / El cliente virtual: un nuevo paradigma para mejorar el relacionamento entre clientes y servicios de información y biblioteca
Satellite Meeting Sao Paulo, Brazil, August 18-20,2004
Edited by Sueli Mara Soares Pinto Ferreira and Réjean Savard
2005. XVIII, 385 pages. Hardbound
€ 128.00 (for IFLA members: € 96.00)
ISBN 3-598-21845-1

K·G·Saur Verlag
A Part of The Thomson Corporation

Postfach 70 16 20 · 81316 München · Germany
Tel. +49 0)89 7 69 02-300 · Fax +49 (0)89 7 69 02-150/ 250
e-mail: saur.info@thomson.com   http://www.saur.de